A WORD FROM HOME
LETTERS FROM THE WAR
FIRST PUBLISHED IN THE
ZION MESSENGER 1943-1946

A WORD FROM HOME

LETTERS FROM THE WAR

FIRST PUBLISHED IN THE
ZION MESSENGER 1943-1946

Compiled and Preserved
By Violet (Fischer) Gaige

Published by Quiet Storm Publishing
PO BOX 1666
Martinsburg, WV 25402

www.quietstormpublishing.com

Cover by Clint Gaige

ISBN: 0-9744084-5X

Library of Congress Control Number: 2003096451

This is a work of fiction. Any resemblance to actual events or persons, living or dead, is entirely coincidental.

Printed in the United States of America

❧DEDICATION❧

This book is dedicated to the memory of our heroes
Jess Bieber
Kenneth Brodbeck
Leon Harrwaldt
LeRoy Breier
Cornelius Blome Jr.
Harold Jasmund
Clayton Seeley
Melvin Dauer
and Delvin Noward

I also dedicate this book to the memory of
Reverend Marcus J. Mueller,
Pastor of Zion Lutheran Church,
Ottawa Lake, Michigan,
March 1941 to August 1946

This book is dedicated to honor
the 170 men and women of the Armed Services during World War
II who were on the mailing list to receive the monthly newsletter,
the Zion Lutheran Messenger

I also dedicate this book to honor
Reverend Dallas Adler,
Pastor of Zion Lutheran Church,
October 1946 to January 1958

❧ACKNOWLEDGEMENTS❧

I would like to recognize and sincerely thank the following individuals who made my dream of publishing *A Word From Home* become a reality; by giving me encouragement, typing, and editing.

My nurses, John and Karen

Brandi Amborski
Johanna Amborski
Janice & Larry Baker
Brenda Blum
Larry Blum
Luann Brodbeck
Rocky Challen
Trudy Colvin
Clint & Darla Gaige
Jean Keim
Jo LaVigne
Bette Nutter
Lois Patek
Danielle Ringler
Mary Schaletz
Nancy Slovak
Jean Thieroff
Crystal Tressler
Mary Tressler
Estelle Verdin

❧Introduction❧

I'd like to tell you about Ottawa Lake, Michigan, in Whiteford Township of Monroe County. This little town, four miles north of the Ohio-Michigan state line is surrounded by ideal farmland, yet is still close to Toledo, Ohio for convenience.

In February 1941, men were called in the first draft from Monroe County. I, having five brothers: Clayton, Clyde, Leroy, Eugene, and Curtis (Olin), was very concerned. Leroy (Pete) Fischer was called in the 2nd draft in June. Our church, Zion Lutheran, had a very active young people's group called "Luther League". As the men & Inez Bieber (a nurse) from our church entered the Armed Services, we had a Farewell Party and a *New Testament Bible* was given to each one. Our service secretary, Geraldine (Gerrie) Schmidt, sent the church bulletins while the rest of us all wrote letters, sent cards on holidays & birthdays, and packages at Christmas.

Also at this time, some of the local churches were sending monthly newsletters. In February 1943, at our Luther League meeting, I suggested that we also have a monthly newsletter to send to our service men and women. The group then responded "If you'll be the editor, we'll do the work!"

Our first issue, printed in March 1943, consisted of 10 pages with 100 copies printed. Reverend Marcus J. Mueller (the Pastor of Zion Lutheran Church, Ottawa Lake, MI) developed a devotional page, which served as the cover of our first issue. Members of the League wrote the current news of our young people and other articles about the congregation and community. We wanted our Zion military

7

family, consisting of 16 men and one woman, to know what was happening while they were away from home.

All letters that Pastor Mueller and I received were printed in this paper, the *Zion Lutheran Messenger*. Later when we knew our service people didn't have time to write to us, their families and friends would share their letters. A list of military addresses, with changes, was always listed at the end of each newsletter. Because of this paper, many of them met overseas. Censorship also had to be watched. If a letter was printed, the address of the writer was omitted from that issue.

In six months time, our printed copy numbers reached 250, and material was submitted by the 10th of each month. Archie Collins, from Sylvania, Ohio, did the artwork for our covers. Lillian (Glanzman) Sieler also drew pictures. Wilma (Brodbeck) Fetzer and Betty (Bexten) Knisel were the Co-Editors. Mrs. Fred Root (Aunt Nellie), from Sylvania, O., wrote poems each month.

To give you an idea of our actual hands-on operation, I'd like to share this excerpt from the August 1943 issue:

Birdseye View of the Messenger Staff at Work on July Issue

"It happened at the Fischer home on the evenings of July 13 and 14. All the materials had been collected; the dining room table had three extra leaves added to make it larger for the typing crew, which consisted of Wilma Brodbeck, Wanda Trombly, Norma Dunkleman, and Violet Fischer who cut the stencils. On a card table in the same room were Betty Bexten and Eldora Fischer very busily drawing the cover page and little figures. In the living room on the table, matted with newspapers was the press (mimeograph) which wasn't given a minutes rest once the gang started running each page. These faithful workers were the following: Herman Nieman, Junior Sanderson, Eugene Fischer, Rev. Mueller, and Eldora Fischer.

In the same room was the decoration crew: Gerrie and Lucille Schmidt and Lillian Sieler who gave our cover page a bit of color.

Everyone worked hard and you should have heard the noise they made. It sounded like a newspaper office.

8

About twelve bells after a little snack had refreshed them the 'Messenger' was ready to be stapled. Some folded it for mailing to you while Norma addressed the envelopes. Imagine Pete Fischer's embarrassment if Norma wouldn't have noticed a slight mistake of title on Pete's envelope. Did you say slight? Just Cpt. (Captain) instead of Cpl. (Corporal).

213 copies were made and we hope to increase this number to 250."

Parents, grandparents, and friends gave names of their loved ones to be put on the mailing list. For the first 3 months the paper was 8 ½" x 11" and it went to 11" x 14".

By 1944, my eldest brother Clayton, already serving in the Army, told me to go to *The Toledo Blade* to get our paper supply from Paul Schultz. Paul also told me to gather the pictures of the 170 military men and women so he could put the pictures on the cover page. He also came out to the church and took pictures of their parents and a group picture of the *Zion Lutheran Messenger* staff and workers. Each month a list of the workers, as well as, people and businesses giving a donation for the previous month, was printed in the next issue. When the service men were home on furlough, they would help, too.

This church and community project continued until the last issue dated September/October 1946. By then 500 copies were duplicated each month. Thirty-one men and one Army nurse served from Zion Lutheran Church, with 170 service men and women on our mailing list. Copies of the paper were left behind in the USOs in many countries; strangers would read it and then asked to be added to the mailing list.

Now I'd like to bring you up to date and tell you how I arrived at the decision to compile and preserve the *Zion Lutheran Messenger* into this book.

In January 2000, I was living at the Lutheran Village of Wolf Creek; Holland, Ohio, and wanted to read all 269 pages of the *Zion Lutheran Messenger* at the same time. Earlier, in the Spring of 1996,

I had looked through this paper and pulled out many of the issues to prepare a history lesson for 8th grade students at Eisenhower Middle School; Oregon, Ohio. My son-in-law, Larry Baker (an American History teacher) had asked his mother, Kathleen Baker, and me to speak to an enriched group of students who were studying World War II. Kathleen and I spoke about the role of women during the war. I took several issues of the *Zion Lutheran Messenger* to use as visual aids.

One day while reading, two of my nurses (Karen and John), seeing the condition of the pages suggested that I create a book to preserve this history. When talking to my son, Al, he said that a videotape could be produced. He and his wife, Jeri, who managed a public TV station at the time, came to Toledo to videotape others and me from Zion Lutheran Church; Ottawa Lake, Mich.

Inez (Bieber) Richey, the Army nurse, was interviewed at her home in Sylvania, Ohio. The next day, in front of the altar at Zion, Al and Jeri interviewed Wilma (Brodbeck) Fetzer, Betty (Bexten) Knisel, and myself. World War II veterans interviewed included: Horace Nearhood, Bert Vesey, Leo Bexten, Ronald Ostrander, Martin Seitz, and LeRoy Bunge. I was so pleased with how the video turned out, I no longer felt the need to write and publish a book.

But my opinion changed when the World Trade Center in New York City and the Pentagon in Washington, D.C. were attacked by terrorists on September 11, 2001. I decided that the book did, in fact, need to be finished to honor all of those who served in the military, as I realized that our little community's history must be preserved.

My daughter, Jan (Gaige) Baker, helped me organize the materials needed so that my many volunteer typists from Wolf Creek and elsewhere, could turn faded printed pages into modern computer discs. This book could not have been made without their time and dedication. Please see the listing of those special people who I would like to acknowledge. I sincerely appreciate their endeavors.

There are a lot of letters that we received from overseas included in the pages that follow. However, due to space limitations, it does not include the news articles of the Luther League, the congregation, and the community.

My parents were Christian W. and Ella (Beck) Fischer. I celebrated my 88th birthday in June and am in a wheelchair most of the time, yet able to walk short distances with a walker. I am blessed to have a loving family who has supported my efforts in publishing *A Word From Home*. My three children are Mel, Jan, and Al.

I would like to thank Mel and his wife, Georgia, for helping me to store these precious documents throughout the years. Jan and Larry were helpful in the editing phase. Larry also gave me the opportunity to share my knowledge with the youth of today, giving me the spark. Al and Jeri lit the fuse by producing the video *Calming the Storm – Morale from the Home Front!*

My 3 grandchildren are Tad, Tara, and Clint. Clint, my publisher and the President of Quiet Storm Publishing, designed the book jacket. My three great-grandchildren include Emileigh, Bryce, and Zoe.

Violet (Fischer) Gaige
July, 2003

❧ EDITOR'S NOTE ❧

This book is an interesting study of the war fought at home and in the trenches. The Zion Messenger was a newspaper published by a small volunteer staff of the Ottawa Lake Lutheran Church. As a boy, my father found copies of the newspaper and read them with great interest.

Forty years later, the opportunity to publish this was presented to me. I, of course, had heard of the newspaper, but had never actually read them. In the editing process, I began to read with great interest the letters from these same men that had fought World War II. I am well aware that no one likes an editor and I wish we could have included every written word, but that was not possible. A book including every single page of every single paper would have exceeded 1000 pages. Instead, what I have attempted to do is remove letters that spoke of personal notes, birthdays, outings in the states and such. I have placed my focus on the feelings of those that served overseas, with occasional notes from those that served stateside. I have not corrected the letters themselves; all I have tried to do is decide what should be included and what should be left out. When you make these kinds of decisions, someone is bound to feel slighted. To them, I apologize.

What fascinates me most is how much I could relate to these stories, especially as a child of the last years of The Cold War. I could identify with the generation of my grandparents in a way that had not been possible before. Sure, I have spoken with them and discussed the issues they faced, but memories fade. These letters were written with the memory fresh and contain vivid details that had never been available to me before.

I hope that my editing efforts serve the memory of those that served, both those that came home and those who did not.

The one truth is that this isn't a Hollywood War. As you read, the death of one of the hometown boys isn't marked with fanfare, or a stirring musical score. It shocked me how sudden death really is. One moment we are reading a letter from a soldier and then suddenly we don't see any letters for a while. Shockingly, the inevitable is shared with us. That soldier will not be coming home.

I also hope you walk away from this book with a better understanding of the time and the people who fought in World War II. These were our Grandparents; these were the people who bounced us on their knee as children. These were the people that held us and gave us comfort. These were the people who fought an ugly war to stem the tide of naked aggression. To quote Winston Churchill, "never has so much, been owed to so few."

-Clint Gaige, Editor

❧MESSENGER STAFF❧

Advisor: Rev. Mueller

Editor: Violet Fischer

Assistant Editor: Wilma Brodbeck and Betty Bexten

Reporters:
   League News: Lucille Schmidt.
   Church and community news: Mrs. Viola Osborn.
   Jokes, scripture verses, and stories: Geraldine Schmidt.

Cover Page: Geraldine Schmidt.

Coloring of cover page for the service men and Inez:
   Geraldine Schmidt and Lillian Sieler

Artist: Mr. Archie Collins, Sylvania, Ohio

Circulation: Mrs. Mildred Shoemaker and Mrs. Elise Dominique

Mimeographing crew: Jr. Sanderson, Leo Bexten, Ronald
   Brining, Clifford Papenhagen, Eugene Fischer, Rev.
   Mueller, Herman Nieman, Mrs. Mueller, and Ethel
   Komsteller.

Helpers: League members.

Proof reader: Mrs. Marcus Mueller.

Treasurer: Mrs. Viola Osborn.

Right Off The Cob!!!!!!!!!!!!!

1943

Ottawa Lake, Mich.
September 1943

TO OUR FIGHTING MEN AND WOMEN:

Greetings! Once again comes the opportunity to say a few words. Some of you have gone across, while others are still on USA soil. Recently a missionary from a well-known battle area lodged overnight here at the parsonage. He remarked that when he first set foot on US soil, the ground looked good enough to kiss. Naturally, he meant that life in U.S. far surpassed the standards of living elsewhere. For that we all should be truly grateful, giving all due praise to the Lord of nations.

From many quarters we hear words of commendation of the paper,—THE MESSENGER. Of course, it surely deserves every support. Yet, to covet any personal acclaim. We have a large corps of workers—perhaps as many as 20. All the work is voluntary, no one receives any pay, and the cost of materials has been fully met by voluntary subscriptions because the obligations that are involved in such transactions are beyond our present facilities. Here at home, the paper is distributed at church usually on the third Sunday of each month. A few copies are mailed regularly to people in the vicinity, who have no direct connection with our church. About 75 copies are mailed to service men and women.

As is evidenced from the letters that we receive, The Messenger serves as a real friendly agent. Naturally, we hope that each issue is a living reminder that this paper is published by eager Luther Leaguers, whose motto still is WITH CHRIST FOR CHRIST. It is in the spirit of Christ that we send this paper on its way.

October 31st, by the way, is Reformation Festival. Some of you may be singing the battle hymn of the Reformation "A Mighty Fortress Is Our God" in or near Germany. It was Martin Luther, you remember, who composed this wonderful and inspiring hymn, basing it on Psalm 46. We point you to this Psalm (the 46th), and say let the Word of God give you strength, and courage, and cheer. The strength of the Lord is our joy; our joy in the lord is our strength.

Cheerio—
Your Pastor and Friend

అఅఅ

SOLDIER FRIENDS MEET ON FOREIGN SOIL.

The good news from letters received by Olin Koester and Mr. and Mrs. George Schmidt tell us that Kenny Brodbeck looked up Howard "Huck" Schmidt on August 27th at his army post over there. You can be assured it was the best news of the month and all of their friends rejoice in their good fortune and hope they can get together quite often.

The following is the letter written by both the boys to Olin Koester:

"Well here we are both together again just like the days back home only one thing missing and that is the rest of the gang.

I got a letter from Huck yesterday and he said he saw some of our trucks around where he is so I decided to look him up and here we are together. We are only about six miles apart at present and looks like we will be together thru the thick of it. Now I will tune in on Huck.

Well, here I am tuned in again. Of all days I would have to be on guard so we are sitting at the guard tent writing this wonderful letter to you fellows. There isn't much we can do, as I can't leave the place to go anywhere so we just have to stick around here. I will let Kenny take over.

Here, I am again while Huck fixes up the guard book. I have my camera with me so we will take a few pictures and I will send them home if I get a chance later on. We are both living in doghouses with the soft ground for a bed. Huck certainly was a surprised boy when I stuck my head out of the tent and said "Hello". I will let him finish this.

Boy, he wasn't only saying it when he said I was surprised when he stuck his head out of my tent. I was in town and when I got back to camp they told me about someone looking for me so I asked them what kind of a built fellow he was and they told me so I thought it must be him so I asked if he was still there and they didn't know so thought he left. I started for my "Dog house" and out he came and so we still are here together and he is smoking a cigar and I am trying to keep the flies off of me."

--Two of the old gang, Huck and Ken.

OUR LEAGUE AND LEAGUERS

On August 26 our Luther League met at the church basement. We entertained Luther Leagues from Maybee, Dundee, and Riga with about 70 Leaguers attending. Junior Sandersone gave a very interesting and vivid account of the Delegates School that was held at Dubuque, Iowa on August 17 to 21. This was for District and Federation presidents. Jr took Trumar Helzer's place who was not able to attend. Eugene Fischer gave a report on the Luther League projects, G.F.O. and the Resolutions at the school. Naturally, it wasn't all work and no play because they had just lots of fur. They had a picnic, a banquet, a play and the people treated them swell. We were glad they represented Ottawa Lake and that they brought back with them new enthusiasm for our Luther League.

After playing several games partners were chosen and each couple had to go through the furnace room which was fixed up as a "Haunted House" with ghosts and everything before getting their eats. Everyone reported a good time and we hope to entertain again.

I though boy could start any car that came along. Anyway. Clifford Papenhagen couldn't find the starter on a Ford the evening at League Meeting. Cliff P. and Leroy Bunge being very nice gentlemen were helping Lucille Schmidt in getting her car out of the car jam in the church drive. Some fellows park their car in the dumbest places, e.g. Don Consear. Leroy yelled for Cliff to move another car Lucille could get her car out and Cliff ready to help opens the car door only to find a man asleep in the front seat. I don't know which one was scared the most, Cliff or the sleeping man. Leroy was of great help as he stood very still. The girls were a great help too. All they did was laugh at the two boys. Anyway, Gerrie and Lucille got home safe and sound and thanks a lot boys. You were a great help. What would we do without our boys?

Betty Bexten is doing all right for herself. She now rides the bike around. I wonder why? It wouldn't be the three gallons of gas.

Elroy Rittner was seen with that cute, dark-eyed gal again. Seems her name is JoAnn and she is the ex-steady of one of our boys by the name of LeRoy. Guess she likes that name.

Who is Junior Sanderson thinking of these cool nights? Come on Junior, stop keeping it a secret.

Clyde Papenhagen had an appendicitis operation last month at the Bixby Hospital in Adrian. Glad to hear that he's improving fast and it will seem good to see him in Sunday school and church again.

Our Luther League is selling Christmas cards again this year.

Well, it's back to school again and we have a good representation at Burnham this year from our Luther League.

Here are some of the names of those attending: Juanita Brier, Ronald Brining, Doris Fink, Joann and Janet Jacobs, Lois Kodelman, Juanita Nearhood, Mildred Faselk, Marvin Fink, Dean Beck, Betty Hammons, Bernice Ahleman and others. Relmond "Chub" Bunge is going to Iambertville High again.

Wilma Brodbeck and Betty Bexten with several friends vacationed at Mrs. Ida Brodbeck. We have organized a regular staff now to make our paper work more efficiently and the "Staff" will appear on one of the pages of this paper.

Melva Hall and Elda Kopp are spending a couple weeks up at Indian River, Mich. with Mr. and Mrs. Harry Smith and Dannie.

TO THE NURSES IN WHITE

This month the "Messenger" is paying a special tribute to the nurses who are serving their country in aiding the boys who are in the armed forces. Every citizen is very proud of them and they can be assured wherever they are stationed our thoughts and best wishes go with them always. That brings us very close to home since Zion has a representative better known as 2nd. Lt. Inez Bieber. We miss her letter this month but realize that duty comes first so will be content to wait until later. The Staff members of Zion, and all your friends wish you God's Blessing and hope that your new location will be as enjoyable as your past in Indiana and Kentucky.

OUR LEAGUE AND LEAGUERS

Mrs. Eldora Fischer was given a farewell party on August 25 before she left for Tyler, Texas to join Clayton. Outdoor movies were enjoyed Twenty-six people attended and the guest of honor was presented with a pen and pencil set by the group. She has arrived in Texas and has acquired a bit of tan. She writes us too that she likes it a lot and is located at 132 South Beckham, Tyler, Texas.

Two Canadian Air Cadets were very nice and posed for Lucille Schmidt when she asked them to. After the picture the boys told some interesting stories of their Army life.

Gladys Fisher is caring for her sister's, Mrs. Goldie Kock, three little girls while their mother is convalescing at the Sanitarium at Howell, Michigan.

Ronald Brining seems to join Bill Brodbeck often in Bill's cow barn. Wonder if they sing like Fritz, Pete, and Olie Fischer used to while they milked. The boys always said their singing kept the cows contented.

Gerrie and Lucille Schmidt and Violet Fischer were guests of Mr. and Mrs. Richard Kummerow in Detroit over Labor Day. They attended Rev. Dodt's church and Sunday school.

There is a committee working on a play to be given sometime in the future. You'll hear more about this play, boys.

We can't say Doris Fink doesn't work. She even broke her glasses when sweeping the floor the other day.

Ronald Brining is in such a hurry to see his hometown that he passes everybody going 25 from Sylvania to Ottawa Lake.

Who is that handsome fellow that walks down the hallways with Joann Jacobs at high school?

✍✍✍

BITS OF NEWS FROM HERE AND THERE

Since our last "Messenger" Erica and Henry Lunde have been really seeing the States. We were very glad to see both of them when they dropped in at the Halter home to visit her

23

parents when they were enroute to Miami, Florida from San Francisco, California. Erica spent a few days at home before joining Henry at Miami. In the meantime Henry was visited by Kurt and then he was sent on to Boston. Since Kurt was coming to Miami for the weekend Erica stayed and saw Kurt before leaving for Boston. While in New York Erica Surprised Mr. Halter who was also in New York at that time. Together they visited relatives in New Jersey. They both seem to like Boston quite well. They have a four-room apartment there.

Paul Freeland, being well known here from his visits in the Halter home while stationed in Toledo, had a ten-day furlough. On his way back from his home in Conn. he stopped in to see "Mom and Dad" Halter and saw other friends here and in Toledo. He looks swell in his dress uniform and has his T/Sgt. Stripes now. He is in the Marine Corps. How is your little car, Paul? He is stationed at Sand Diego, Cal.

Burt Vesey, son of Mr. And Mrs. Wade Vesey, had a fifteen-day furlough from Camp Crowder, Missouri where he is in the Signal Corps. He likes his work very much. He attended school for six months. His camp has about 65,000 soldiers in it. He has been in service eight months now and they are right in the "Heart of the Ozarks".

All of Joe Steiner's friends will be glad to know that he is out with his company again and writes that he'll be having a seven day furlough soon. Hope you have a good time, Joe.

The following bit of news was in a clipping from the Monroe news: Private Floyd Gray, Jr., son of Mr. And Mrs. Floyd William Gray of Route 2 Ottawa Lake, has arrived at the University of Cincinnati for Army specialized training program basic engineering work with the 1555th Service Unit. Private Gray attended Burnham High School. Before being assigned to the University of Cincinnati, he was stationed at Fort Bragg, North Carolina.

In a recent letter from Arnold (Barney) Kummerow he enjoys the paper a lot and wishes to thank the Luther League for sending it. He works at the U.S.O. at night. He went out to

Cape Cod swimming and the waves came rolling in four or five feet high. He's fine and hopes everybody in Ottawa Lake is too.

Sam Felt writes from Topeka, Kansas that he has been receiving the "Messenger" and enjoys it a lot and wishes to thank all those who help make it possible for the boys to receive it. He's fine and likes Kansas real well.

Lt. And Mrs. Franklin Kummerow is now stationed at Boise, Idaho.

"Petty irritations are like a bee's sting—only a fraction of an inch long; the rest is imagination."

Bits of news from Edgar Strable
written at Peoria, Illinois

Dear Mom:

I received all your letters and I am sure glad to get them.

I got my copy of the "Messenger" two days ago. I think it is a fine paper. This month they have two more of my buddies' addresses in it. Now I can drop them a line.

I have a pass this weekend to Ft. Wayne, Indiana. Thought I could get a pass for Toledo, but that was too far. They will not issue a pass that far away. I only have from 4:00 P.M. Sat. until 12:00 P.M. on Sunday, so you see it didn't give me too much time.

I had a fairly good time at Ft. Wayne. I met a civilian couple by the names of Max and Gladys who are married. He is one day older than I am and he leaves for the army in a few weeks so we had s party Saturday night.

I got up early last Sunday morning and went to church. I went strolling down the avenue and went to the first Lutheran church I found. It was a Salem (Swedish). They have a lot of different ways, so different than ours, but I guess it all meant the same. I found out where St. Paul's Lutheran Church is. It's not far from the Hotel and I'm going there next Sunday.

We have been very busy here lately. They sure are giving us a lot to learn, in a short time. This course used to e for 12 weeks and now it is cut down to six so you can see how we are rushed but I guess I'll make it.

We are still as busy as can be. We have only two more weeks here and then I may get to see you all. Some of the boys from another camp have received their furloughs already so I'm keeping my fingers crossed.

Well, Mom says "Hello" to everyone. I'm O.K. and gaining weight, I'll try to see you all soon.

--Your loving son,
Ed (Edgar Strable)

Parts of letters from William DeNudt to his wife, Bernice:

"I received the "Messenger" and was very glad to receive it and see where all the boys are stationed and their news. And now I am also receiving the A drain Telegram but it doesn't come very regular. When I receive it I get it all in one bunch, seven to eight papers at a time. And then it keeps me busy to keep caught up with what is all going on around home. These days we are pretty busy. We get up at two o'clock in the morning and go to work. Hope you like the pictures in this letter. We are doing our own developing."

Fort Lewis, Wash.
August 31, 1943

Dear Mother and all,

Just a few lines tonight before I go to bed. Hope this finds you all well and happy. Well, Mom I got my pay today. $38.25, gee, isn't that a lot for a month's work. I am going to have to save all I can because I lost $15.00 when I lost my bill fold last month. Have you got my pictures yet? You should have by now. I must close. So long and may God Bless You all until I can get home to see you.
Hi Dad and kids.

--Your loving son,
Malcolm Gray

&ej &ej &ej

Del Rio, Texas
August 8, 1943

Dear Friends:

Well, believe it or not it's really me writing a letter, but really we are busy and its so awful hot here that when a person gets off of work, all you feel like doing is hit the sack, "bed".

Well, I made another stripe now, and that means just some more work and what a job. I'm Asst. Line Chief with just 2 50 men to take care of.

By the way I haven't lost the weight I put on while home on furlough. I'm very glad to hear that Mrs. Mueller is home and feeling better. I got a letter from Doris today, she is on furlough in Louisiana with her Uncle and Aunt, but will be back soon.

Well, it's about 2:30 in the morning and I have some forms to check so I'll say so long for now.

Sorry to hear about Carl Beck.

--Sincerely,
T/Sgt. Frank Schumacher

ꙮꙮꙮ

Miami Beach, Florida
August 26, 1943

Dear Leaguers:

I received an August copy of the messenger, I didn't know the Luther League was printing a messenger and I was very much surprised when I opened the envelope. Thanks for sending it as I appreciate it. I have enclosed a contribution towards this messenger.

I have been here a month, and I don't consider the basic air corps training here though, although, I don't have much free time. We have lectures concerning camouflages, nomenclature of rifles, and chemical warfare. We have schooling of a soldier one hour every day on the drill field. Every Wednesday we have to strap on our gas mask for the day and enjoy the period spent on the beach. We have calisthenics for about an hour and then we are allowed to swim in the ocean. Sometimes the waves are quite high and it is fun riding them. Unlike the cool lakes of Michigan, the water is warm.

These hotel rooms are nice to stay in. The showers in them are very handy. It is much easier to keep one of these hotels clean than a barracks.

One Saturday afternoon I saw a naval airplane fall into the deep blue ocean. The pilot bailed out and the wind drifted him in over the beach.

Every soldier who has never been on this beach before is amazed at this romantic playground of America. The moon over Miami is beautiful. I never saw so many beautiful hotel building before. Between these hotels are many tall palm trees.

I will soon be leaving here, and I hope I may be able to return as a civilian in the future.

We have to turn our lights out at 9:00 P.M. so I will have to lay my pen down.

--Sincerely,
Bernard Myers

এড়এড়এড়

Sheppard Field, Texas
August 31, 1943

Dear Friends:

Things have shown little progress here at Sheppard Field. In fact, everything has slowed up considerable—even the temperature has dropped, but that only slightly.

To fill in time while awaiting shipment to some technical school from here. I am now working nights as a filing clerk here at Headquarters in the school assignment section. I tried the other night to hunt Wesley Van Dyke and Frank Schumacher's file cards, but apparently they have been put away in a composite file of those who went through here quite some time ago.

Since the Physical Training School is temporarily closed while moving, I have been reclassified into weather observer school. When and where I'll ship I don't really know. But I'm hoping it will be soon, for a place does get monotonous after a time.

We have yet to see a good rain here since I came here the first week of June. (It did rain one night shortly after I arrived, but that didn't even settle the dust of the old "cow pasture", our physical training field.)

No, there's not much to say, so I'll say adieu, and hope to have a change of address by next month.

I am fine and hope all fronts are the same.

--As Ever,
"Olie"
Pvt. Curtis D. Fischer

ৡৢৡৢৡ

Sheppard Field Texas
August 1943

Dear Friends:

I wish to thank you for sending me "The Zion Lutheran Messenger", and have enjoyed it very much as it brings me all the news from back home and that is about all we can look forward to while we are here in camp.

I am very sorry that I didn't get to thank you sooner but since I received my first messenger I have transferred into the air corps. I have been classified as air mechanic and aerial gunner and should be leaving soon for school but I am hoping that the messenger will follow me through.

I was very sorry to read of the death of a good friend of mine, Carl Beck, "But the Lord knows best".

Thank you and the one's that make the messenger possible and I'm sorry I didn't get to thank you sooner.

I remain,
A Hometown boy,
Harry W. Hill

North Africa
August 24, 1943

Dear Leaguers:

Well, I haven't much to write about for this time, but will do my best. It is kinda hard to write letters when you can't think of much to talk about and that is my trouble. You know I don't get around much anymore, and that leaves me just looking at these Arab's and they can't talk so I can understand them and if they try to tell something I just don't catch on.

You look out towards the fields and all you see is grapes and hills you can't see how the corn, potatoes, wheat, etc. Grow because they don't grow any that I have seen. I have seen some wheat fields so I can't discuss our crop situation over so you know how I stand, there isn't much I can talk about that I haven't already written to you about.

I wrote letters to Pete and Ken the other day, I don't think Ken is very far away from me. I found out where his outfit is but it seems I never get a chance to go over there. I can almost see the place from where I am at and I still have my fingers crossed that I can get to see him. Boy, we will have a lot to talk about whenever we get back to good old Ottawa Lake again and I hope it isn't long until we do because there isn't a place better than being back in good old U.S.A. again. I couldn't wait until I got over here and now I can't wait until I get back.

I hear Lucille has her car all fixed up now so she doesn't have to worry about it; but the only worry she has is getting gasoline to drive it.

Well, I see where they have Olin in Texas, almost the same place Peco started from. I wonder how he likes Texas. I always wish I was back there again. I would never holler about it like I used to. Boy, I thought that was some place to be but I will take it back again.

Well, I guess I will have to close as I am running out of words.

So long and God Bless You.

--As Ever,
Howard Schmidt
"Huck"

❧❧❧

Fort Leonard Wood, Mo.
Sept. 5, 1943

Dear Mom, Dad, and brothers and sisters,

Well how is everybody at home? I hope O.K. I am just fine. I just got back from seeing a show. It was "Heaven Can Wait". It was really a good show. I just finished writing Elwin Beck and Don Hart. I just received a letter from Grandma Briggs and I received one from Grandma Nearhood last week.

By the time you get this letter you should have received the pictures I sent of Fat and myself. Fat had a pass yesterday and today he just got back about an hour ago. I get a pass next week and I'd like to see several things while I'm in town.

We have a new General in charge of the 75th division. He has been in the Army for 31 years. The other General has gone overseas and we have a new Regimental Commander also. That is about all I have to say for now.

--Your son,
Horace Nearhood

❧❧❧

Camp Murphy, Florida
August, 1943

Dear Friends:

Well, here once again is a little news from the land of sunshine, and believe me there is quite an excess of it. I have a slight revision to add to the washing method explained a few issues ago by Olin, I believe. Anyhow, the new army method is as follows:

First find a good brush and some soap and proceed to the shower room with the dirty clothes. Next insert yourself in them, and get some nice lukewarm water from the shower. Next insert yourself with the clothes to be washed on you and using soap and the shower and brush as a combination go to work. They say it works swell.

The army is sure a queer place. First I write to Wilbur at Miami and get an answer back from Lincoln, Nebraska. Anyhow, I told him I'd come to see him but now I've changed my mind.

I have quite an incident happen the other day though. It was this way. I was quite simply doing nothing one fine morning when I was supposed to be working, and so was another fellow, so the conversation drifted. I told him my name was Durst, and he said he used to know w fellow by that name and wondered if we were related. After a time it became evident that we went to Burnham together. His name is Sullivan; maybe some of you know him.

I thought good fortune had hit me when my sister and Brother-in-law came to Miami. Henry was going to school there and Erica came down to stay. It looked good till the navy decided to transfer him to Boston and not let him go to school.

I have a very severe complaint to make on our little camp. It isn't passes, because we get them every night till one. Of course, there's no place to go, and the beach is closed after dark, but that's the army. My main complaint though is that at

5:00 A.M. they throw us out of bed. Next place I go I hope they let me sleep all night.

Well there's one thing I believe we can all say, it doesn't matter where in the world we are, the place that rates tops is a little place called Ottawa Lake.

--Bye for Now,
Kurt

৵৵৵

Dear Readers of the Zion Lutheran Messenger:

I received the July issue of your monthly paper, and really enjoyed reading it. I have been wanted to write to you before, but it seems as though I just never can get caught up with my regular correspondence.

I am still here at San Luis Obispo and it is a mystery as to when we will move, if we move, and where we will go. Part of our Division has moved out to parts unknown.

For some reason or other I would like to describe the scene of the writing: It is 9:15 P.M. and I am seated at a small table beside a burning stove. The light is shining directly over me and as I listen to the fire "Crickle" it sort of carries me back home to those winter nights when it was really cold outside, and I used to stand over a hot fire trying to pop some corn. Our huts are approximately 15' square and there are six of us that stay in them. I would like to stress the fact that we are able to carry with us memories of the things we enjoyed so much years ago.

When I mentioned about "Memories", before, I also had in mind the swell time I had last weekend. Saturday afternoon I went to Santa Maria to visit my relatives. They are beginning to feel like part of the family to me. Sunday morning I went to S. S. and Church with them and in the afternoon they held their annual S. S. picnic. It was the first picnic I have been able to attend for a long time. After the meal the men and us fellows had a ball game and some played horseshoe. We also enjoyed contests. In one of the contests we had to put a grain of rice from one plate to another with a toothpick, only one grain at a time of course. I didn't do so good at it, but enjoyed myself anyway. It reminded me of the S. S. picnic we used to have in Schroeder's Grove every 3rd Sunday in June. The people there are all so friendly and they really make you feel at home. I have attend Services there several times and heir minister, Rev. Meiger, is a swell speaker and is really doing his part in making the boys in Service feel at home. Every Sunday afternoon they entertain service men and then have super for them.

I enjoyed myself so much last weekend that just had to pass it on to you.

--Your fellow member of Zion,
and your fellow Leaguer,
"Pete"

ళళళ

Camp Fannin, Texas
Sept. 12, 1943

Fellow-Leaguers:

We are now about to open our cycle here at Camp Fannin. Already we have had about a week of pre-cycle training for our men. It is greatly different to be a leader and instructor rather than a trainee. Now I must tell others how to do things, show them how to do it, and make corrections. To our men now in the service I am known as a Cadreman. Some may like their cadreman while others look with scorn on their instructors and corrections. Nevertheless they are working for the interest of the trainees and they can appreciate the position of the trainee for they once were in their training days.

It is grand to have my wife at Tyler near me. However, the army is still busy place and so I cannot spend much time away. The barracks is a beehive at the opening of the cycle for there are so many things that must be shown to the trainees.

I have been assigned to the 4th platoon and men in our group are 35 years of age or over. These men are somewhat different than men in their teens and training will be a little difficult at first.

I am feeling fine and hope that my buddies are also enjoying good health wherever they may be.

As ever,
Clayton Fischer.

ৎৎৎ

North Africa
Sept. 1, 1943

Dear Folks:

There isn't much to say as things are about the same. We work, eat, and sleep and go to some French peoples house to eat.

I was one last week for a chicken supper and am invited back again tomorrow night with another fellow. I don't know for sure if I will go or not as I have a two-day pass coming up starting tomorrow but don't know if I will go any place or just stay here.

They have their potatoes all dug, threshing done, and even have their corn husked over here.

Yes, I received the package a while back. Everything was in good condition. We don't have to cook but when we are hungry about 8:00 P.M. then we cook stuff to eat.

I haven't seen anybody that I knew here yet outside of our own bunch. Did they have Sports Day at the Lake this year? I sure am missing out on a lot of them but will try to make the one next year.

Well, I guess I will close for this time, so tell the people "Hello" and write when you can.

Your Son,
"Spud" Raymond Shanly

෴

August 15, 1943

Dear Leaguers:

Just a line to let you know I am busy nowadays back down here in those hilly midlands of England. It is like "Deep in the Heart of Texas" only we don't have the hot and dry weather as a year ago. Crops are good, no corn. The farmers are busy harvesting wheat now.

I received several nice birthday cards from the U.S.A., thanks a lot! It was quite warm here on the 30th. A hard day of duty and slept in the guardhouse over night. I received that picture of Inez O.K. that you sent also the July issue of the "Zion Lutheran Messenger".

We cannot buy ham, eggs, and steak here like we could in Ireland.

Was invited out to neighbor camp service, Cavalry (Mecg) Colonel D.W. McGowan Commanding, Capt. Don H. Heard, Chaplain, from the pan handle country of Texas.

One of the Lieutenants is going to be baptized this evening.

Yours sincerely,
Elg.

৵৵৵

Dear Leaguers:

They say better late than never. For over a week I've planned to write this letter but really and truly I've been very busy. Kurt Durst wrote to me trying to make arrangements to meet me in Miami, Florida but the army had a different idea. They sent me here.

Our work is progressing very well here and after I had written to about everyone I knew what I was doing here, we had orders to tell nothing. Our work is supposed to be a military secret. They don't want anyone to know about it. I had to laugh when I heard the order as the day before I read my letter in the "messenger" and the remark about the 250 copies being sent all over the world. I hope our General doesn't get a copy or it will be the guardhouse for me.

I enjoyed those letters and my copy of the paper very much. It seems to take away that feeling of being all-alone. You know where the other boys are and what they are doing. It brings you back to where we started from and one becomes amazed at how far this war has separated us. What stories some of us shall have to tell. I hope it may be possible to have a reunion after this is all over. I know I should look forward to such a thing.

I have been kept busy even on Sundays we have to work to catch up. It seems the Army always picks Sunday to move men around in camp. Two Sundays we have been doing that. Today our passes into town were all jumbled up and I was trying to straighten that out. I did manage to get into town around 11:00. What a relief to get away from camp.

   Must close now.

   As Ever,
   Wig

✌✌✌

KENNETH B: " I bumped into Huck Schmidt on the street in town yesterday ".
PETE FISCHER: "What did he have to say?"
KENNETH B: "Nothing. My truck knocked him unconscious."

✌✌✌

Texas Tech.
August 17, 1943

Dear Friends:

   Have received your second paper, and am sorry I haven't answered before but I have been pretty busy. I went from Toledo to Columbus, from Columbus to Koosler Field, Mississippi, I was there thirty-seven days, and what days they were! All work and very warm from 105 to 125 all the time. Now I'm here at college in Lubbock, Texas. It's swell here, good eats, and a lot of school. We are studying math, English, physics and history. Besides physical exercise and drill. They take good care of us but are very strict. We get only ten hours flying time here. We will be here from three to five months. From here we go to Santa Ann California. If we pass there we will go to some flying field. It's quite a job to do but we all expect to make it. All we can do is try. The weather here is swell. It's very warm

39

but you don't sweat much. Well, as for news I guess there is nothing to say.

Very truly yours,
Art Loomer.

❧❧❧

Somewhere in the South Pacific
August 24, 1943

Dear Violet and Leaguers:

Will write a few lines to thank you all for the "Zion Lutheran Messenger" which I have been receiving for the past two months. I have started to write to you before but something always turns up and I would put it off. I hope today I will get it done before something turns up again.

Although I don't belong to the church I enjoy reading the Messenger very much. I have not been around Ottawa Lake and Sylvania for the past seven or eight years but there still are a lot of old friends of mine that I have lost track of and through the Messenger I have found out in what branch of service they are.

As my sister, Doris ahs probably told you I am in the Seabees of the Navy, and stationed somewhere in the South Pacific. The weather is fine. Just about like what they have in California. The only difference is it rains every two or three days. I will have to stop now. This V-mail doesn't give you much room for writing.

Sincerely,
Dale E. Viers, Sea 1/c

❧❧❧

Somewhere in Alaska
August 10, 1943

Hi Leaguers,

Well, I finally have time to write, but I don't know what to tell you because I can't think of anything to write about.

Anyway, I am somewhere in Alaska. Undoubtedly you would like to know where and I would like to tell you but can't because of the censorship rules.

I am right near to the best town in Alaska, at least I think so. They have a nice U.S.O. where they hold dances and parties at least once a week. They also have a swell Lutheran church. We go there with a lot of civilians. It seems nice to step in a church with some native Alaskans. It is a lot better than going to a place where you are among a group of soldiers. But after all a good Christian organization is the best thing a soldier can have.

I have seen some beautiful scenery since I left the States about a month ago but Ottawa Lake still looks best of all.

Cheerio,
Verne Jacobs.

✤✤✤

Somewhere in the Pacific
September 1, 1943

Dear Violet and Leaguers:

I received a copy of the "Messenger" and I enjoyed it very much and want to thank all who helped in any way to send the paper to me.

I am in the South Pacific. I cannot tell the place just yet but will in the near future. I never realized that the ocean was so large nor that water could be so blue. I never missed a meal from being seasick. Some of my mates were very sick. When we crossed the equator we had quite a celebration, which I can tell you more about later.

I like the navy and my work very much. My course I took in Diesel Mechanic is helping me and I am getting lots of experience, which will help me when I get back.

We have good food in the Navy. We get ice cream every day and can go to a show every night if we ant to. They keep us very busy and the hardest job is scrubbing our "whites." I will be a good washwoman before this war is over.

Thanking you again for the paper.

Goodbye,
Alvin C. Miller

ๅๅๅ

Alameda, California
August 16, 1943

Dear Friends:

I have been receiving the "Messenger" for the past few months and it has added greatly to refresh the memory of the fellows and girls I knew back home. It is hard to express the appreciation I feel, however, it means a lot and I wish to thank you all.

I am still in Alameda, California where I have been for the past four months. I am working in a dive-bombing squadron and the work is quite enjoyable. We work long and hard hours, but there are no complaints as we realize what the other fellows are going through.

The weather here has been excellent and most of my liberties have been spent at San Francisco beach.

Tell LeRoy Bunge he should be more careful while riding on a motorcycle.

As time waits for no one I must end this letter and get back to work. I would appreciate greatly to hear from some of you and again I thank you for the paper.

Sincerely,
Franklin Fry

TRIBUTE DUE

Herbert Pattison serving in Uncle Sam's Navy is reported killed in action at the time the "Quincy" ship went down. He attended Lambertville High and was well-known in this community.

A telegram was received Monday by Mr. and Mrs. William Moore of Sylvania from the War Department confirming the death of their son, Lieut. Don Moore, who had been reported as missing in action four weeks ago. Besides his parents, Don is survived by his wife, the former Miss Doris Troutner, and a child born on the day he was reported missing. Also sisters Mary, Mildred, and Sally, and brothers George, Paul, Robert, and Ben. Don graduated from Burnham High School.

September 4, 1943

Dear Friends,

How are you all? I am swell. Just got back from Kisha. We were rather surprised them we got there to find the Japs had decided to give us the Island without trying to save their faces as they call it but were glad for the troops we were landing. Kisha isn't a bad place. It is one of the nicest islands up that way if it wasn't for tat heavy fog around those parts. We are very busy. Don't think I will be in the States long. I have reached the Officer stage now. I received my certificate for a birthday present the 30th of August.

How is everything going around Ottawa Lake? Sure would like to see it again. I wish I could take all of you on a trip with me sometime so you could see some of the sights I have.

I get the "Messenger" and enjoy reading it. It is so nice to know what you all are doing. The best of luck to you all.

Garld "Chub" Holmes

Cornelius "Junior" Blome was in Sicily just two days after the invasion. He found the Italians a very friendly people; they even offered the boys wine. Nothing convoy and they brought back 20,000 Italian prisoners. They were very glad to get out of the German's hands. He read in the "Messenger" that some of the boys here are stationed at several places he's been but he hasn't seen anyone he knows so far. He gets the "Messenger every month and wants to thank the entire staff for printing such an interesting paper. He gave a generous donation to help meet expenses. He's fine and hopes when he gets his next furlough he'll see more of his friends here.

Alliance, Nebraska
September 22, 1943

Dear Millie:

Well, I feel a little better now after getting a good nights rest but I am still a little tired. I got my three day pass for Sunday, Monday and Tuesday so I went out to the ranch and helped Jimmie round up and drive his 300 head of cattle home from their summer pasture. I will tell you all about it.

Jimmie and I left Sunday afternoon about 12:00 o'clock. We took the horses out to the range where the cattle were. It took us four hours to get there and I sure was tired after riding twenty-five miles. We took a count of the cattle and then went up to some people house by the name of Hanson. It was about three miles from where the cattle were. We were to have supper with them and stay all night. After we had supper Jimmie, Hanson and myself went to see the man that Jimmie owed for the feeding of his cattle for the four months. After we got back to Hanson's we went to bed about 9:00 P.M. Jimmie said that I made so much noise that he could sleep, but I guess I did O.K. for when I hit the bed I was out.

We got up Monday morning at 4:30 and had breakfast and was out with the cattle at 5:30. It was still dark and cold. We got all the cattle together by 6:00 and started them home. We had a hard time holding them back for they were full of pep. Hanson helped up until we got them slowed down. After a couple hours they came down to earth and took their time. They went along O. K. until we came to sand hills and then we would have to push them over. All the time we were driving them through other cattle and we had to cut them out so that they could not get in with Jimmie's cattle. That sure is a job.

By 11:30 we were about eight miles from home and it sure was going slow by now. The cattle were so tired (and so was I) that every time you were not pushing them they would lay down. And to top everything else Wilma missed us and we didn't get any dinner.

Along in the afternoon I was riding a black horse that Jimmie had gotten and was leading him other horse, Penny. The black got a funny spell and gave a big jump. Penny would not move and she pulled me off my horse and did I hit hard. I thought that I lost my teeth. Boy! Did Jimmie get a kick out of that? Well, we got home at 5:00 o'clock and when I got off the horse I couldn't walk. We had something to eat and I went to bed at 7:30 and didn't get up until the next morning at 8:30. I got awfully tired and lame but I would like to go out and do it again. It was an experience that I won't forget for some time.

Love,
Bill

❧ ❧ ❧

Camp Fannin, Texas
Oct. 3, 1943

Dear Folks and all,
    I just received my rating yesterday. Eldora is sewing on my stripes for me. I'm sure glad she's down here to do that for me. Now it will be a little easier to give orders to the men for before they didn't see why they should take orders from me when I was only a private like themselves.
    There isn't much news here. I go into Tyler whenever I can and Eldora's working in the store to pass her extra time away.
    Our men are on the rifle range now and so we have been getting up at 4 and 4:30 A.M. Then the men work on their equipment until about 10:30 or 11 P.M. This makes a long day. It will let down a settle in a couple of days.
    We had heavy rains here early in the week and the sand at camp nearly washed away.

Your son,
Clayton Fischer

❧❧❧

North Africa
Sept. 3, 1943

Dear Violet and Leaguers:

After a wonderful ocean voyage arrived with our group in French North Africa. Must be near some of the other League member but unfortunately couldn't find their addresses in the last Messenger so don't know where or what outfits they are with. Was very happy to receive the "Messenger" just as I left the U.S.A.

Enjoyed being at sea on a well-equipped ocean liner. Really had all the comforts of home with plenty of delicious food, a daily wireless newspaper, and laundry service. We also had church Sunday morning and evening and daily devotional meetings. Every afternoon and evening we enjoyed programs of singing and other entertainment. Our group of nurses were the only gals aboard ship so I need not say we were well cared for with a shipload of soldiers. We went most of our time on deck watching the water. It rained one fore moon and this was the roughest the water got all during our trip, but it wasn't so rough that only a couple got seasick. We all enjoyed taking our turn of duty on the hospital deck of the ship.

Since our voyage has ended we are now happy in our new tent homes in North Africa. We live four or five to a tent and have nice cots and one electric light bulb in each tent. The country is beautiful, people are friendly, buildings are attractive and best of all is the perfect beach just a little ways from our tents.

Best regards to all,
Inez Bieber.

French North Africa
September 19, 1943

Dear Violet and Leaguers:

How are you and everyone at home? I'm O.K. Today is a pretty warm sunny day after a couple of real rainy ones like we had last spring, remember? Three of us girls went swimming this afternoon and we had more fun jumping to dodge the high waves.

A couple of nights ago I went to a dance with a fellow from East Toledo. He has been here over a year and was so glad to see my cousin and I, as we know lots of his friends from Toledo.

Received my first over sea letter yesterday and was glad Jess had a chance to get home and that everyone was well. I am unable to write about our work but as yet we haven't had much to do.

I am enclosing a piece of our money here thinking you might like to have it. It is 50 Francs, equal to our dollar. It looks exactly like our people here. Have seen several veiled ladies downtown. Three of us girls went shopping the other day but of course it amounted to mostly window-shopping as most of the things they have to sell we just wouldn't want. We also stopped at our Red Cross Club and had a large dish of chocolate ice cream and cake. It was so good as it is the first we have had since we've been here.

The other day when it rained we girls caught rainwater in our helmets and the next day it was sunny and warm we gave each other shampoos and had lots of fun.

The girls that I live with are so nice. Two of them, Miss Lee and Queen, are from Kentucky and the other Miss Magin is from Georgia. We have so many good times together and we decided one day that every morning when we were all together we would have a short Sunday school class. We read from our Testaments and discuss it and sing some hymns and sometimes other girls stop in too. Our short periods sometimes amount to at least an hour or more.

We have services here every Sunday in a large tent but not until 1:30, as that is when our pastor can come. I heard him say last Sunday that he delivers six sermons so he is very busy but we enjoy them so much.

Will close for this time with best regards to all, especially Rev. and Mrs. Mueller.

Sincerely yours,
Inez Bieber.

ஐஐஐ

Lincoln, Nebraska
Oct. 5, 1943

Dear Luther Leaguers,

This will have to be short, as I have to hurry up for chow. I received the "Messenger" and was very surprised to hear some of the news that was in it. How people do travel from month to month. You think of them here and they are there. I'm glad to see that a few reunions are taking place, as I know how it is to be miles from home and no one to talk about the things at home. I am still at Lincoln doing the same job. We do have hopes though of an early termination of our job. What follow we don't know. Today I have to go up for reclassification. I don't know what they will offer. I heard though that Permanent Party will not be sent to any of the Air Force Technical Schools. I'll probably be sent to some place where the wounded are being treated for recuperation. Those are mere rumors. Those who are in the army know how we live for those rumors. Probably I'll spend the winter in Lincoln.

I've been going to a Lutheran Church in Lincoln every Sunday. As my duties make it necessary for me to be back on the Base at noon I have to go to the nearest one in town. That church happens to be a Missouri Synod. Church. I've been in at the Lutheran Service Center in town a number to times. They certainly have a swell place and they really treat you nice. I enjoying to the Service Center so much and sometime I'll describe it to you.

I just heard the call for chow so I'll have to beat it. Write me all of you Leaguers!

As ever,
Wig (Wilbur Facklam)

᪥᪥᪥

O.A.M.C.
Stillwater, Okla.
Sept. 22, 1943

Dear friends,

I have just received the September issue of the "messenger". I really enjoy reading it, even though I don't know everyone. It is good to know what others are thinking and doing these busy war days. I think that your endeavor on behalf of the service men is more than appreciated, especially by those who spend long hard hours in combat areas.

For the past several issues I have been reading news of what everyone else is doing, never thinking that others might want to know what we boys in the Army Specialized Training Program do to keep busy.

First of all, I am located here on the campus of Oklahoma Agricultural and Mechanical College. The campus is beautifully landscaped and is located on the northwest side of the city of

Stillwater. Stillwater is a quiet, small sized college town of about 10,000. It is also the County seat of Payne County, Oklahoma.

We live in Murray Annex which used to be a girls dormitory. The living accommodations are excellent. These dormitories are comparatively new and are built with a "Georgian Colonial" style architecture, as are most of the dormitories on the campus. We have WAVES living next door in Murroy Hall. Across the street in Willard Hall is another group. The sailors are in a large dormitory on another section of the campus. We also have a large Air Corp training detachment here.

My day begins at 6:20 A.M. when the first call is sounded. We have five minutes to fall out for the morning report. Incidentally, it has been necessary for me to learn how to go down steps two or three at a time—no one need worry about my slipping, that's just an excuse for getting to the bottom faster. We eat breakfast at seven. Classes begin at eight and continue until one o'clock in the afternoon. The next thing on the daily program is the call for "Chow"— I needn't mention how important that is to a soldier. There is still one more call that is more important and that is mail call. We usually have this after the noon meal. Two afternoons a week are study and three are physical training.

At 6:00 P.M. we fall out for the evening retreat ceremony which usually marks the end of a soldier's day, but not ours; at 8 P.M. we fall in to study till 10:30 P.M. when the lights go out. Sometime between 6:00 and 8:00 P.M. we eat at the college cafeteria. We are off from 3:20 P.M. Saturday until 6:00 P.M. Sunday when we form for the evening meal after which follows an evening of study, preparatory to another week of work.

What do we do to keep so busy such long hours? The several subjects which we take are mathematics, trigonometry, physics, chemistry, history, English, geography, and military science. Our company has a Military Band, Dance Band, and two baseball teams. Most of these are keeping the boys busy with their extra time. I play in the Military Band which is the only extra activity that is allotted time for rehearsal during the regular workday.

One might wonder what we do with free time. I know that letters, four pair of shoes and full field equipment occupy a good portion of mine. The later two of these items have to be kept in good order because we operate on a Cadet system. If we receive too many "gigs" our weekends are filled with details that are conducive to the pleasure and comfort of the rest of the boys; for instance polishing floors and washing windows.

When the weekend rolls around most of us take full advantage, because of the strenuous program during the week. There are three theatres and a skating rink to provide us with relaxation and entertainment on Saturday evening. Sunday morning I attend St. John's Lutheran Church. It is a Missouri Synod Church. The pastor is Rev. Schulte who is newly ordained. He was installed here last May. His home was in Detroit.

I guess that's all I have for new. Here's wishing the rest of the fellows in the Service and those who keep the home-fires burning, God's richest Blessing.

Sincerely yours,
With Christ and For Christ
George Dannecker
(Son of Rev. and Mrs. Theo. Dannecker, Maybee Mich.)

❧ ❧ ❧

THE FOLLOWING ARTICLE WAS IN TOLEDO BLADE WITH BATTLE ON MUNDA

"During the battle of the ration dump, Pvt. Blair Hertzsch who had a noncombat assignment, voluntarily armed himself with an automatic rifle and worked his way forward despite intense enemy fire and continued to blast away at the

Japanese positions until reinforcements arrived. Pvt. Hertzsch is the son of Warrant Officer Otto Hertzsch, 556 South Detroit Ave. who also was in the Munda Battle. More than 200 Toledo servicemen helped capture Munda. The victory may not have been as decisive as the allied victories in Tunisi and Sicily; it may have lacked the glamour of Guadalcanal but as a triumph of American soldiers over the Japs in jungle warfare at its worst it has not been surpassed in the Pacific war. It has earned for Toledo a campaign ribbon the city can be proud to wear."

PARTS OF A V-LETTER TO HIS FOLKS

Dear Folks,

Received a letter from you a few days ago, also one from Jean that I should answer today. We had a personal inspection today and they have given us the rest of the day off. I guess they wanted to see how we looked after a year overseas. Today is our first anniversary here and we are having a party tonight in the area. It has been raining quite a bit lately but it isn't so cold. How about sending three or four spools of thread in one of my packages? I'm going to send home some Yank magazines in a couple of weeks. I'll put in a piece of heather from Scotland.

Wesley VanDyke

November 1943

John Fisher also enjoyed several days at home with his father visiting friends and relatives. John is still stationed at Medford, Oregon.

Bert Vesey, son of Mr. And Mrs. Wade Vesey was home on a three-day pass from Fort Monomouth, New Jersey and enjoyed hunting on day. He's looking fine and says, "Thanks for the Messenger. I like it".

Olin Fischer was home on his day off Nov. 8. He came from Chanute Field, Ill. Where he is in weather observation school. And guess what! The little mustache—well, it isn't any more. It was cute but you look years younger, Olie.

Arthur Shanly was home from his post in Canada recently and looks fine. He was able to attend the annual Homecoming at Bowling Green University where he attended college.

Also Richard "Dick" Fisher from Sylvania was also home for a few days from Milwaukee, Wis, where he is attending school. He's in the Navy.

❧❧❧

Cincinnati, Ohio
Nov. 4, 1943

Dear Mom,

I got your letter yesterday so I will answer now. I don't have much time to write, as we are so busy studying all the time. Sometimes it is hard to get enough sleep. My friend Jimmie Smith has been shipped out. I don't know how much longer I will be here. I don't know when I will get home again. It probably won't be until the end of the term sometime about the first of Dec. So long for now.

Your loving son,
Floyd Gray, Jr.

❧❧❧

Violet: "This is a wonder value—worth double the money. Latest pattern, bright fast colors, holeproof, won't shrink and it's a good yarn."
Customer: "Yes, and very well told besides."

അ അ അ

Oct. 20, 1943

Dear Violet and Fellow Leaguers:

I suppose that this letter will come as a surprise to you and I don't think some of your members will remember me but maybe you can tell them, Violet, that I was that little fat fellow from the Maybee League. My sister Ruth (Mrs. Kenneth Olrich) to you folks got a copy of your August Messenger and mailed it to me. It arrived yesterday and after reading it through I decided to write, as it was certainly worthy of a thank you letter. Our league sends me a copy of our monthly paper too but it is not near as large or complete. I can see that someone has to put in a lot of time in preparing a paper like that. I enjoyed reading the letters from some of the fellows in the service and I do remember some of the boys personally. It took me back to the days when we used to those good old softball games and other get together.

I will try to tell you folks of a little of my army life and especially my experiences since entering Foreign Service. I entered the Army in April 1942, and after about a week at Camp Custer where I received shorts galore and examinations and so forth I was sent with a large group of other Monroe County boys to Jefferson Barracks for my basic training. While at J.B. they told me that I would have my choice of becoming a link trainer or a meteorologist as a result of my exams I chose the latter and May 26 I left J.B. for the sunny south to take station training in weather observing. I was stationed at Hendricks Field, a new base near Sebring, Fla., a small city of about 2000 population and the home of Rex Beach. I had the pleasure of meeting Rex and enjoying a steak roast at his home. There were some very scenic spots in the vicinity and I tried to visit all of them. The tropical gardens were beautiful and it is here that the "Tarzan" pictures are filmed. During this time I qualified as a weather observer and I volunteered for Foreign Service. On Oct. 25 I got my orders to go to New York with two other boys from our station. We knew that our wish had come true.

We spent about a month is New York being prepared for foreign service which included more clothing issue and more immunization but they did give us some leisure time and we managed to get to New York City and enjoy ourselves.

We came over in a large convoy and landed at Casablanca where we stayed as a group for about 2 weeks. After that we were divided into groups large enough to man a weather station properly and were all assigned to different cities and airports. I was fortunate enough to be in one of the stations that did a lot of traveling. We went from Rabat where we were located near the Sultans Place, to Tindouf, way down to the desert where we stayed in the French Garrison that was mentioned in the story "Beau Geste". After a couple of months in the desert we were transferred to a small city near Oran. We were housed in a lovely building at this location and it was quite a treat after the way we had roughed it at our other locations. From here we went on a long trip to a camp near Sousse. On all of these previous trips I had gone by plane but on this trip one of the boys and myself drove our jeep. I was glad for that as I am sure we seen enough things of interest to offset the terrible sunburns that we received on the trip. We traveled nearly one thousand miles along the coast of the Mediterranean and passed through Algiers, Constantine, Kairogan, and many other pretty cities. We seen some of the ancient Roman ruins and I saw the large Coliseum at Ed Jem. I want to hitch hike to Carthage on my next day off and than I will have seen most of

N. Africa. I guess that covers all up to the present. Write Please.
We enjoy letters,

Carl Schmidt

ন্থেপ্থেপ্থে

September 24, 1943

Dear Violet and Leaguers
    Just received mail for the first time in a month and was
very pleasantly surprised to receive the Messenger. It is a great
paper and very interesting. It made me feel pretty swell to be
remembered by the people around Ottawa Lake. It has been
almost six years now since I have been away. Although I haven't
been much on corresponding I have thought of all you people
many times and wish to take this opportunity to say hello to all
the people who remember me.
    As you probably have read (about a year ago) about our
great successes with the encounter we had with the Japanese I
won't tell much more except it was an experience I will never
forget. I thank our God above that I was not one of those who
gave their lives that night for the home and country that love.
Each one died a hero.
    I am sorry I didn't get a chance to see all of you when I
was home last December, but it had been 5 years since I had
seen any of my folks that I just couldn't find time to get
everywhere I wanted to go. I suppose you all know that I have
been happily married for the last four years and have two perfect
children. I haven't seen much of them since the war because
except for the time we spent in Philadelphia my stay in the
states has been very very short. But I really have something to
look forward to when I do come home.
    We have been in the Mediterranean area for some time
now and have taken part in every major engagement.

As my space is running short I will bring this to a hurried close hoping you all the success in the world with the Messenger, I remain an old friend and Leaguer

P.S. I have just received another advancement to Chief Perry Officer.

Lester L. Knuth C.S.F.

က္ခက္ခက္ခ

Somewhere in England
October 18, 1943

Dear Violet and Leaguers

After reading the Sept. issue of the Messenger this evening I am in the writing mood. Am quite busy now days at this center. Am looking forward to a four-day leave soon.

We have a rack built in our tent for our clothes and equipment, a good heating stove and a kerosene lamp. I was out to that country home again last Sun. and had some good home made cookies again, those with raisins in.

I went to town last evening to get my torch from the repair shop and brought back two packs of fish and chips for the boys in my tent. They gave me a leg of a rabbit which they caught and No. 1 fried egg for breakfast this morning in England. My fatigue pants now have one big picket on each side and too bad for those Jerries now for I have hobnails in my shoes now.

Today was ration day and a shot in the arm, not so bad yet.

Cheerio
Pvt. M.E. Bieber

က္ခက္ခက္ခ

Somewhere in England
October 15, 1943

Dear Violet and Leaguers
    Received the Messenger today. Thanks a lot! I haven't heard from Pete for quite a while but a letter from my folds said he has gone overseas, so I don't suppose I'll hear from him for some time. I sent a letter to him about 10 days ago so that will be sent on to him. I just got back from my first furlough. I went to Scotland which is a 20-hour train ride from here. I went on a Red Cross tour and saw most of the historical sights in the city. We also went out to the Firth of Forth.
    I saw where Huck and Ken got together in North Africa. I still haven't seen anyone over here from back home. I hope everyone in Ottawa Lake is getting along okay. Thanks again.

    Sgt. Wesley VanDyke

෴෴෴

Winnipeg, Manitoba
Oct. 15, 1943

Dear Violet and Staff:
    A short time ago I received a copy of the Messenger and, believe me, it was good to get a condensed letter which was packed with information about friends who lived so close to home.
    It's almost incredible that from such a small area these men can be scattered to such far-flung places. I could hardly believe that Al Miller was "somewhere in the Pacific".
    Your copy was handed to me, as I was about to take off on a routine flight so I took it along. Reading as much as I could, we soon had traversed two hundred miles and it was

time to land. However, I finished it a little later on in the evening. It was one good evening well spent.

In closing let me say that I hope to be seeing you all before very long and thanks again for the copy of the Zion Messenger.

Sincerely Yours,
Pilot Officer A. R. Shanley
R. C. A. F.

৵৵৵

Oct. 31, 1943
S. England

Dear Violet and Leaguers:
I have been quite busy and had a four-day pass this last week. I spent it with Emil Yoch a boy from Iowa. We made a round trip to London and saw what we missed before. We stayed at the Victory Red Cross Club. We saw the Madame Tussaud's Exhibition which is a wax exhibit of all well-known people. We spent sometime in St. Paul's which I saw last Feb. We saw the change of the guards in front of the Buckingham Palace the other day just before we left. We saw a couple of good shoes and spent sometime dancing at Covered Gardens.

On our way back we stayed over night at Oxford. We spent sometime walking about the College area and along the Thames River. We stayed over a couple of hours in Bristol. We spent the rest of our time sight seeing about Bristol by bus and saw lots of bombed area which isn't so pleasant. Also met some people who haven't any home to go back to now.

Cheerio,
M. Elg Bieber

ৡৡৡ

Out at sea
Oct. 23, 1943

Dear friends

Just a few lines to let you know I am thinking of you all. Haven't much to write about. I cannot tell you where I am or what I am doing. I can tell you that I have crossed the equator. It's been a year now since I was home. Boy, what a year! I've seen so much, both good and bad. It's raining and cold on topside tonight but we are warm and comfortable. It's time to darken the ship. So long for now.

As ever,
Garld Holmes

Toledo Man Gets Silver Star

Pvt. Blair F. Hertzsch, infantryman of the Toledo area has received a Silver Star award for gallantry in action at New Georgia in the Solomon Islands in July according to a report from Army headquarters. Pvt. Hertzsch is a driver in the maintenance section. When an enemy detachment surrounded the ration dump killing and wounding several of the garrison. He armed himself with an automatic rifle and, according to the report, contributed indispensably to the successful defense of the ration dump pending arrival of reinforcements. In addition he assisted in the recovery of a fellow soldier's body killed in action. His father Chief Warrant Officer Otto L. Hertzsch is serving in the same company. Pvt. Hertzsch lived at 556 South Detroit Ave., Toledo and is a friend of Melva Hall.

Oct. 6, 1943

Dear friends,

I'm finally getting this little task done. I meant to write you sometime back and tell you what a wonderful job your League is doing. Ralph and Lillian Sieler have sent me two copies of the Messenger and I enjoy reading them. It is a very good way to learn about the boys from around there and some of their experiences. I would like to write a detailed description of this place and about the many things I've seen but the censorship is very close so there isn't much one can write without having it all blacked out. Therefore I just wont try.

I have noticed in the Messenger that the boys over seas write much shorter letters than the boys in the states. The reason probably being censorship. Thanks for the Messenger. And keep up the good work I know the boys all appreciate your efforts.

Yours truly,
Woody Reed

മ്മാമ

Buzzards Bay, Mass
Dec. 11, 1943

Dear Violet and Leaguers,

Just a few lines to let you know that mother sent me the paper that you people in the league put out for the service men. It is really a swell thing you are doing. I know if they all enjoyed it as much as I did, only knowing a few of the fellows, I know that you can feel that it does help a lot. It shows a lot of work and all who help put it out deserve more credit than anyone can ever say. I want to thank you very much for thinking of me and giving the paper to mother to send to me. It really was swell.

Although I didn't know a lot of the fellows, most of them in fact, I did know quite a few. I think I about read the print off of it. Any news from home you know is always welcomed by any one who is away. I don't believe I missed one article in it. I've sent it on to my brother in England and I'm sure I can speak for him that he will enjoy it as much as I did.

There isn't much to say about any of my experiences as I haven't had very many. I've more or less been in this same location since I came in. So it has more or less been routine with me. Some thing all the time. However, I am fine and like this branch of the service very much. I expect to go to sea any day but never can tell when the exact time will be. I was put here 4 months ago on temporary duty awaiting a new ship. Well I'm still waiting.

One experience I'll never forget though is the night I attended a dance at the U.S.O. here. To see anyone from home was my farthest thought, when I received one of those good old slap in the back and turning around who should I see standing face to face with but Kenny Brodbeck. We both were as surprised as we could be. We had made plans to meet on one of my liberties but never got to it. I understand Kenny is overseas now. Wherever he is if this letter should happen to reach him I know he'll remember that night. It sure is a small world. I haven't said much here but I do want to thank you ever so much for thinking of me even though I am not a member of your organization. It was really swell. Good luck to you in your work and I'll take this time to wish all of you a Merry Christmas and a Happy New Year. Thanks again.

Yours truly
Charles McConnell

Hawaiian Islands

Readers of the Zion Lutheran Messenger;

First of all I want to thank all of you who make possible the publication of such a wonderful paper. It not only brings your home and home friends to you through news, but through it makes possible the meeting of home fellows on foreign soil. Now to make it a little clearer, it was through the Messenger that "Woody" Reed, formerly of Blissfield, came about looking me up last Sunday. He saw my address in the paper, and knowing that we were over here and favored to look me up. It so happens that I was in front of the barracks waiting for church to start, as it was being held outside, and he thought it was me so he came over and asked me if I wasn't Leroy Fischer. I told him I was, and he asked me if I recognized him. After meeting many fellows as we do, we remember most of their faces, but it is hard to connect the names. He told me who he was and that it had been about five years since we had seen each other. Sunday night we went to one of the theatres to see a USO show and while we were waiting we talked over the past. So you see this is still a rather small world and it is full of surprises.

Before I go any further, if this just isn't what it should be, it will be partly due to the fact that it is 2 A.M. and I have only been up a couple hours after an hour or so of sleep. I am CQ here from mid-night until 8 A.M. I am really behind on my letter writing and thought now I could get caught up. So far I have written three letter and still six house to go.

I suppose some of you were surprised to see or hear where I am. I got a day pass a short time ago and visited Honolulu and Waikiki. We saw some beautiful buildings and took a few pictures. I am going to send all of them home that I can, and if any of you would care to see them you can do so by stopping in at home. Of course there are some things we aren't allowed to take pictures of over here.

Most of the people here seem to be independent and it is really hard to get acquainted. I went to church in town one Sunday morning, but they aren't nearly as friendly as they are back in the States.

You can buy almost anything you want over here as they are behind with their rationing, but they get a good price for everything. They have good bus service here and you can do almost anywhere you care to.

We have been moved several times already since we have been here and will continue to move often the way it looks. Now we are staying in large barracks. We work and sleep on the floor and the two rooms are aside of each other. They are both small and we are really crowded. Have wooden double decker beds and sleep on cots. I was on guard the other night, the first one in almost two years, and what little sleep I got was on a table. A fellow can sleep almost any place if he has to.

We went roller skating the other night as we have a cement rink here. Also went to a wrestling match and a USO free show this week. It was the first wrestling I had seen in quite some time, and I really enjoyed it.

As time will not permit me to thank each of you in an individual letter for Christmas cards I received from you, would like to thank all of you now. I have received a number of cards already, also a number of boxes. Am feeling fine and hope all the fellows are too. Keep up the good work with the paper.

Leroy "Pete" Fischer

ഏഏഏ

San Francisco, Calif.

Dear Violet and Leaguers;

Just had a very pleasant visit with Leroy. It's the third time I've seen him in the last week. It sure is nice to see someone from around home. Leroy is the third person I've run across in my short stay of eighteen months here, that came right from home. I meet many fellows from Michigan but when you haven't known them before it doesn't mean a thing to you. Thanks to the Messenger for making it possible to find Leroy. Hope you have everything under control back there. Merry Xmas to you all.

Woody Reed

&&&

Lincoln, Nebr.

Dear Violet and all;

Here I am back in Lincoln after a very well spent furlough. Now I hate to go back to work. I really and truly had a very enjoyable time. I was different from other soldiers. All I did was cat and sleep. I believe I ate four meals a day. In fact I gained 10 pounds on my furlough. Now I'll have to work that much harder in P.T. to take off that surplus.

Thank you for the lovely birthday card. I believe that everyone in Ottawa Lake signed it, didn't they? Would you please also thank the Ladies Aid for the swell box they sent me. The things that they had in there we can't get in camp and I sure like hard candy and nuts. I'll hide that so I can enjoy it alone.

Was I tickled that I could attend the Luther League Play this year. You don't know how much I enjoyed it. How I tried to help with the mistakes and how I applauded. It brought back many memories. It was a swell play and as usual Wilma and Fritz took very good parts. That is one thing I hope the Luther League never give up doing as a home talent play is different from a movie. I'm sorry I couldn't have seen Clayton though. I got a card from Kurt Durst and I see he is to stay in Florida though he has moved. He sure is a lucky boy.

Well I must close now to write a few more letters. Tell hello to everybody. Write soon.

As ever
Wilbur Facklam

ৰেৰেৰে

Italy
November 9, 1943

Dear Violet and Leaguers,
Well it sure was a long time since I've written and I sure don't know what was the matter with me but just plain lazy. Isn't that what you say about it?

I just finished my supper "Chow" as we call it in the army and we had a fairly good chow we even had homemade donut's and they surely were nice the fellow that does our baking know how to do it he would make a good house man for some women that doesn't know a anything about baking.

The weather is kinda of cold now here in Italy it almost feels like good old Mr. Winter is here for to stay but I sure hope not anyhow. I haven't heard or seen Kenny Bsinco we left Africa I don't know whether he was on his invasion or not if I haven't mistaken I think he was I made it we landed the ninth of Sept. it was a little tough if you asked me.

Boy I sure am making some mistake in my spelling but I guess you will be able to make it out at least I hope so.

I hear they have Pete overseas now boy it sure would be nice if we three fellows could get together once it sure would feel like old times again so let hope we all met here back home would be the best place to met but that will come later an and I hope it is soon I am getting kinda tired of this life.

I still am getting the League paper, and I sure do enjoy it, it sure is a swell paper to read I wish I could come home once just to see how much hard work you gals do to get all those copies out to all the fellows in service it sure is a lot of work to do all of them. We had a church sermon last Sunday and the Chaplain sure had a nice sermon it pretty hard to go to church over here so the Chaplain came around and we have church in the house, we are going to have a Thanksgiving program over here so if I got a chance I am going there is going to be a little church sermon, the Chaplain will give he sure is a nice follow.

Well Vi that is bout all I can think of for this time so I guess I will have to close hoping to here from you soon, but until then

As always,
Howard Schmidt

ৎৎৎ

Alaska 11/25/43

Hi folks,
All is well with me tonight. It's Thanksgiving and I am thankful for a lot of things. Chiefly that I am well and safe even if I am a long way from home. I would have liked to have been closer home but things can't be that way. We had a good dinner today, turkey with the trimmings and also ham. I can't complain. I must close for now with love to all.
Harple Gray

ৎৎৎ

Tyler, Texas 11/26/43

Dear Leaguers,
Here we are back in Tyler and about to report back to camp and consider my first furlough as history. The first

experiences are always novel and this was no exception and so we will have to write you about it.

My furlough papers were slow in coming from Regimental Headquarters and as a result we had less than half an hour to finish packing, purchase our tickets and get to the bus. This meant a lot of rushing around and as a result we looked our of place carrying an overcoat under one arm and have beads of sweat gathered on my face. Foolish as it appeared the overcoat came in very handy when we were home.

Our trip as far north as St. Louis was very pleasant. We had a seat together all the way. Some fellow soldiers were less fortunate when they boarded the train at Little Rock. Their seat had to be improvised by parking on their suitcase placed in the aisle. Some became overcome with sleep in the wee hours of the morning and made a bed by placing papers on the floor in the aisle and sleeping there. One of the fellows was aroused toward morning by one of his buddies announcing that the sleeper was to be on the famous K.P. for the day.

Our trip back from Toledo also had plenty of amusing things to keep from becoming dull. Eldora was able to get a seat when a kind-hearted soldier gave up his seat to her. I made my seat on our suitcase. In St. Louis again it was a rush to try to get a seat. We were fortunate in getting a seat but you will laugh when you hear where it was. This train had a Ladies' Lounge and seats there for about half a dozen people. We were the last to get seats there. We shared it with 2 soldiers, one from our regiment at camp and the other also in the Infantry but now at Camp McCoy, Wis.; a sailor who was going to his home in Texas on leave; a newly married couple who were going visiting in Houston; a girl from Ill, who was going to visit her soldier friend in Houston and a civilian also going to Houston. The dullness of the evening hours were brightened by music and singing for the bridegroom played a mandolin. Now we must return to work and wait for our next furlough.

As Ever
Eldora and Clayton F.

❧❧❧

To our servicemen and women:
Ottawa Lake, Michigan, January 1944

Greetings from Ottawa Lake and a happier New Year to you all!

How we wish we could utter those words with a hearty handshake, face to face! But not just yet. Perhaps the joys of a glad reunion will find such expression soon. May god grant it!

It is always heartening to us when we receive letters from you folks. Two things always receive immediate attention, when a letter comes, namely, the date and the signature. Write whey you can!

A leading national weekly recently carried a noteworthy article entitled: "The Church Came Out To Us." The writer tells how in the North African desert campaign some of "the boys" on Sunday were in Foxholes during a downpour of icy rain. Dive-bombers were strafing constantly. Naturally, on such a Sunday, the soldiers couldn't go to church. But the Chaplain carried or sent Testaments to the foxholes. He said: "Read the verses I have marked and then pass the Testaments on to the next foxhole". The writer concludes "— and so the church came out to us." The Chaplains are indeed right out there with the armed forces. We know from the letters that come home that the Chaplain means much to you. And so it should be.

Your Chaplains brings you the message of the Eternal One...."The things that are seen are temporal, but the things that are not seen are eternal."

Surely a midst all the wreck and ruin that some of you have seen you have harbored such thoughts as expressed by the hymn writer —

"In the cross of Christ I glory,

Tow'ring o'er the wrecks of time;
When the woes of life o'er take me,
Hopes deceive and fears annoy,
Never shall the cross forsake me:
Lo, it glows with peace and joy."

Now, finally, may the last two words by your keynote for victorious living in 1944. Only the Lord Jesus can give you true and lasting inward "peace and joy."

Cheerio,
Your pastor and friend, Marcus Mueller

☙☙☙

Home on furlough

We were glad to be able to talk with Bob Dietsch while he was here on furlough. He's at Greencastle, Pa. Now.

Olin Fischer was home for a week while he was being transferred from Chanute Field, Ill. He looks fine and guess what, No mustache!

Donald Hart visited his parents recently.

We're mighty glad to see Stanley Kastel home for a week. Those desert maneuvers weren't much fun out there in California. He'll return to Indio, Calif.

Don LaPointe came to his home with his wife who had been visiting him in S. Carolina. He spent a few days here and is now at a new camp.

Kenny Schmidt is expected for a few days from Camp Beale.

Burt Vesey was able to come home to attend both of his grandmother's funerals, Mrs. Harrawaldt and Mrs. Vesey. He's looking fine and enjoys the "Messenger". We're sorry you trip had to be made under the circumstances but glad that you were able to attend their services.

Charles "Chuck" McConnell was seen around Sylvania. He's looking fine and glad you got home Chuck.

֍ ֍ ֍

Parts of Edgar Strable's letters:

Dear Mom:

Just a line to let you know I'm O.K. We are on the Rifle Range. I made a score of 190 out of a possible 220, so I made sharp shooter, 5 more points and I would have made expert, but I got a silver medal anyway.

We are going on Maneuvers Friday morning. We leave at 4:00 A.M.
A.M. for Middletown, Pennsylvania, we stay 10 days then come back here. Will be back in Virginia for Christmas.

We are all very busy getting ready for this trip. We had to get my Truck's ready, that's greased, oil change, battery charge, general check on tires, load all our trailers and get the men ready, now on our way. We arrived in Middletown, PA. O.K. and are at a very nice place only 6 miles form Harrisburg, and that is a large city.

We have 400,000 square feet of landing mat to lay, while we are here, so you can see we will be very busy for the few days we are here. Drove thru by truck, sure saw a lot of mountains, & dangerous roads. We have a swell U.S.O. club here. I like to over there, it stays open till 11:00 P.M.

Sat. was the first time so far this winter I saw the ground covered with snow, it's much colder here then in Richmond, Virginia. It's been down to zero that's a great change from what I've been used to and so far haven't even had a cold. I sure have been getting cards and letters lately everybody and his brother thought of me.

I'm at the U.S.O. ion Harrisburg and this Sunday. The law is no shows here on Sunday, everything is folded up on

Sunday, but they make up fir it during the week. This U.S.O. is in the Y.M.C.A. and I just came out of the swimming pool. It was nice and warm. I was in about an hour. I feel swell now.

We got back to Richmond, Va. Last Thursday nite about 6:00 O.M. that sure was a long ride as I had to ride 260 miles in a jeep, and it was cold. It has rained for the past two days here, it was nasty for us today. We had to fire the carbine rifle on the range. We were out there all day even though we had on our raincoats and boots on, we just couldn't keep dry. I qualified with the carbine rifle, now I'm entitled to wear an additional silver bar link in my sharp shooter's metal.

We had a fine Christmas dinner. I went in to Richmond in the afternoon, there wasn't much doing as most business places were closed.

We moved into tents this coming Tuesday that's supposed to be maneuvers it is sure rugged out there. Candles for light, a hole in the ground for toilet and we have to use our helmets for washbasins. Yes it's just like the real thing.

Here we are living in tents. I'm trying to write this by candlelight. We are sure on maneuvers now, we green the far end of the Base, living just like we would have to live if we were in real combat. We have six man tents, dirt floors, a little stove, that's out every morning. We wash out of our helmets, eat out of mess gear, today makes 4 days in a row that my clothes haven't been off, it's to cold here that we go to bed with our clothes on, even our socks to keep our feet warm. We have no place to clean up, as our water is limited. We haul our water 9 miles, so you see water is scarce, we got a quart of water a day; to drink, wash and shave, so if we get thirsty, we don't wash.

Well I haven't drowned in this mud and water we are living in, yes we are still roughing it, but I don't mind it so bad now, maybe I'm getting used to it this dirt and grime. I spent a very quiet New Year eve. I was wading mud almost to my ears trying to set up an electric generator run by gasoline engine, so we could have some light in our tent. We got it up, now we have lights in our humble tents, called home.

I felt ornery the other day, so I painted a sign and nailed it to the tree in front our tent door, this what it reads, "33rd. Street & Broadway Smokey Joe's". Even the C.O. got a kick out of that, you know Mom for all the grief, we put up with we have just as much fun too, so it isn't so bad.

Must close for now. Say "Hello" to everybody. I'll write when I can and as often as I can.

All my Love

You Son, Eddie

&~&~&~

From Peter Fischer
December 15, 1943,
Hawiian Islands

Members of Zion, Leaguers, and readers of the "Messenger".

Howdy folks, I tried to cover all of you when I used that saluation, but in case I didn't I didn't mean to leave anyone out. I meant to write this letter sooner so that it would get there in time to be published in the December issue, but here it is the middle of the month already and I suppose that the December issue has already gone to press. So it will no doubt be in the January issue, which by the way, will be the first issue of the new year of 1944.

I received the November issue a couple of weeks ago and was really glad to receive it again. I really enjoy reading this publication and know that it requires a lot of work in publishing it and means a lot of cooperation on the parts of some of you, but don't think for a minute reading it as much as I do. I would like to keep the paper from one month to the next and keep them all in one big binding. But we have been moving around so much that we always like to travel as light as possible and just haven't the room for everything that we would like to take with us.

I have only been able to see Woody Reid a couple of times in the last month as we aren't close together again. He never moves, but we surly do our share of it. We were just moving back and forth between the two different places, but now we have a new place that we are in. We are quite a ways from a town and about the only time that I could see him is during the evenings, and the transportation is no good here at all in the evenings. There are a couple of other fellows from near home that I am going to try to locate if I can and maybe the time will come at that. I was so surprised that Sunday morning when Woody came up to me, that I am keeping the lookout for those other fellows all of the time as there just isn't anything impossible and we may run across each other that same way.

I haven' been on a pass for a couple of weeks or so am going to try and go the first part of next week. We have been quite busy so far this month as we moved the first part and then right after we got here we had to get the monthly payroll made out and go to the company and get it signed.

This place is a woody area and when we first got here it was really a muddy mess. It rained for the first few days and it was really hard to keep the building as well as our clothing clean. After it dried up a little bit they got some stone in and we had to build walks to our buildings.

We have a small theatre here where they hold Church Services every Sunday Morn. Our chaplain holds the services here on Sunday, but the rest of the companies have their services at any time possible for the Chaplain to hold them.

Great Falls, Montana,
January 5, 1944

Dear Fellow Leaguers and friends:

Now that I'm a bit organized here that coveted time off. I find time has passed so fast this may even be too late to make the January Messenger. I hope not!

To all who I was able to see in that "all too short" time at home, let me say it was really great to see you all and talk to you brief as it often was. To any I may have missed seeing—well, we'll have a standing date for furlough. Yes, furloughs are one of the army's best institutions – ha !.

But here I am in Montana, and the most surprising thing of all is how warm it really is here. Thus far the temperature has always held at least 50 to 10 degrees about that which Chicago has at the corresponding time . it hasn't hit zero here yet, but old mercury is due to fall way below any day now.

After drawing 4 shifts here in station they took 20 of us for 2 weeks course in further study of surface observations and Northern orientations, when we will leave here we get 2 more bags of fur-lined equipment, so we shouldn't have any difficulty with the cold up there.

Naturally I can't say where we might be going, but this I know; some of the boys back have come from posts where mail service was as infrequent as every 6 weeks. These posts are few, however, if I should draw one of those posts, letters would become as diamonds—and as a hint to any would-be letter writers-o-I sure would like to be a rich man.

A round our base here are several ranges of mountains. They are about 40 miles away, but don't look over 2 or 3. With the unusual cloud formations and the effects of the sun on them with the mountains, we have many very beautiful sunsets. The dark Blue Mountains are covered with traces of snow and are very pretty in themselves.

And now it's time for me to say good-bye. Best wishes to all in this present New Year. Bye for now.

As Ever,

Olin (Curtis D.) Fischer

❧❧❧

From Mrs. Hein (Mrs. Mueller's mother)
Columbus, Ohio

A Happy New Year to you, and to the Messenger Staff, God grant you good health, and strength to carry on the good work that you all have been doing.

We talked to Bill over the phone the other night. He moved from Daechart, Texas to Wichita, Kansas and then to Bruning, Nebraska, during the holidays. He said they are living in a fine building, he sleeps in a food bed, and the eats are very good. Also they have an excellent flying field, and there is plenty of work to do from morning till night.

He is expecting to come home on furlough for a short time in Feb.

❧❧❧

Word has reached us from Morgan Mehan's folks that he is now moving to some front line, and that when they get through there they will be sent home, and that we would not hear from him for some time

Somewhere in Italy,
Dec. 7, 1943

Dear Violet and all,

Are you surprised when you finally hear from me? Seems the days are not long enough to get everything done and it isn't because we don't begin early enough in the morning. How are all the folks at Ottawa Lake? I'm O.K. except for a little cold. I've had one letter from Kenneth Brodbeck since I've been here and he wrote that he was going to try and get a pass and stop out, as he knows where our hospital is. Today I rushed off duty at 2 P.M. and got ready and rode into town with two other nurses to go to the Symphony. This is the third one I've attended and its just amazing to think we are able to hear such wonderful music for only 40 lire or 40 cents. I counted over 65 pieces in the orchestra, most of them violins. They usually have a couple of numbers with singing. After Xmas they are going to have operas here. It is quite warm now and I was plenty warm today with just my suit on. For the first time since we've been here we had a Sunday chicken dinner and it was swell! I worked from 7 a.m. until 2 p.m. so I went to the Sunday services held at 2:30 Sunday afternoon. We are living in tents again since they need more building for patients. We four girls that lived together in Africa are in our tent. Our floor is tile and we have an electric light and nice furniture and a stove. I am enclosing a small remembrance (Cameo stone) from here and hope you will like it.

Sincerely yours,
Inez Bieber

Nov 14, 1943

Dear Grandma and Grandpa; (Ellinwood)
    Just a line or two to let you know I am just fine. How is everybody around there? Sure would like to get back and see all of the folks and kids again. Seem like ages since I was there last. I heard from Frank the other day, everything is fine here. Keeps us busy these days, always something to do.

Love and best wishes,
Robert "Bob" Creque

    From India where Leroy Gray is still stationed comes this bit of news written on Dec. 22nd: "Joe E. Brown has just finished his tour in China and is coming here Xmas Day. Christmas Eve they are going to have a songfest at the club. I believe they intend on making a tour to the hospital to sing for the patients. Naturally, I'll be on hand. The Indians for the most part don't observe Xmas that is especially true of the Mohammedans and Hindus. They do have many holidays. The main one is Dwali which they claim is something like our Xmas but to me any resemblance to same is purely coincidental. I am not acquainted with all the facts but it appears to be a festival of lights in honor of the goddess of light. At least during that time this year the town was pretty lit up with literally thousands of lights. All these festivals appear strange to us Yanks as well as Rebels but to those people they have a definite significance."

    Pete Fischer ate his Xmas dinner in Hawaii and the next day was able to see Woody Reed and have a good time together.

    The Nearhoods are fine and still in the S. Pacific. We hope to hear more from them next month.

Dear friends, - - from Frank and Esther Kummerow.

I have been doing plenty of moving around lately. I am duty officer tonight so again I am trying to catch up on my writing. Esther and I have a five room house here and we enjoy it very much. Even have a little kitten, which we named fluff and it is a lot of company to Esther

I suppose it is cold back home by now. It freezes hard here but we haven't any snow except in the mountains. The flu is pretty bad around here also. Esther was in bed two days with it but it is much better.

I suppose you all had a nice Christmas. Esther and I went to church here Christmas Eve and heard and saw the children speak. It took me back to Ottawa Lake when I was on the church programs for Christmas. We both enjoyed it very much.

Well, I must close for this time. Write when you can and I will try to do better. Hope you all are in the best of health and may the good Lord keep and guide us.

1944

Camp Fannin, Texas,
January 2, 1944

Dear Leaguers,

We are now opening the last week of the training of the men in this present cycle. Already the men have made applications to the transportation Officer to make arrangements for travel home while they are in route to their next station The men naturally are very anxious to get home for at least four and in some cases six months.

The men have just returned from a two-week bivouac. The weatherman was not so kind to them for it rained a great deal of the time. The first week it was fairly dry but acid. During this period they slept in double pup tents. It was in this phase of the training that they ran the battle courses. The course consisted of the Close Combat Fighting; village fighting and infiltration. All of which I had completed at Robinson on last July 4th, a nice hot Sunday. In addition the men had to cover a night infiltration course and an overhead fire course. Since I had not completed these courses before, it was also necessary that I run them.

On the night infiltration course we approached an improvised enemy line, which was reinforced with barbed wire and had machine guns firing over it. As we were crawling under the barbed wire the machine guns fired tracer ammunition over our bodies and they glowed as falling stars as they passed between three and five feet above us. This is one of the times when old mother earth feels good and you know you are safe as long as you keep down. In the overhead fire course the troops would advance in formation at a signal everyone would hit the ground right on your stomach and face while 105 mm bullets went over you head and would land a few yards in front of us.

In addition to helping in the supply room I have been the Company Mail Clerk since the middle of last month. Christmas business was good almost all of the packages arrived while the men were on bivouac. Rather than have the men have the packages scattered in the field we held them all in the supply room until they returned the day before Christmas. They had a nice large pile when the packages were all together.,

During the second phase of the bivouac the men had to spend the evenings in foxholes and so since they were drenched in the rain it was far from pleasant. The condition was made worse when the temperature dropped and it froze. The men returned tired and cold and nothing except home could have seemed as good as the barracks which up to this time have been considered as ugly places in which to be housed.

May the year 1944 be good to you wherever you may be and may we all hope and pray to be together before the year closes.

As Ever
Clayton Fischer

෨෨෨

Somewhere in Sicily,
December 1943

Dear Folks and All

Just a few lines to say. I'm still very much alive and feeling pretty good and hope this finds you folks the same and please write often. I received your Nov. 16th letter the other day, but don't think I answered yet. You see we are pretty busy around here with our regular details now. While a couple are on detached service. I kinda wish I was on detached service yet, but then I now see, stay and eat with those boys in Palermo.

When I go up with the patients I go up there often and visit Gale Smith after taking the men to the hospital and picking up reports.

I was up there yesterday and it was a rather nice one. Gale works under Gen. Patten and is a S/Sgt., but he never flies like I do. Well I guess I'll have to eat dinner soon as I've got a duty from twelve till six so I'll eat early. Must get my rations now.

Harold Jasmund

࿊࿊࿊

We have dreaded the time when we would have to write the following news in our "Messenger" but since so many of you boys have been personal friends and even pals to the boys listed below we want you to know about them. As the Messenger goes to press we find that the parents of Corneleius, Jr. Blome have received word from the War Department that their son is reported missing. Jr, is the brother of both Mrs. Herbert Papenhagen and Mrs. Harvey Lievens. We hope and pray that he will be found and will return to his family and friends.

Lt. Kenneth Shull, husband of Laura Griffin Shull is reported missing. He is in the Air Force Ground Crew.

Lt. Robert Wood from Sylvania also is reported missing in action in the Central Pacific.

Memorial services were held in t he Community Church, Sylvania, Ohio for Lt. Jim Randall, Sylvania, Ohio who was lost in the plane crash in Sacramento, Calif. On Jan. 6.

Eddie Howard, son of Edwin G. Howard, Sylvania, Ohio also is reported missing.

࿊࿊࿊

February 1944

A death certificate was received by the family of Cornelius, Jr. Bloome. His death occurred on Dec. 2nd, 1943 at a port in Italy. He was guard that night on his boat when a German Bomber came over. Our sincere sympathy goes to his folks, and his sisters, Mrs. Linda Papenhagen and Mrs. Bertha Lievens. May God comfort you in your sorrow.

We're glad to hear of the promotion of Sgt. To Edgar Strable. Good work Ed and we wish you all the best wishes possible.

Mrs. Henry Lunde is still in Norfolk, Virginia. She's busy scrubbing and cleaning a new apartment that she is occupying there. She wrote her mother she was really glad that she had taught her how to scrub as she had plenty of it to do in her apartment. Henry doesn't know where his new "parking place" is yet. Hope he likes it as well as Erica.

We're sorry that Howard Hotchkiss is still in the Naval Hospital in Chicago at this writing. Howard had scarlet fever and the flu and is now recovering from pneumonia. We hope that you're feeling a lot better and that you'll be out of the hospital soon.

In a recent letter to his folks Howard "Huck" Schmidt wrote that he's back in N. Africa now in a hospital because of ear trouble. He flew from Italy on a Hospital ship. We hope that he too will be feeling much better.

Tampa, Florida
February

Dear Friends:
Since my last letter quite a lot has happened. In fact, what we all like to see happen. I came back to see dear Old Ottawa Lake, and it sure looks good. They can fight wars, and change cities, but Ottawa Lake will always be the same. Of course things do seen a little dead there, but wait till we all get back and that will be taken care of in short notice.

Now I'm in the Gulf of Mexico, side of Florida, and there is as much difference in Florida as between a graveyard and a nightclub. Well I'm in the graveyard. Tampa is an old city with nothing to do, and no place to go. Palm beach was clear, active and full of life. Lots of people down here are Spanish, and when you go some places, you begin to wonder if you'll get out alive, and then we only have about 25 soldiers here for every civilian.

The main thing we do here is move. I've moved seven times in the last two months, and my company now is broken up, so I get kicked out again. The funny part is I'm still within blocks of where I started, and never get any farther away.

We have our little difficulties here as well as you do at home. The weather is funny. In the morning you freeze to death and in the afternoon it's too hot, and there's nothing we do about it. Then for about a month awhile back we couldn't buy soap (a schoolboys dream if there ever was one), then over Christmas for two weeks the city was out of gas, so those little A coupons didn't do much good, you walked anyhow. Butter is a thing of the past now.

Right now I'm writing this sitting on a cot trying to get a little sunshine. In front of me is what's left of the fireguards tent. They were all out looking for fires last night, when their tent burnt down.

Do you mind if I go eat now? That you know is the favorite pastime of 99.9% of the army. The other .1% must be sleeping – Pastime No. 2.

So long for awhile,
Kurt Durst

Clewiston, Florida
Dear folks:

There is not much news from around here but everything is going to schedule and of course things are just fine. I drove to Miami early Saturday and came back Sunday evening. No one else went along with me and I spent quite a little time working on my instrument rating. Attended services at the Lutheran Service Center in Miami and also had the Lords Supper there. This place is advertised in the Mighty Fortress.

The last few weeks have been grand for me, as I did a lot of cross-country flying. Made four trips to Haines City and Wimauma and that took me right over the Singing Tower at Lake Wales and then over to the West coast close to Tampa and St. Petersburg. At Wimauma we landed in a small auxiliary field and just across the road was a large orange grove. That was really something for the British cadets and of course I did not mind it either. Now that that particular trip is over with and when we practice aerobatics you are very apt to see oranges and grape fruit whiz by your head in all directions. Also made four trips to Sarasota and Okeechobee. At Sarasota the Ringling Brothers have their headquarters and all their equipment and animals are kept there for the winter. That place is also right across from the airport and of course I had to take my boys to see the monkeys and elephants. With the airplane that I am flying now you can really go places in a hurry and at almost a few hundred miles an hour the towns and cities go by almost like magic. Some of the trips are made at quite a high altitude and then again you will go on a trip at low level just about skimming over the tops of Palm Trees. On these low level trips you see very few landmarks and your destination will loom up suddenly when your estimated time of arrival is up and provided that you have figured your course correctly.

Things have not gone so well here the last few weeks because there have been quite a few accidents. Have had at least four cases where landings were made without the wheels being down. One cadet had his arm broken when he made a belly landing away from the field and down wind at that. Every now and then someone will come in and forget to lower his wheels. That is definitely bad and there is no excuse for that at all. Last week we also lost two British cadets. They were on a night cross-country trip and they apparently flew into some bad weather. They were found the next day in their burned

AT-6 near Ft. Meyers. Night flying over the everglades is not exactly a lot of fun. The ship I am flying now has full radio equipment and that means everything in the world to me. The other day a cadet (Danforth) that I knew quite well at Dick's place in Tonawanda fell out of an AT-6 at 9000 ft. and of course landed by parachute. He either forgot to fasten his safety belt or unlocked accidentally while doing aerobatics. He may be eliminated for that because he wrecked a swell $30,000 airplane.

Everyone is in fine shape here and I hope that all you folks are enjoying the best of health.

Love,
Dan Mueller
(brother of Rev. Mueller)

&

Del Rio, Texas
Jan. 12, 1944

Dear Violet & Leaguer's:
Well here we are in the New Year already, in fact twelve days gone already, time sure does fly. It won't be long until I've been in this man's army three year's. Sure doesn't seem that long.

I received a large picture of James & Barbara. James sure is a big boy. Say Violet did I ever thank you people for the last copy of the league news, if I didn't, thanks a lot and I enjoyed it very much. And also thanks a lot for the xmas box.

We have been so busy here I don't know which way to turn. We are trying to change to eight hour shifts on the line and what a job that is.

I understand my young brother is getting married. Doris is still down here with me.

I received a letter from my mom the other day and she says that you people haven't had much snow this winter. Well the other night we got four inches of that beautiful snow. Sure made me home sick. The people said that was the most snow in forty years, they even let out the schools for it.

I took my 64 physical the other day, so I may see foreign service yet. By the way I received a copy of the League news the other day, sure enjoyed it. Thanks a lot!

Well I have to get back to work, so I'll sign off for now. Write soon.

As ever,
Frank Schumacher

ᏚᏚᏚ

Somewhere in Italy
Jan. 28, 1944

Dear Rev. and Mrs. Mueller,

The war news has been very encouraging lately so we are all hoping to be back before too long. Today is my day off duty so am doing a little letter writing this morning and plan to go on a little sightseeing trip this afternoon. Yesterday afternoon I went to an Italian Variety Show with some of our patients. The orchestra was very good and they played most of the favorite old songs. Later in the afternoon we took pictures of some Arab patients on our ward.

It is remarkable so many days without rain. Perhaps the so-called rainy season is over. The days are brighter and much longer but it's still quite cool. We are restricted from going into town because of typhoid fever epidemic among the civilians. The armed forces are protected with shots to prevent contracting this disease but precautions must be taken. Best wishes to all.

Sincerely,
Inez Bieber

Jan. 11, 1944

Dear folks,

Well, I have a little time before chow and I will write a few lines. There isn't much to write about as things here are about the same. It sure is swell out today so I did a little washing. It sure seems funny not to have Arabs to do the washing for you but I guess I will make out alright. All we do is put them in a pail of water and cut up soap on them and boil the dickens out of them, then scrub and rinse them. They come out pretty good but I still don't think I will take in washings when I get home.

How is everybody around there? Tell them I said "hello" and that they should be over here then they wouldn't have to walk through snow but have nice sun shiny days.

As always,
"Spud" Raymond Shanly

❧❧❧

Italy
Jan. 13, 1944

Dear Rev. M. Mueller,

I've intended writing you for sometime to thank you and the Luther League for the Messenger that is being sent me. I enjoy reading it and the letters that some of the fellows write home that I know. I'm only sorry that I don't know more of the fellows because I might have a chance of meeting them over here. My luck so far in doing same hasn't been too good because since my being overseas 20 months I've only met one fellow I knew from home and the 13 months I spent in the States I didn't meet anyone I knew. So although some of the fellows say it's a small world because they have met someone they knew overseas, up to date I'm afraid I can't agree. I hope my luck changes because I sure would enjoy seeing some of the fellows from around home.

I don't know whether this will be of interest but I will give you a few of the places I've been since leaving the States. I've been fortunate and sometimes unfortunate to see the following: Labrador, Greenland, Iceland, Scotland, England and then we went to North Africa where I visited the cities of Oran, Biskia, Constantine, Tunis, Tripoli and other smaller cities too numerous to mention. I also was at Sicily and Sardinia before coming here. I can't say how many miles that would cover but I sure would like to know.

From the letters I read that the fellows wrote most of the above places have already been described so I won't attempt to say anymore about them.

I sure miss the enjoyable evenings our League would spend with yours and vice versa and also the conventions that the Leaguers were able to attend. A person doesn't realize how precious things like that are until it is taken away from him as it is when you leave the States and I think that the fellows from your League who are overseas will agree with me.

It is going to be a very happy day for me and I know millions of others too when we all put foot on the good old U.S.A., the grandest country in the world. A person realizes it after you see how other people live.

Again I want to thank you for the paper and I want to say hello to all who remember me.

Sincerely,
Wilbur R. Schneider

(V-mail letter from Worthy White)
Somewhere in Australia
Jan. 3, 1944

Dear Leaguers,

I am sorry that I haven't written sooner and thanked you all for sending me the Messenger. But I guess it's better late than never so I am thanking you now. I like to read it very much as it contains so much news from so many people that I know.

I have been in Australia quite a while now, as you probably already know. Things are quite different than back in the States, such as driving on the left hand side of the road and the money is in pounds and shillings, and etc.

Well, this seems to be all the room to write on this skimpy v-mail so will have to say so long.

As ever,
Worthy White

Kessler Field, Miss.
Feb. 6, 1944

Dear friends,

I'm stationed in the sunny south again. I never had the opportunity to enjoy summer sports during the winter season until I arrived here. This weather makes me think of May or June. After having a shower this morning the sun is shining brightly.

I have been going to school nights. The time flies by so fast. Reveille is at 9:00 A.M., and then the next morning at 1:00 A.M. I hit the bunk for a few hours of rest.

The A.M. students are allowed one 24-hour pass a week. My day off is Tuesday. Last Tuesday I went to "Paris of America". I had a swell time in New Orleans, Louisiana. I would have had a better time if my chum would have gone with me as we had planned. New Orleans has plenty of scenery and I'm going to go there again when I receive a chance.

The fishing season in the Gulf of Mexico near Biloxi usually starts in April. I'm waiting for the chance to go fishing in one of the schooners. About 15 fellows rent a schooner together and that way the cost for each fellow is lowered. Maybe when April arrives I won't be here but I'm looking forward to it.

Sincerely,
Lernard Meyers

৵৵৵

Fort Lewis, Wash.
Jan. 17, 1944

Dear Violet,
I thought I would drop you a line. I haven't written for I don't do much writing any more. They keep us on the go from 6 in the morning til 6 at night.

One thing I am writing for is to see if you will send me Olin's address. I saw in the paper he is in Montana. There is a boy in camp here with me that has a brother in Great Falls. He ask if I would get Olin's address so he can tell his brother to look him up. He and his brother are from Carleton, Michigan and that isn't very far from home. I thought that both of them being from Michigan that they might get to know each other.

The weather out here is very rainy now and it gives a fellow a good chance to get the flu. I suppose it is cold and a lot of snow back home now.

Well, I have to write to mother yet tonight so I will sign off. So long and God bless all the folks back home. I enjoy getting the "Messenger" and thanks a lot.

Your friend,
Malcolm Gray

 educated

April 1943

NEWS ABOUT THE BOYS!

In Kenny Brodbeck's letter of March 28th he wrote how he'd be helping his Pal, Joe Steiner soon, Kenny's really talking daggers. In his letter of the 23rd, he wrote that he had met Bill Winelander in New Bedford, Mass. Bill is the son of Rev. and Mrs. Winelander of N. Blissfield. Bill's either in the Navy or Coast Guard. You'll have to ask him.

Kenneth's letters are now being censored so he can not say whether or when he is moving. The weather is very much like spring in Mass. The boys have instruments in camp. One of these is a guitar and of course, Ken makes use of that. Good luck, always, Ken, and we all think of you real often.

Andy Ery, who is in the Navy was unable to tell his folks of his planned trip to Africa before he left the States but after he returned, he rated only a 72-hour pass and you bet he came home. It was a happy household when he got home April 7 even though he had to leave again April 9.

Eugene Hart's wife and mother drove to Texas a couple of weeks ago to visit him. His wife will make her home down there. His brother, Donald Hart, is at Camp Hulen, Texas.

OUR BOYS IN BLUE:

San Diego, California
April 1, 1943

Dear Leaguers!
We finally got here in San Diego, California. We were a day late though as our train was six and one-half hours late getting to Los Angeles. It was a good thing Henry had a day to spare. We were on the way from Ottawa Lake four days and three nights, and we got pretty tired the last few hours. But everything is so pretty here that it was worth it. The country here is the most beautiful land that we have ever seen. It is more beautiful than any pictures can show. So different from what we've been used to. They have all kinds of pretty flowers, shrubs, and the palm trees are lovely. The orange groves are just like you see them in pictures. This is paradise. The land between Los Angeles and San Diego was the most beautiful of the whole trip. The states we passed through before getting into California were mostly desert. Here everything is green and the trees and flowers are in bloom. The houses are mostly stucco. The city is very clean, part of it is built on a hillside. We have had sunshine nearly every day. It isn't real hot but it is nice and warm. It gets cool enough to use blankets at night.

They have a nice down-town district. Many of the folks that live here are originally from different states and have come out to visit people and have come back to live here and make their home.

One of these days we're going to find out if we can cross the border without any trouble. We are just 14 miles from the Mexican line. There are so many places and things we would like to see and do while we are here. Most of the busses, streetcars, and taxis are driven by women. There are quite a few Mexicans around. Henry likes his school real well so far. He will have quite a bit of short-hand. Henry comes home every night and it makes the day seem so much shorter.

We are living in a three room apartment which is completely furnished with our radio we have one in every room.

Our apartment is quite a ways out of town but it is nice out here. The Pacific Ocean comes right up to our front yard. Here is our home address so if any of you happen to come to San Diego, please come and look us up.

Erica and Henry Lunde

✍✍✍

Dear Luther Leaguers:

All is pretty quiet here for now since I have had sort of an accident and am laid up with a broken arm and a few other things. Just got out of Sick Bay and it's pretty dead in that place I can assure you.

Would be glad to hear from anyone of you who has time to write me, letters certainly are always welcome at a time like this.

What I wouldn't give to be able to be at one of the League meetings once again and see you all there. I often think of that little church at Ottawa Lake. So many things I would like to write about but some other time.

Where I am now it is a very pretty place. The people are all very nice to us Sailor boys and try to make us feel at home where ever we go. When we are on the beach of all the places I have seen Michigan and Ohio still looks the best to me and it will be food when this war is over and we can return home again.

We are going into dry docks again for a couple of months and may get to come home on a fifteen day furlough. So maybe I'll be seeing you all before you know it but in the mean time I'd appreciate some letters from all you Luther Leaguers.

Well, so long for now gang.

As ever,
Garld Holmes

OUR BOYS IN ARMY DRAB.

Bernice DeNudt received many nice snap shots from her husband, William, who is still somewhere in Alaska. One of these had a decorated Christmas tree with gifts around it so I guess Santa Clause found the boys up there too. Bernice and her family received Easter cards from him too recently.

Here is what was on a diploma that Bernice received from her husband:

"This is to certify that Corp. William DeNudt having visited Alaska and fulfilled all the requirements of this order by tracking a salmon to its den, eating a totem alive, digging ice worms, dehorning a mosquito and by salting the tail of a Kodiak bear, has been granted membership for ten years to life in the mystic and Aurual order of Alaska Cheechakos and is entitled to all the benefits and detriments thereof. Any tales told by the brother are to be believed without the slightest doubt and when he tells stories of palemate dogs, deaf-mute totems, forbearing fish, twenty-five hour days, long dark nights, perfumed Eskimos, reindeers, and Santa Claus "it is to be just as though Chief Muck-much himself hath spoken only not as loud." Dated somewhere in Alaska, this 8th day of April 1943.

Somewhere in Africa

Dear Luther Leaguers,

I left New York around the fourth of August for across. After sailing for a period of time I landed in England. We didn't stay there very long and that was alright with us. Our next convoy was to parts unknown and were at sea for over two weeks. We were on one of those old English tubs. The eats were terrible. Being seasick wasn't enough they had to feed us food that was spoiled. Our eats were pretty good while in England tho.

After we landed in Africa a few days I received all my many months mail, packages and so forth. By the way, I also received the package from you Leaguers and it certainly came in handy. Boy, is it ever nice to get mail and packages at a time like this. Being near Xmas when we landed our Xmas dinner was same as usual but in the evening we had a party and that was very unusual for us.

The climate here is agreeing with me. It is a little wet but has warmed up some so I can feel at home. We are sleeping in tents and I like it very well, at least you can go to bed without someone disturbing you. The dust blows most of the day and night and the beds feel of good fresh sand, just blown from some Arabs sheep pen from across the fields. It would be a good idea if our dug-outs were farther under ground and again when it comes to digging – I believe it's deep enough.

We are getting good old chow now, all American rations, plenty of fruit, eggs, and chicken. We buy them from the Arabs and cook them ourselves. As yet we don't know much about the war over here and are pretty lucky at that. I do need a good French-English dictionary or something so I could talk their language.

I don't have much to tell or say except next to the good old U.S.A. I guess this is the place to be. I'll sign off for now and pick up my pencil again as I have so many letters to answer I don't know just where to start in at.

As ever,
Cpl. Noble Woodyard

❧❧❧

It is expedient for us, that one man should die for the people, and that the whole nation perish not. John 11:50.

Miami Beach, Florida

Dear Leaguers:

I have a few moments of leisure so I shall start this letter. I've taken upon myself the job of writing letters for the "jeeps", the boys I teach. The last few nights they really had me humping. I wrote twelve letters night before last. Boy, they all just flock here. You see they won't go to everyone as they are afraid they will be laughed at. You see having them in my class they have confidence in me. You should read some of their letters. I get a big kick out of writing these letters.

Well, as you see I'm Pfc., now. Was made it the first of April. Sure excited about it. Now I have to sew on my stripe. You should see my sewing. I sure love to sew – in a pings ear! It took be one hour to sew on one stripe and there are two to a shirt.

It sure is a beautiful day here. The sun is so bright after a foggy night. The day is like a day in June. Of course, it is so monotonous to have the days all alike. I wish I could feel just one night of frost.

Well, here it is Sunday and I've got to finish this letter or bust. It sure is a wonderful day here. The wind is quite strong today and blowing from the north. Of course, being a north wind it is quite cool. I went to church this morning at the Band Shell. We have an Episcopalian Chaplain.

Haven't received many letters this week and I'm out of form in writing letters. You see since I've been writing letters for the boys in my class and they have been pestering me. I've been writing on the average of three or four a night. By the time I finish with them it is too late to write my own correspondence. Today I was going to answer all my letters and here comes on of my "jeeps" in. I finally got rid of him after I wrote two letters for him. Very <u>nice</u> letters to their wives and sweethearts.

One of the boys from our town is down here in Miami Beach. He had been coming over to see me every Sunday. Last Sunday we went on a boat trip in Biscayne Bay to see the beautiful homes on the bay. Quite a few rich people up north have winter homes on or near Miami Beach. You can't see them from the land side but from the water they are beautiful. Today we're going over to Miami and take a bus somewhere. Well, I'll have to close now. I'm sorry I can't write more. Write, kids!

Your Leaguer Pal,
Wig.

వావావా

Camp San Luis Obispo, California

Dear Leaguers and all,
I received your paper, "Zion Lutheran Messenger" and certainly appreciated it. Well, I'm back in an army camp again and it really seems swell. We traveled on day and one night to get off the desert and come to Camp San Luis Obispo. From the looks of things this is going to be just the opposite of what we had out in the desert. This morning we had to come to work with our woolen uniform, with a tie and had to get our shoes shined. One good thing there isn't as much sand here and they say it rains quite a bit but I think their rainy season is over by now.
I suppose we'll have to do a little more soldiering but I know this is going to be a lot better than where we were. The camp is located between tow or rather three hills or mountains. It has a lot of nice green grass and all hard roads. We are sleeping in huts, which have six in each hut. They have oil heaters in them. If I owe some of you letters please excuse me as I have been very busy making out insurance for the fellows but should be caught up soon. I received many nice birthday cards and thanks for sending them.

It seems good to go to church in a Chapel again and it is pretty close to my quarters.

Got to go to San Francisco the weekend of the 4th and had a good time. I wonder if I acted like a country boob in the big city. About all the news for this time and write when you have time. Sure enjoy your letters.

Just,
"Pete"

❧❧❧

Alliance, Nebraska

Dear Leaguers:

Suppose by this time you all have heard the news we weren't able to come home just yet. I called Mom and Dad one night at 12 bells to tell them of the change of plans. Yes, they were surprised. They laughed when I told them it has been 25 to 27 below zero but I would like to have them send me my summer duds. Well, we've moved into our "apartment", only it didn't turn out to be an apartment. Our landlady couldn't get anyone to cut the door so it is just one room. It is very large and has just everything in it.

One Sunday afternoon recently Bill and I went out to the post to see a mass jump put on by the paratroopers who have been shipped out here. About 90 men jumped from 9 planes. They also dropped supplies like they are trained to do and they have a German police dog that jumps. It was quite a sight. We were allowed to take pictures so I took advantage so I took a whole roll. About all the news from these parts at present. We're fine and hope all our friends back in Ottawa Lake are too.

As Ever,
Mildred and Bill Shoemaker

Atlantic City, New Jersey
April 5, 1943

Dear Leaguers:

Hi, kids, guess where I am —— in a hotel in Atlantic City, New Jersey. Everything's grand so far. I'll start at the beginning of my trip and tell you the details. As soon as we got to Detroit from Monroe the first thing we did was eat and we haven't stopped yet. They passed candy bars and oranges around on the train. Fort Custer was good but this is really the life. We are living in a large hotel here. I'm in the Air Corps, signal corps. We certainly were given a lot of clothes.

I wish I could tell you all about the view from the hotel or a little more about it but I will sometime. The room we're in was $20.00 a day for civilians. We certainly are getting a lot of food here, for supper we had – beef stew, mashed potatoes, pineapple, fig bars, milk, cocoa, spinach, and pickles. We had Swiss steak for dinner. I'll have to cut out eating so much or I'll be getting fat.

They publish a weekly paper for us. There is plenty of entertainment. We have both salt water and fresh water to bathe in. Coming from Fort Custer we had a special train all the way. They didn't tell us where we were going until we came through Philadelphia. We went through Canada too.

About all the news for this time and I'd enjoy hearing from all of you.

One of Uncle Sam's boys,
Kurt Durst

Del Rio, Texas
4/2/43

Dear Leaguers:
Received your paper the other day and say, I really enjoyed it. It got here the day we went on a cross country to Fort Wayne, Indiana and I read it on the way down there. I think the paper is a very fine idea. That way we know what you all are doing back home.

We certainly have been busy keeping these planes in shape to fly and then fly in them. I sat down the other day and added up my hours for the month and I have over a hundred, that makes me over five hundred hours in the air.

Doris is planning on coming down the sixth of this month. I don't know how she'll like it here in Texas because it has been quite hot here.

We are supposed to go to Florida this afternoon and come back tomorrow night. In the past six days I've been in about fifteen states so you see I can't sing that song, "Don't Get Around Much Anymore".

Well, kids, I'll sign off for this time. I think I'll see you all in May. Bye, Bye, for now.

As ever,
Frank and Doris Schumaker

❧❧❧

Ft. Benjamin Harrison, Indiana
March 27, 1943

Dear Leaguers and congregation:
Received you "Messenger" and enjoyed it beyond my telling.

I am in the letter writing business this morning. It is now just 4:00 A.M. I've been on night duty ever since I've been here and in the mornings I'm sleepy so I go to bed early and think I will get up early in the afternoon and write and what do I do but sleep until 5:00 o'clock so I just have enough time usually to get my room in order and myself ready to go to chow at 5:45.

We have close to 1000 patients here and at night we usually have a couple of wards so I have on the average of 50 to 60 patients to over see. The majority return to duty. I don't have so much to do because on each ward there are ward students who are also soldiers in white uniforms who have had some lessons on nursing care. I have two on each ward and they are very good and go ahead with their work. I have to pass out medicines, which aren't so many, and the most important thing is our reports. I have to check on the students work and try to keep them busy and help in case there are patients that are seriously ill. I have to also carry the keys which seems important. We are warned never to give our keys to anyone except perhaps another nurse for many reasons. A few reasons is that we keep all medicines locked and all the soldiers clothes are locked. The kitchen door and the linen room door is locked too. So many of these patients are up and around and if they could get to the medicine they might decide to help themselves instead of asking us and get the wrong kind. We keep their clothes locked because they might decide to just leave us although we try to be good to them so they don't feel that way. The kitchen usually has lots of milk and fruit juice in the refrigerator and if we left the door open I'm afraid the patients that are up and around would get more then the sicker patients who are confined to bed.

We have to check on the patients very close. Every night after 9:00 o'clock when lights are out we have to count to see that everyone is in and if someone isn't you have to account for him and officers usually come around a couple times and anything off line is then reported. All those fellows know what it would mean probably better than I if they didn't obey the rules around here so I've never had any trouble yet. I have a lot of fun and lots of these patients are just beaming with little tricks.

This is one trick they played on me the second night I was on duty. The lights were out about one-half hour and one of the fellows came out and wanted some medicine for a headache. I took my flashlight and started back to the medicine cabinet, which is in the ward, and tried not to make any noise and just then I kicked against some wash basins one of the fellows strung along the floor. Some of the fellows just about died holding back the snickers, they thought that was a real joke. I acted real mad and said I'd give the person who did that 10 minutes to get them back where they belonged. They all waited but I didn't do anything more about it but counted it as a joke.

The first thing they ask you here is what state you are from. Everyone seems to like Michigan but the girls from Kentucky take a beaten. They have that cute southern accent so they don't even have to say where they are from.

I now have only seven nights and then I'll be back to normal living again, sleeping nights and working days. I always enjoy letters so drop me a line.

Sincerely,
Inez Bieber

ೋೋೋ

News about Andrew Ery:
Since Andy is in the Navy his folks hear form him about every seven weeks. His trips, which are all convoying have been mostly to Casablanca, North Africa. They get very little time off when they are across and when they get back in Port here usually they rate just a liberty, which gives them a few hours around their port. Andy's port is usually New York. When they

are in port they have to fix their boat, if damaged, and Andy is on a destroyer. The only furlough he has had was a 72 hour pass, which gave him two nights at home. His traveling time comes out of that time also. He was home last on April 7, 1943. His rate at present is Fireman 1/C but is due for another promotion.

His letters are censored as well as those he receives. Thus far his boat has never been hit but he has served in at least three major sea battles including the landing of troops in Casablanca. He has been on the same boat since he joined in October 7, 1941. He had six weeks basic training at New Port, R. I.

అలఅలఅల

May 4, 1943

Dear Luther Leaguers:

Just a few lines to say "Hello" to you all. Haven't much to write about. I am back at work again and feeling fine. Sure was glad to get back on the job. Never liked to work so well. Ha! Ha!. Time goes very slow if one is not busy.

I received my first class sea-men paper in March. Would like to tell you all about our work but that's out. I had hopes of seeing some of you about three weeks ago. But my plans were sort of shattered. So guess I'll have to forget about the furlough for sometime again.

Had hopes of seeing some of the guys. The other day I thought sure I was going to run into Pete for some reason or other, but I didn't. I'm the funniest guy. Always straining my eyes for someone I know. But so far no good.

Will write again next month.

As ever,
Gerald Holmes

అలఅలఅల

San Diego, Calif.
April 28, 1943

Dear Folks:

I read in the Sylvania Sentinel that Pete is out here in California. Where is he located? Paul Freeland, the Marine that used to come out to our house all the time while he was stationed in Toledo is stationed out here just a few miles from us so we see him a lot.

We drove up to Los Angeles last weekend and visited Henry's grandparents and aunts. California certainly is a beautiful place, at least around here where we are.

We have a nice big yard here and I planted a garden. I pick strawberries just about every day. I wish we could stay here longer, it sure would be fun to use them.

We went to a Lutheran Church downtown Easter morning and really enjoyed it very much. It was a small church and we were surprised to find one so small downtown. We went to the early service.

Then on Easter afternoon we went to Mexico. It is quite a place. Nothing is rationed down there, but they are kind of particular what you bring back across the border although I thought they were pretty lenient at that. Each person is allowed as much canned goods as you want to bring back also 4 ½ pounds of meat, but no coffee, sugar, beans or rice. We brought back some meat. They still have silk stockings and most everything else down there but the price is plenty steep. We were in Tijuana, Mexico. The place itself is old and dumpy looking. It is just like a movie. Men riding down the street on horseback and all kinds of peddlers along the street trying to sell you something or wanting to take your picture sitting on a donkey. We would have had one taken but I knew Dad would have said, "It's a good thing they get hats on so you can tell which on is which."

Hope everything is OK back in the ole community and we'll be seeing you soon I hope.

As ever,
Erica and Henry Lunde

❧❧❧

NEWS FROM ONE OF OUR LEAGUERS WHO IS IN CAMP ROBINSON, ARKANSAS

Clayton writes that they are in a new section of the camp. They are busy cleaning it up. It is red clay and they have a lot of rain too. For the past week they have been on the rifle range. When he first started out he didn't do so good so he had to do a lot of practicing. Monday and Tuesday they were firing for records. Said his score was average and that he made a score of 153. That was 13 points above the number necessary and that gave him a rating of marksman.

They have a Lutheran Chapel there. The liturgy of the Chapel is very similar to our church and so that makes him feel very much at home.

The weather there is like in July here and he said it seems odd to hear that folks back here are still having a furnace fire.

They go through the alphabet for K.P. duty, which means that every fellow gets a chance. He has had it for the second time now. Says he has also been table waiter and has learned to wash his clothes. Says he uses super-suds and a plunger. Best of luck, Pal. We sure miss you in church, at our League meetings and other activities.

❧❧❧

N. Africa
April 17, 1943

Dear Leaguers:

Received my first copy of the Luther League Paper, even though I hardly know half the names I really must compliment you all on the good work. It really is nice. Am sorry that I don't have much to write you myself, but I know you'll understand that I don't have much time. And there's very little that I'm permitted to write.

Our boys had their first real action by air the other day and they really done a good job. Everything done up right and most all the planes returned. I'm what you call a ground Mechanic. I like my work a lot. Don't know of anything else I could pick that would suit me better.

We don't have much reading here, I do get the Stars and Striped and a few other magazines, that's where the League paper comes in handy. Have subscribed for the Stars and Stripes for Lovetta for a year. There's a lot in it that wouldn't be in your paper probably, it explains the war action much more clearly, and every little detail small or large is published.

Still haven't gotten my French-English dictionary and am still having quite a time with my hands making them understand over here what I want.

Will be looking for the News from Ottawa Lake again next month, so until next time.

As ever,
Noble Woodyard

᪥᪥᪥

Lincoln Air Base
5/9/43

Dear Leaguers:

I received the "Messenger" OK, my opinion of it is very high, it not only keeps us in touch with all the folks at home, but it gives us the latest addresses of all our friends, that we can sit down and write a letter to anyone of those in the service.

I like the small notes each one writes that way we know what the other fellows are doing and of their experiences. I really think that paper is a fine thing, the Word of God, and the prayers that are found in it help to console a soldier. Especially in the time of need, although we have our Bible. I'll say "keep it up home front, your doing fine" and a million thanks for my copies.

We have been very busy in Motor Transportation. Causal movements, and supplies keep us very busy, in that manner I hardly find time to write Norma and Mother but I do manage to send them a line once in a while, so keep your chin up friends, I'll manage to find time someday, (I hope).

I'm OK, doing great, and feel the same. I sure hope I can stay this way now. I've had enough hospital.

One of the old gang,
Edgar Strable

ജ്ഞൈൈൈ

THE BOYS IN ARMY DRAB—

The "Messenger" found its way up (Somewhere) in Alaska and shook hands with Willie DeNudt because he wrote his wife Bernice he had received the paper the League was sending him and he said it was very interesting to read the news of the boys and where they are stationed. He is in service two years the 23rd of April and he hasn't been home for a year and a half. Bernice is getting very anxious to see him home but he says there's no furlough for him in sight yet. They are keeping him pretty busy and he has won several medals from the army for bravery. He isn't able to write much news since all his letters are censored.

Dear Mom,

Just a few lines to let you all know that I am well and hoping you are the same. I am sending you a couple of table cloths and a pillow case and films to be developed.

Keep the letters coming because it seems good to hear from all of you. Some of the boys got a week-end pass. Hope Horace and I get one for next weekend. About all the news for now.

Your son,
Forrest Nearhood

ঌঌঌ

JOE STEINER writes from NEW GUINEA.

Several of the people here have received letters from Joe in the past two weeks. In a letter to Orville and Ruth Fischer he wrote that he felt like a cat tied to a tree. Also that you really learn how to pray and believe different than you ever did before. Fred Fischer's also received a letter.

In letters to the Christ Fischer family he wrote the following bits, on April 22, 1943:

"How's everything back there? Nothing ever happens to me. I just go on doing a lot of nothing and there is no place as dull as New Guinea. Nothing ever happens down here. We ran out of Jap's. I've had a few plane rides and a lot of boat rides but for social life, there just isn't any.

I am looking forward to that paper you sent but it takes quite a long time for something like that to get here.

I am having Xmas. My Xmas packages are coming in and I have a little time to relax now. So Merry Xmas to you all.

At one time here one of the guys offered an Australian $15.00 for a box of candy and the Australian would not sell.

About all the news around here.

As Ever,
Joe

❦❦❦

Ft. Benj. Harrison, Indiana
April 23, 1943

Dear Leaguers:

I received my prize from the "Guess Who" column in you "Messenger" and thanks very much. Each letter I received while I was in isolation with the measles was really treasures.

Yesterday my nurse use the heel of my bedroom slipper to pound pins and pinned all my Easter and get-well cards up on the wall in my room. I have 14 all together.

Imagine me getting ready to enjoy my first 24 hour pass after finishing night duty – then to find myself getting redder and redder with a rash resembling measles so I soon landed in an isolation unit in the hospital instead of a pass.

I had the three day measles and the regular measles at the same time and really looked a mess for a week or more. I was quite sick for two days and was feeling fine when I developed tonsillitis. After a few days of that I developed some sinus trouble so that is why I have to stay in bed now.

I've been out of isolation quite a while and am beginning to get bored with staying in bed so I guess I'm getting better. I hate the idea of being here Easter Sunday, but if nothing else turns up I think I will be out of here the first of next week sometime.

I think it is good experience for us to be a patient at least once to perhaps remind us of some of our short-comings. I've had wonderful care since I've been sick here. One of my several doctors is one of the first doctors that left from St. Vincent's Hospital in Toledo to enter the service. He is Chief of the Medical Service here and was promoted from Major to Liet. Col. Last week.

Elg sent me a Easter card and enclosed an Irish coin. It has a harp on one side and pigs on the other side. Seems to me like a crazy combination but maybe it stands for something. I have also received three V-mail letters from him lately.

May 1, 1943

Dear Leaguers:

Received my second copy of "Zion Lutheran Messenger" and was glad to get it. I certainly was surprised to find the Bieber's all done up I poetry. Was equally surprised to read my own letter.

Have little in the way of news to write.

In the past couple of weeks during my excessive spare time I've acquired the reading habit. It is a pleasant past-time when "things to do" are scarce.

Just thought and thought but couldn't figure out who the "guess who" might be so will be anxious to see the next "Messenger" and hope the winner will enjoy receiving his prize as much as I did.

This is Saturday morning, which means general inspection. The inspectors haven't come yet but everything seems to be in perfect order and clean as all the help have been busy as bees all morning.

Sincerely yours,
Inez Bieber

Some of you remember Dan Mueller, brother of Rev. Mueller. He's the one who came by airplane from Niagara Falls with his sister, Helen, one day last year. He parked his plane at Franklin Field overnight, visited for an evening in the parsonage and then flew back to Niagara the next day. Well, Dan is in Florida now – instructing RAF cadets. Says he: "Things are going as good as can be expected out here. The job is quite a headache. Traffic is rather heavy and to send the students up solo is a mental strain as far as I am concerned. I have only three students now as one of them just could not make the grade. They have to learn to fly blind under the hood, know day and night cross country navigation and also do a fair job of aerobatics. Started several of my boys on aerobatics last week and already I have been blacked out when the student fell out of a half roll. A person will black out when recovery is made from a steep dive or where excessive speed is involved...

We are expecting a lot of bugs and insects here this summer so Jack and I have just completed a nice screened-in porch for our trailer. The end of the war can not come too soon for me.

Love,
Dan

❧❧❧

Kansas City, Mo.
April 22, 1943

Hi Leaguers:
I got my copy of the paper today, and thought it was swell. I have been trying to figure out how I could keep track of the girls as they got married anyhow. No kidding though it's a swell paper.

Well, since then I've moved westward. I think we have about tops here at Kansas City. I have a nice semi-private room in a small hotel. What I enjoy most is the maid service. No making beds, cleaning rooms or washing towels for us.

We have a pass which entitles us to eat in a downtown restaurant and order what we want and as much as we want. Just like back in civilian life, only they don't give you a bill.

I'm going to Radio Aviation School here. We get to sleep till 7 AM if we wish. We go to school seven hours a day and one half day on Saturdays.

We do the rest of the time just as we see fit. We can go and come just as we please. Our hotel is civilian operated, our restaurant is, and our school is so we actually never see any officers.

Our course here is thirteen weeks, which will run to the end of July. I wish it lasted thirteen months instead. All the fellows I've talked to that are leaving wish they could stay.

There are not very many soldiers here for a city of 500,000 and there are just as many WAACA, besides the other girls, and there are lots of them.

The civilians are swell too. Whenever we want to go anywhere we never have any trouble getting a ride.

They were nice enough to give me a rating of Corporal when I got here. I was made P.F.C. just three days before, and hadn't even gotten time to sew my stripe on when I got another. Now I'm Sgt. Besides all the other things, the government gives us $2.75 a day to pay for our hotel and meals. We have a flat rate of $1.90 and so we get .85 a day over our pay. All I can say for my army life is – well I never lived like this before. It suits me swell. The school is sort of tough but the top of the class always gets awarded in more ratings so that's something to work for.

Tomorrow is opening day for summer uniforms. I pressed my own at the Kansas City Canteen yesterday, no kidding, they look pretty good for my work. I got my camera from home today so I'll be sending some pictures. Well, Kids, I guess I'll be saying so long for now.

As ever,
Kurt Durst

ഛഛഛ

Zion Lutheran messenger
Ottawa Lake, Michigan 1944

To The Men And Women In The Armed Services:

Undaunted in the face of bitter odds! Why not? While there is life there is hope—hope of survival. That is a truism all over the world in peace and in war. A crisis in life calls for extra reliance upon the "inner resources" of life. You cannot draw money from the bank. If, you did not first deposit it there, Neither can you lean much upon yourself in the spirit of self-confidence, unless you have the firm assurance that there is "something within: upon which you may rest.

True confidence and courage are born of God. By nature we are creatures of fear. This is due to the inescapable sense of sin. But thanks to god, by our new life in Christ, his victory becomes ours and in his strength we have new courage and bold confidence in the face of all that is evil and unhuman. Before the next issue of this paper reaches you Easter, 1944 will have come—and gone. May the deep joys of that first Easter be abundantly present in your hearts. Though the noise and drone of guns and planes should broadcast death on all the battlefronts of the world, yet permit God's Gospel of the "EMPTY TOMB OF CHRIST (Mark the 16th chapter) to enlarge your spiritual vision. "This is the will (of God the Father) that every one which seeth the Son (Jesus Christ), and believeth on him, may have everlasting life: and I (Jesus) will raise him up at the last day."

"Yea, though I walk through the valley of the shadow of death, I will fear no evil for thou (Jesus) art with me..." Thus Psalm 23:4. At all costs hold the front line of faith

Cheerio

Your Pastor and Friend

Marcus Mueller

❧❧❧

Somewhere in Italy,
Feb 1, 1944

Dear Violet & Leaguers

Have a special message to you right fresh off the Press. This morning while I was off duty, and was writing a letter to Elg I happened to glance up and to my surprise thought I saw Kenny go past our tent. I hurried to the door and sure enough, Kenny was on a pass and stopped by and talked about being glad to see someone! We visited for a while and then had dinner together and then went for a short hike to do a little sightseeing.

Kenny sure looks fine and I think he has even added a few pounds. He had on his new scarf and sweater and really looked swell.

I had to go back on duty from 2P.M until 7P.M. but we had supper together and spent the evening together. Kenny said we must write to you and that was a very good idea so I'm on my half. Even though I'm a poor cook, we had some cocoa. He didn't have to go back to his outfit until Wednesday, so I had him sleep in the hospital so we could climb the famous mountain tomorrow, because I have the whole day off and believe me it will be put to fullest advantage. Kenny won't be able to say he's never been in the hospital—here's hoping the night nurse doesn't get her bed numbers mixed and try to et him to take some medicine. At least he can speak English

117

instead of French, so think he'll be able to defend himself. Think I'll rest my hand a while and give Kenny more room to write.

I don't know so much about these night nurses giving me any medicine. It sure was a grand meeting we had putting all jokes aside. You should have seen my dear Lt. when she popped her head out of her tent door. She sure was speechless for a few minutes. I am proud to say that she is looking very lovely and has put on a few pounds herself. She also has some very nice girlfriends that stay in the tent with her.

Really how I happened to be here is due to the fact that I was lucky enough to draw a five day pass to the rest center, which is only about the same distance as Adrian is from home (from rest center to the hospital). It took me no time at all to pick up a ride in to the hospital. I have my camera with me and will try and take some pictures of the two of us before I return to camp. I hope we can send you some of them in the near future.

This makes the second time I've run around with a dear friend since I left the states. I hope it happens more often. I have just about spilled my wad so I will let Inez finish this letter

Seeing Kenny seems so good I just can't believe we are so many miles form home. In fact it's the nearest I felt like being at home for a long time. (Kenny said I should add that the feeling is mutual). Wish we could run across Huck and we would have a gay time reunion.

We will write again soon and let you know all about our mountain climbing tomorrow

Best wishes from Italy
Sincerely,
Inez and Kenny

❧❧❧

Somewhere in Italy,
Feb 15, 1944

Dear Violet:
    I finally got around to drop you a few lines and let you know how Inez and I made out the next day after we wrote that letter to you. She more than likely has written you before this but never the less I promised.
    We done some mountain climbing all right and had a swell time took up three rolls of film and hope they turn out good. I received a letter from her the other day and she said she was a little stiff, after the walk but was ready for another one anytime.
    She sure looks swell and has a nice cozy tent for a home. I've never enjoyed two days more than I spent with her. It seemed so much like home. I sure wish I could drop in for supper some night kid. I have a lot of things to talk about. I am waiting for My January Messenger, and hope it arrives soon. I hope this find you O.K. I am O.K.
    As ever,
    Love, Kenny

Dear Clyde (Pagenhagen)
    Received your V-Mail and I am okay. Have been restricted to tent city since the first of the month. It was a real treat to go dancing again. We have some good shows in our mess hall some evenings "Silver Skates," Lady in a Jam".
    They served us two oranges for Sat. dinner the last two Saturdays a real treat and a chicken dinner today. We get ice cream now for supper. Uncle Sam is sure treating his nephews if they are far from home. My name is Matt in the army. It takes nine days for a letter to come from Inez.
    Over sea's duty hasn't been too bad so far lots of nice dances. Most of the people are in a uniform to help win this

war. W.L.A. is the Land Army Women, which really work hard on the farms. Sending my best regards and hoping to see you soon

Cherrio
Pvt. M.E. Bieber

ୡୡୡୡ

MEMORIAL SERVICE HEALD FOR CORNELIUS BLOME, JR. HELD AT ZION, SUNDAY MARCH 12TH

This service is held in memory of Cornelius Blome, Jr, who on December 2, 1943 died in the service of our Country.

Cornelius was born in Toledo, Ohio on Feb 1, 1921. he was the son of Mr. and Mrs. Cornelius Blome, formerly of Ida, Michigan.

He received instruction in the saving knowledge of our Lord and was confirmed into the Lutheran Church in Deerfield, Michigan.

Cornelius enlisted in the Merchant Marine in March 1942 and served as cook. While in the service he made three crossing of the Atlantic, one to Russia, one to Sicily and the last to Italy. Twice he was home on furlough. His death was the result of an attack on the ship on which he was stationed.

Surviving are his parents of Blissfield, Mich., and four sisters: Mrs. Betty Heck of Monroe; Mrs. Haxel Brodbeck of Toledo; Mrs. Linda Papenhagen of Ottawa Lake; and Mrs. Bertha Lievens, Riga.

May the God of all comfort, console the bereaved hearts.

We think of the noble lines of Tennyson's "Crossing The Bar".

> Sunset and evening star,
> And one clear call for me!
> And may thee be no moaning of the bar
> When I put out to sea,
> But such a tide as, moving, seems asleep,

Too full for sound and foam,
When that which drew from out the boundless deep
Turns home again.
Twilight and evening bell,
And after that the dark!!
And may there be no sadness of farewell
When I embark;
For though from out our bourne of Time and Place
The flood may bear me far,
I hope to see my Pilot face to fact
When I have crossed the bar
                    Alfred Tennyson.

NEWS FROM ZION AND COMMUNITY

Somewhere in New Guinea,
Feb 10, 1944

Dear friends back home

Well, here we are safe and sound in New Guinea. Our trip over was rather smooth although I did get a little sick the first couple of days out; I never thought a large ship could toss around like it did. We crossed the equator and they had a little ceremony that lasted a few hours. They held it on deck and not being too tall I had a hard time to see. They selected a few from each company to go through this treatment. They had them put on bathing suits; smeared grease on them on their face and chest, cut some of their hair and then dumped them in a tub of water. They used large scissors to cut their hair so that it looked like a lawn mower was used. We lost a day while crossing the international date line and we had a hard time keeping track of the time. The day that we lost happened to be Sunday so we had our services on the boat on Monday. The first services they held in the Officer's Mess, and it was conducted by both the ship Chaplain and our regiment Chaplain. Then on Monday evening we had about an hour of singing and I really enjoyed that. We have a fairly nice set up here considering the fact that we are out here in the jungle area. It is cleared up quite a bit now. The natives are really small bushy-haired fellows and are really dark. They are working on the roads here. They seem to be plenty dirty and I think that they are diseased. They don't wear hardly any clothing at all, only a small piece of cloth around their waist. Some of them can speak broken English but they have a language of their own. The first night I saw them they were loading up on a truck after a days work and they started to sing. They seem to be happy little fellows. They do a lot of work for their size.

Before we left to come over here I got the Messenger and was I really glad. The first night that we were on the boat I took it out of my duffle bag and read it form one cover to the other. I really enjoyed reading it, in fact, I read it several times coming over and towards the last it seemed as though I knew just what was coming in the letters so it wasn't so interesting any more.

I will appreciate all the letters you folks can write as it looks like our activity over here will be limited to a great extent.

I'm fine and I hope this finds every one in service and back home the same. I'm looking forward to seeing you all again and let's hope and pray that it will be soon.

A fellow Leaguer,
"Pete" Leroy Fischer

Lincoln Nebraska,
Feb 13, 1944

Dear Leaguers:
Thank you for the lovely note and the Valentine. I'm so anxious to hear about the boys. We sure get scattered don't we. Gosh Olin in Alaska, Clayton in Texas and Pete in Hawaii. How war chases us around. I would have gotten a valentine for the League, but war does funny things. Thursday we had a terrible snowstorm so we were restricted to the Base Thursday and Friday night. I wasn't able to get any valentines until Saturday and of course they were all picked over. I decided to send a letter instead.
Last Saturday we were placed on the alert for shipment. I was to be allowed to go to school. We were to leave Wednesday. I was to go to Fort Logan near Denver. Tuesday I was scratched form shipment. The school has been closed. I was turned Air Corp unassigned and allowed to hold my rating of a sergeant. Now here I am supposed to be shipped but not shipped. My job is finished. Nothing for me to do here. Don't worry the army won't allow that long. I'll probably be shipped this week. Where I'm to go I don't know. I hope I can go to school. Probably the next time you hear from me; I'll have a different address. But keep writing to mew at my present address, as I may be here a month or more.
I want to thank the Luther League for the nice Valentine and also Gerrie for sending me the papers and the valentine.
Hoping to hear from you soon, I remain as always.
Sgt. Facklam
In other words
"Wig" (the immortal Sgt.)

Dear Violet & Leaguers:

Here we are settled once more in this fair city of the sunny south (what a city, and I haven't seen much of the sun either). If you live here very long you have to be a duck to like such sloppy weather as we have had so far.

They may be fighting World War II everywhere else in the world, but these poor people down here are still fighting the Civil War with us.

Outside of people shoving their elbows into my ribs, cleaning their shoes on my stockings, and walking all over my feet (but that's all right I walk on them too) on the street cars. I managed to get along quite well.

Was talking to an English sailor the other evening and when I told him I was from Michigan he said, "oh, the people from up there are tough." I asked him where he got that idea and he told me how he read in the paper that they were always fighting there. Don't know what paper he reads, but I guess he must have read about the strikes and race riots.

We like our apartment very well and if any of the boys are ever shipped to Norfolk they are welcome to drop in anytime, and if you girls ever get the urge to see thousands of sailors you may come to Norfolk and visit us too.

Give our regard to all those who help to make the messenger the welcome end interesting paper that is. We look forward to receiving it as it is the best way I know of in keeping up with the people we know "from back home".

Love:
Erica & Henry

Somewhere in the South Pacific
Feb 22, 1944

Dear folks:

I received you box and it came in pretty good condition except that bar of soap you had in it sort of flavored the candy. Ha! But we ate it anyway. I received the box from the Ladies' Aid too. Fat received his a couple of days ago. I was on K.P. the other day. It isn't so bad over here as you just have to wash the pans and take the garbage to the garbage pit.

I was on the Fiji Island for about two months. It was really nice there. We slept in a barracks and there were two theatres that we could go to they had a Red Cross too where we were able to get good meals. We were stationed in the Capital of the Fiji Islands. The name of the city was Suva. It was a nice place and we went swimming in the ocean once in awhile. There were two P.X. in town where they sold ice cream, cigarettes and many other things. We really had good chow on Fiji. I was on New Caledonia for a little while but I didn't like it there so well. The natives were pretty friendly on both Islands. There were white people of both Islands. French people on New Caledonia and English people of the Fijis. I have seen an active volcano. It is a big high mountain and the smoke just pours out of the top.

Your loving son,
Horace Nearhood.

❧❧❧

Dear Rev Mueller:
With much gratitude I am answering for you kind consideration in sending me the Zion Lutheran Messenger. It's

the first one of its kind I've ever seen, and a mighty nice one at that. May God bless it to the needs of many hungry souls.

Have been stationed at Camp Parks, California for six months. Strange as it may seem the scenery is very beautiful. In Michigan one would think of snow and very cold weather, and everything dead for the rest of the winter. Here in Calif. the mountains in all their splendor are very neatly capped with snow while beautiful green grass is growing along the incline. With the sun shining on them, they are the most beautiful scenery one would wish to see. California is beautiful and has pleasant weather, with it all I'll settle for good old Michigan.

Our Battalion will be leaving the States ion the very near future. I'll write you again when we arrive at our destination I can't say where it will be, because we don't know that ourselves. I am almost sure it is to the South Pacific.

It's almost time for lights out, so I'll close for this time. May the peace of God rest and abide in your heart now and until Jesus comes.

Sincerely yours,
Edwin Schieb S1/C

ҩҩҩ

Somewhere in England
Dear Violet and Leaguers: (from Vernon Packard)

At last my army career has brought me to a foreign shore. Am now stationed in England. I like it here. The landscapes are beautiful and the English people are very hospitable to all. Have seen the river, which we read of back in the states. I am planning a visit to London soon. There I plan on visiting all the old famous churches and other historic landmarks. There is a decided difference between England and the U.S.A. We are very changeable, always attempting improvements. The English love tradition and are conservative in their likings. Also we in Americans emphasize size more than our British brethren.

Everything here is on a smaller scale. The British "tummies": are nice fellows once you gain their confidence. They are more reserved than we are. When they see we desire their companionship and conversation they join us gladly, In their smaller more crowded country they administer Caution to us not to intrude on another's privacy. It is my sincere hope that this conflict, and our forced unity with other people in a common cause, will bring to our people a realization of the necessity of human brotherhood, and love. If so then our sacrifices will not be in vain, but bear everlasting benefit to all mankind.

A friend,
Vernon Packard

જીજીજી

Somewhere in New Guinea,
 February 14, 1944

Dear Violet and Leagers:
    Just received the December Messenger a little late but very welcome never the less. I certainly do enjoy reading it I have read it through twice already. Keep up the fine work on a truly fine paper.
    As you see my address has changed again. Yes I am back on the other side of the world again. I think I left Africa just a little before Inez Bieber got here. It seem as though I am always just missing people. I see by the Messenger that a lot of the young people are in several places I have already been. In the six years I have been in the Navy I haven't run into anyone yet that comes from around the Lake. I guess its because I don't stay one place long enough.
    I see Pete Fischer is in the Hawaiian Islands now. I spent two years there before the war I wonder if he finds them as interesting ad I did? My stay in the States was very limited this time only 18 days to be exact. I believe that was the fastest

18 days I over spent in my life. My family has moved back across country now to Portland, Oregon. Sure hope to be able to join them soon.

I showed our paper to the Chaplin aboard ship and he thinks it a very remarkable piece of work, we have our church service every Sunday. We just received a portable electric organ and it does help with the singing.

There doesn't seem to be much to write about. I can't give much information as to what we are doing due to censorship regulations, but I will say we are always ready willing and able to fight for our God, home and country. Let us hope and pray that this war will soon be over so we can all settle back down in a free peaceful country to live our lives and worship our God the way we choose.

I will bring this to a close wishing you all a belated Christmas and continued success with your great work I remain, As always

Lester L. Knuth

&&&

"GOD BE WITH YOU ALL UNTIL WE MEET AGAIN"

Clewiston, Florida
Dear Sister Helen:

Have received both of your letters in the last few days and of course was very glad that you are able to come to pay us a visit. In another week or so we will start night flying and that will mean long night cross-country trips. I'm very glad that the advanced airplanes are equipped with radio. This fog problem is really something in Florida. A ground fog will appear in almost no time and it is very nice to follow a radio range to some other airport that is open. The last class lost two cadets when our field was closed in by fog, as they returned from a long cross-country trip. They wandered off towards Ft. Meyers and apparently tried to let down thru the fog. They crashed into some trees and burned.

One of my cadets had a very close shave the other day and he was eliminated for Italy. He was on a solo flight when flew into a large flock of birds. I'm enclosing a card, which shows a picture of these birds. Those birds called Ibis, are bigger than a chicken and he hit at least eighteen of them. He tried to talk his way out of it, but he must have been going at a very high rate of speed because there were holes as big as you r head in the leading edges of the metal wings. One of the birds went thru the windshield (side panel) and hit him on the shoulder. The airplane, inside and outside, was the dirtiest mess that you could ever hope to see (cadet also). The engine cowling and the space between the cylinders was packed full of dead birds and the engine was very much overheated because of this. Men at the field had to work several hours to pick bits of meat from every crack and crevices. Repairs to this ship will amount to at least four thousand dollars. The student's theory was that he made a simulated forced landing and hit the birds at about 120 M.P.H. However, everyone at the field believes that he was diving at the birds and was going well in excess of 200 M.P.H.

Well, I guess that is all for now and I hope that you are perfectly at ease about making this trip.

Love,
Dan Mueller
(brother of Rev. Mueller)

Camp Fannin, Texas,
March 5, 1944
Dear Members and friends of Zion: -

As I look at the addresses of those of our number now overseas, I cannot help but notice that we are now disbursed into every major theatre of operations. Then we also have members who are helping to bring supplies wherever our members maybe. It also is interesting to note that the greater part of our number now is overseas. It can't be said of Zion that they are not doing their part.

Our members overseas will have great experiences – some good – some not so good. There is only one thing to keep every before us and that is that our Providential God will stay by your side whether it be in Italy, on a lonely island in the South Pacific while you are patrolling on a gloomy night, in the cleared spot of the thick jungle of New Guinea, on board of an ocean convoy, in the snow bound artic station, or just on maneuvers in Great Britain keeping in shape for the opening of the great European front, or in t he training station here at home. Now is when you faith may be tested. Rely on God, He will see you through.

Things here at camp are as usual. We have just experienced the rainy season with a downpour most every day. Today has been a change and we have had a grand day. Perhaps the rain is all over now. It is indeed very unusual ot see most of the trees in blossom and some even more advanced with the leaves better than half developed.

I don't want to take too much of the space of this issue to tell you of the common everyday happenings of training camp for most of you can recall your basic training days and with that I think I have said enough – how you hated to have the non-coms always trying to see what they could find wrong with what you were doing.

I think if each of you often and wonder just what portion of the training you will retain to help save your life while in close combat if that should be your lot.

All we can do is hold fast to our Christian Faith and pray for a close of this conflict so that each and every one of us can return home safety.

As ever,
Clayton & Eldora Fischer.

This letter was received last week form a soldier in the Southwest Pacific who was awarded a Silver Star in the Battle of Mudna. He also was in the battle of Bouiganville, it reads as follows:

Dear Meva:

First of all I want to thank you for donating your blood to the Red Cross. Melva, if you would see some of the wonders that blood transfusions do you will feel well repaid. I have seen fellows brought in that I wouldn't give a plugged nickel for their chances of living. Give that one or more transfusions and they are back to life. Some cases out here have been kept alive for three days on someone else's blood allowing them to finally replace their own. I have no doubt that canned blood (plasma) has saved more lives then any other single thing or medicine. Pvt. Blair Hertzsch has been overseas two years and belongs to the 37th Div. He is the son of Mr. & Mrs Otto Jertzwch, Toledo.

Parts of the letter written by Raymond "Spud" Shanly to his folks dated Feb. 12: " I did a little washing the other day and it came out pretty good. I try to do it once a week or so then I don't have so much at one time. We have about two shows here a week and some of them are pretty good. We even had a good old Western the other night and the boys really whooped and hollered. I haven't been to a town for so long that I don't know what one looks like, My A.P.O. has been changed to No. 650."

William DeNudt writes, " will be in service three years on April 23rd. I sure traveled quite a few miles and had only one furlough. I just had company. It was the inspecting officer. He inspected the quarters and rifles. Everything passed good. I am still in t he same place yet but now I have a new address. I guess they think we will get tired of always having the same address."

ഔഔഔ

Fort George G. Meade, Md.
February 10, 1944

Hi Violet & Leaguers,

I enjoy the Messenger. Every once in a while a person starts reminiscing about old times, all those enjoyable Rallies, Conventions (Texas Minn., Maryland, Colorado) banquets-plays-and all those grand get together that were had by so many leagues in the District. You start wondering what all those lads and lasses are doing these days. Being away form home now a year and a half, losing all contacts. It is nice to read little tidbits about the fellow leaguers you use to know.

I had a perfect Christmas this year I was home, had eight days which all went much to fast, didn't get around much. I had been in her Hospital here for a week, just before my furlough. So had to take it pretty easy at home. I was a little afraid I'd miss my furlough, so I came out of the hospital too soon, gut you can't get a good horse down.

The gals are still in there plugging and doing a grand job, you probably seen in the papers, that more and more WACs are leaving for overseas. So maybe my chance will come soon. Have anyone in Alaska I can look for you?

The WACS on this post are constantly increasing and taking over more jobs. The Army ground Force Replacement Dept No. 1, is just like a railroad station around there, coming and going. Boys getting ready for shipment and boys coming back from overseas assignment. We also have an induction

132

and reception center her. So we have the green rookies. The expectant and the well-seasoned soldiers and they are all an interesting lot of course the boys returning from overseas. The ones being gone for 15 to 24 months are very interested at seeing their first WAC. It is a little surprising to see. Who have seen 18 months of service. We've thought that everyone knew all about the WACs.

Our gals sure have a full day working long hours with special classes and duties after work. Our basketball team has had a grand time this season, playing the WAVES SPARS MARINES and other WAC'S outfits. Most every camp around here now have WACS stationed there. We have our own bowling league, alleys, on the post and bondy. We have one team that is in the past league and we can give them some stiff competition.

Guess my rambling has gone on long enough. Give my regards to all the old gang, and I'm looking forward to a grand get together.

When Johnny and Janie comes marching home again. So till another time.

Always—Lorene Flege

Lorene is from St. Mark's in Toledo and well-know here. Her brother Alvin is one of the Scout Masters who has visited our S.S. & church with their troop.

We're happy to hear of the recent promotions: Russel Crecue has become a Private First Class and Howard Gross of Sylvania received his commission of 2nd Lt. On April 8 at Ft. Sill, Oklahoma.

જીજીજી

Somewhere in New Guinea,
March 24, 1944

Dear Fellow Leaguers:

 Sorry I haven't written a letter to you all before, but we have been busy most of the time we have been over here. Then, too, I suppose that you have been hearing from me, indirectly through the Folks and the Messenger. I received both the cards that you sent me, and thanks a lot for sending them. I especially appreciated the Birthday Card, as it makes a fellow feel good to think that someone remembers their birthday date, I almost missed it myself this year, as I always thought that the day was Wednesday instead of Thursday the 16th and my birthday. It wasn't until about noon that I realized that it was Thursday instead of Wednesday. Dates, days and time doesn't mean anything to us, as there is only one day that we are interested in and that is the day when this thing is over with and we can all get back home for good.

 I still haven't received the February issue of the Messenger as yet, but it should be getting here soon. The latest letter that I got was the 9th of March and that was a V-mail, while the latest Airmail was dated the 4th of March. I think that the V-Mail is the faster of the two coming over here, but the Air-Mail is no doubt the faster going back to the States, surely miss the Messenger and can't wait until I receive it. It is always good to hear just what the rest of the people are doing and where they are located. This isn't such a large world after all, as I think that we are almost half way around it. Now that I am over here, I would like to go back to the States by the way of the Atlantic, so that I could say that I traveled around the world.

 We moved again the weekend before last, and have just nicely gotten set up again. In fact, there is still a lot of cleaning up around and floors to be put in our sleeping tents, so that will give us something to do for a few days. The lumber is scarce over here, but may be we will get some later on. We cut some trees up the other day to get some blocks for the foundation, so that we would have that much done when we got the lumber.

We have a nice area here where we are, as we are right along the water and have a swell beach here. It was jungle area until about a month ago when the companies came up here and cleared most of it off for us. From what they say, there must have been quite a few fallen coconuts here and I guess that they had plenty of work. There are really a lot of coconut trees here, and they are plenty tall. We have to be careful when we walk around so that some of the coconuts don't fall down on us. We have eaten quite a few of the coconuts and drank quite a bit of the milk out of them. So far we haven't gotten tired of them. We are allowed to go in swimming every day between the hours of 11AM until 2:30 PM and from 4PM until &PM. If we stay here very long I should be able to swim. I can swim now, but not too much.

It is still plenty warm over here, in spite of the fact that we are having fall now. It is plenty wet here too, and they say that the rainy season hasn't started as yet. We haven't much fresh water around here, so every time that it rains we take off our clothes and take a good bath. Then we catch as much water as we can so that we wash our clothing. We find that it isn't such a bad job to wash the clothes now that we are able to get rinse, and there isn't as much tatle-tail-grey as there used to be before we were able to get it. Back there is washday generally on Monday, but here everyday and any is washday for us.

The other day I saw a couple of native women, and they were the first I have seen since we have been over here. We see quite a few of the men and talk with quite often. Some of them speak fairly good English, too. I suppose that some of you will remember the pictures and lectures that the Missionaries showed and gave at the Church a few years ago, so that will give you some idea of what it is like over here. I think that the Natives are more civilized now than they were then. I haven't seen many of their huts as yet, but hope to go to one of their villages soon so that I can see just what they are like.

I can't seem to think of anything more to write about, so will have to close for this time. Will be glad to hear from any of you if you have time to write, and will try to do my best in answering your letters.

I suppose that there will be quite a number of marriages this summer, so I want to take the opportunity now to congratulate you newly weds to be, and will eat a piece of your wedding cake after this is over and I get back home.

I'm feeling fine and hope this finds you all the same.

A fellow Leaguer
"Pete" Leroy Fischer

❧❧❧❧

Somewhere in New Guinea

Dear Violet and Leaguers

I received the four copies of the "Messengers" yesterday. I certainly do appreciate them very much. I don't know so very many of the boys in the service but some of them I've often wondered about, and now through the "Messenger" I know about where they are. Sure enjoyed reading Inez letters. She and I graduated together from Blissfield. Those were the days

I'll try to tell you something of the war on this side. There isn't many Japs right here now. WE have them more or less surrounded. With their supply lines cut and are just gradually closing in. I haven't seen any for a few weeks but those that have say that they are in pretty bad shape. Half starved and clothing in almost shreds. So you can see we are giving them a pretty bad time. Although they are in a bad state of health they certainly show a lot of fight, and they just won't give up. We have wonderful air support and also naval support.

After living in the jungle so long I'm getting so I like it. Some of the most beautiful sights never would be seen in any other part of the world. And these fuzzy-wuzzies)(natives) are sure doing a great job in winning this war. Most of them talk fairly good English. They are starting a ration plan in sending us home for a furlough. Just a very small percent goes at a time. But then after two years overseas it certainly is something to look forward to. So maybe I can see you all very soon.

Thanks again for the "Messenger".

Sincerely

Morgan Mehan

అలలల

Somewhere in Italy,
March 19,m 1944

Dear Ethel & family (Ethel Komsteller)

By all means I must writ to you and hope you folks are all well. I received the V-Mail with t he several little notes form everyone and really enjoyed it.

I have been on night duty for one week and 7 more nights and I will be finished with my two weeks of nights which we all average about every 4 months. It isn't so bad abut its an awful job keeping awake and we work 12 hour duty form 7PM to 7AM. I though I'd get caught up on letter writing while I was on night duty but this is about the first I've written because it seems when I am not busy I've been too sleepy to writ4e letters or even read. It is now almost 5:00AM, so another night is almost over and the ward-boys will soon wake the pts. To take early morning temperatures at 5:30 AM. The night nurses must censor all the pts. Mail so that takes a little time to read letters for about 130 patients.

Yesterday our Chief Nurse brought each of us nurses little wool knitted foot warmers that the Red Cross sent to us. Mine are made from dark green wool and they are so cute.

The other day I decided to get an Italian permanent wave because my hair was quite long and stubborn. It was an experience I'll never forget, quite unlike our American Beauty Shops, I'll have to admit, but my hair has some curl and doesn't look too bad so all is well. Ethel, you wouldn't recognize me as a nurse because you know overseas we don't wear our nice white uniforms because they just wouldn't be practical. We usually wear a brown and white pin stripe seersucker with caps to match, gut at night we can wear wool khaki pants and wool skirts. Maybe we don't look like nurse, but we keep nice and warm.

Happy Easter to All
Love,
Inez Bieber

ഔഔഔ

Camp Fannin, Texas,
April 7, 1944

Greeting where 'er you be; —
The Lenten Season and Easter 1944 are now history. For some of us this was the first Easter away form home and for others the first Easter from our homeland. In spite of all this most of us have been able to celebrate this event under Lutheran auspices. It is gratifying to read from Inez and Kenneth that they have a Lutheran Chaplain in their midst and Leroy writes of going to a Lutheran service in New Guinea. We know that these church services help bridge the numerous miles between you and the church back home.

It has been unusual to see roses in bloom at Easter but here they are. No doubt this area will have roses in bloom until the frost comes in the fall. Likewise the fast growing grass here reminds one of the times that should be spent on lawns back home.

Today I had the experience of riding with a lady bus driver for the first time. It appears that they are breaking in ladies to drive busses between Tyler and Camp Fannin.

We are both fine and we hope that all our acquaintances in the services are likewise in good health. If we will not be considered too late we want to wish you and one and all a Happy Easter.

To all the folks back home that remembered us with Easter Greetings we wish to say "Thank You".

As every,
Eldora and Clayton Fischer

ৡৡৡ

Somewhere in Sardinia
March 18, 1944

Dear Violet and Leaguers,

I guess that I don't have to tell you how much mail does to cheer us fellows. Our mail service here in Sardinia is very irregular. I hope and pray that this thing can all be cleared up soon and we can all return to our homes once again.

It is two years since I have seen anyone from Monroe County and I have been overseas for 16 months. I have 4 nephews and nieces that I have never seen yet.

It is Sat. night and I am at the weather station doing my writing. I am not on duty now but we have better lights and facilities here than we have in our tent. We are having communion tomorrow and I intend to attend. We have a fine group of young men and I have one friend who always attends services with me. He went to the Lutheran Church in San Antonio and he said the pastors name was Fischer.

We have very little entertainment here in Sardinia. An occasional movie is just about the only thing. The villages have little to offer. The stores are all empty and the natives are poverty stricken with hardly enough to eat and all are poorly clothed. When we go to town on a pass we are not allowed to buy food at the restaurants. In view of all this, our officer has made arrangements to have us all spend about one week at a rest camp. One of the boys has just returned and another is about to leave. I hope to go in about 2 or 3 weeks. They say it is very nice. Hotel accommodations and all.

It will be my first vacation since entering the army. I have never even had a 3 day pass. I guess that is about all for this time. I will write you again after my vacation. I am enclosing a couple of pieces of Italian money as souvenirs.

A Maybee Leaguer,
Carl Schmidt
(Mrs. Ruth Olrich's brother)
Sunny S.England (sometimes)
April 16, 1944

ههه

Somewhere in India
April 14, 1944

Dear Violet and Leaguers,
"Flash!" Somewhere in India and it's a nice place over here. The facilities are good, have movies, a PX, nice chow hall and showers.

Sorry that I haven't written sooner but I'm fine and hope you all are the same. We are organizing a baseball team and this afternoon we played our first game and won. After the ball game we had a big shower and right now it is so windy that the wind is blowing the candles out and the lantern doesn't work very well.

Was sure surprised when I saw the first native and the way they dress and their ability. They are hard workers. All their work is all done by hand. There is very little machinery. Everything they carry is carried in a basket and then put on their head and off they go. The heavy things are drawn by oxen. They steer them by the tail. If they want them to go right the ox's tail is pulled right and etc. Incidentally, we are using India currency and did it puzzle us a bit. No longer nickels and dimes, it's rupees and anna's. One rupee is worth and thirty cents. One anna, a little less than two cents; one pice is one quarter anna; one lakh one hundred thousand rupees is thirty thousand dollars and one crore one hundred lakh is three million dollars.

I was where Worthy White is for awhile. I was also very close to where Pete is. I saw their locations in the Messenger. Well, there is so much to say which I would like to say but that will have to do as you know it's one step closer to victory.

Your friend,
Martin "Marth" Seitzie

৵৵৵

Ontario, Calif.
April 18, 1944

Dear Violet and Leaguers,

Just a few lines to say that I received the paper today. Sure surprising to see where all the fellows are at and what jobs they are doing. Sure takes a lot of branches of service to win a war. Sure would like to see everyone at home but not for a few more months I guess. I just finished Primary at Memet, Calif. Now I'm at Basic at Cal-Aero near Ontario about 35 miles from LA It's very nice here and we have a lot of flying and studying to do. It's sure a long hard grind to get your wings and commission. I've been in about eleven months now and about four and a half to go. Twenty weeks so they say. We get night flying and instrument flying here, about 80 hours all together. We study code navigation, weather maps and charts, besides P.T. and drill so along with flying you see we are pretty busy. My wife Ursula was in Hemet for two months. She went home Sunday. I'd sure like to see my little boy. But I guess everyone else would like to see someone too. I never seem to run into anyone from home. L.A. is quite a place and so is

Hollywood. Have seen quite a few stars but I'll take Sylvania or Toledo for mine. Good luck to all and keep them flying!

Your friend,
Art Loomer

ৡৡৡ

Corsica
April 16, 1944

Dear folks,
I had a day off a couple of days ago and did my washing, shaved and took a shower in the morning. After chow another kid and I went for a walk along the creek and took some pictures.

We met come women along there that were washing clothes and so we took some pictures of them and also had our pictures taken with them. I guess they haven't washing machines as they bring their clothes down to the creek and start a fire under a tub and boil them and then scrub and rinse them in the creek. They come out pretty clean though.

I got a good conduct ribbon the other day and also have three stars for my campaign ribbon for three major campaigns that I have been in so I guess I am getting to be a veteran.

Your son,
Raymond "Spud" Shanly

ৡৡৡ

Somewhere in the S. Pacific
April 4, 1944
(from Harold "PeeWee" Bunting)

Dearest Ma & Pa, (Mr. & Mrs. John Wahl)
Well, this is Tuesday evening and I feel just fine and am in good health. I hope this letter reaches you and finds you in

the same manner. How is everything going with you and the folks around the lake? I hope fine.

We have my truck all painted except for a few numbers yet to put on it. It really looks nice. My assistant and I are going to put our sweetheart's name on the front of it. It really will look nice with the girls names and a heart under their names. If we were allowed to have a camera over here I would have my picture taken by it and send it home to you. Then you would understand why I write so much about me and my truck.

I do miss being home with you folks. I never thought I could miss home so much as I do. But I guess the reason for that is because there isn't anything to do over here in the little spare time we get but write letters and think of home. Often at night while I lay on my cot I think of you and home. I think how we used to work out in the field.

୬୬୬

N. Africa
April 6, 1944

Dearest Mom and Dad,

I'll give you a brief account of my activities since I wrote on Monday night, but I must do it quickly because I'm sleepy and tomorrow may be a harrowing day. Tuesday morning at about nine o'clock, five of us shoved off to see the Roman ruins at _____. The drive required about three hours and we arrived just before noon. The first thing we did after getting there was to eat the lunch that we had taken with us. After devouring the spam sandwiches, hard-boiled eggs, doughnuts, fruit cocktail, and grapefruit juice, we proceeded to tour the ruins. I found them exceedingly interesting and quite worth while. The old Arab guide who led us around, spoke English, but he was a bit difficult to understand, and I couldn't find out just everything I wanted to know. I gathered that this Roman city was destroyed by an earthquake in the seventh century; some of the ruins are still unexcavated, but the city as it is, seems quite complete. Someday I wish to do a bit of reading on the subject. One can get a fairly good idea of the decent sewage and heating systems that were used so long ago, far more efficient than one would think. We saw the amphitheater (I was immediately reminded of ours in Walbridge Park) market place, library, forum, etc. everything that one would expect to find in a city of reasonable size. The streets are practically intact, and one can see the deep grooves made by the wheels of Roman chariots. In the city proper, there was a huge temple built to the Roman God Jupiter, and that structure, as well as many of the others, made me wonder how the Romans were able to construct such building incorporating gigantic stone pillars without the use of modern machinery. A couple of hundred yards from the main town, is the Christian section, and we looked at what is left of an early Christian Church.

The sun was blazing hot down there, and after tramping around for an hour and a half, it was a relief to enter the small but cool museum where we saw some beautiful and very ancient mosaic work.

The museum also harbors displays of less intriguing items such as bits of jewelry, needles, hairpins, lamps, etc. For a small sum, I purchased four supposedly authentic Roman coins which the guide said are probably 2000 years old. They don't look like much—heavily corroded, lopsided, no dates, or anything to identify them. One day I'll try to clean them up a bit. I borrowed a camera and a roll of film from one of the boys, it I don't know whether or not the pictures will be any good. We had no sooner started the tour when our old Arab guide snatched the camera from me and he took most of the pictures.

Your loving son,
Vernon Bauer

❧❧❧

144

Drew Field, Fla.
April 29, 1944

Hi Violet and Leaguers,
Don't give me up for lost yet. I try to eventually answer my letters, although such processes are a little slow at times. In short I guess I'm just too lazy at times. You know born lazy and had a relapse since. Well the gossip around here is pretty slow at present. In fact there hasn't been a good rumor in quite a spell now.

The weather now is hot. The main recreation is swimming. The suntan I have now is more then I ever got up north so I guess I'll have a head start on everyone up there when I get there. The last two Sundays I've been swimming at Clearwater which is about 30 miles from Tampa on the gulf of Mexico. It's a wonderful beach and not crowded. In fact it's one continuous beach all along the gulf, so it would be a little hard to crowd.

My little camera has been busy, and if you ever drop around come in and see some of the pictures. I expect to do the same myself some time. I haven't seen some that I think were pretty good. I imagine Clayton has a real collection by now. We'll have to get together and compare notes sometime. I wouldn't mind taking a few of those Texas shots myself, he is still in Texas isn't he? I have some Texas subjects on my pictures myself, if you get what I mean. My next section of the country will be New Jersey and New York City. Now how about fixing me up for a job in Chicago?

It's Saturday now, but I don't have much ambition to go any place this weekend. I've been everyplace of interest within 100 miles or so, so there is no place left to explore. Well since the weather is getting rather warm I'll drop you my next line from a little cooler place—our dear old north. (subject to change according to Uncle Sammy)

Bye now and take it easy,
Kurt Durst

Somewhere in Italy
April 15, 1944

Dear Violet and Leaguers,

I have a picture of Inez and myself I am sending you in this letter. It isn't too good but I guess you can tell who it is anyway. I got a pass the first of this month and was able to spend a day and a half with her but it rained all the time and we had to stay inside most of the time. Inez took a few pictures when I was there the first and I hope they turn out good.

We are having a nice spring day today. It is warm enough I can sit here and write with my shirt off. The country is really beautiful now with the fruit trees all in blossom and the others starting to leaf out. The wheat is knee high and the planting is all in progress. They turn all the ground over with a shovel. The whole family takes part in the spading from the father to the kids big enough to handle a small shovel. I will have to hurry or I won't get this finished before I have to all out for guard mount. I received the fine Easter card you and the folks sent me. I wish to thank you for the fine verse it had in it.

I received my March Messenger about a week ago and sure glad to see it come. I am waiting for the next one now.

I had a fine Easter but didn't get to church as I was on guard when services were held in my Bn. I hope this finds you well and write when you can.

A fellow Leaguer
Kenny Brodbeck

Somewhere in Italy
March 26, 1944

Dear Rev. and Mrs. Mueller,

Glad to hear from you and thanks for the pretty Easter Greetings. I've been well and we are all enjoying the nice summer weather lately. The country is really beautiful with the leaves just coming out and many in blossom. According to the censors we can now write that we witnessed the eruption of Mt. Vesuvius. Last week my girlfriend and I saw the opera "La Bohme" and today I purchased tickets to see "Madame Butterfly" on Saturday evening. Once a week we have movies in our ward for bed patients that are unable to have much in the way of entertainment and they are greatly appreciated as you can imagine. Will close with Good Luck and Best regards to all.

Very sincerely,
Inez Bieber

છીછીછી

Somewhere in Italy

Dear Violet and Leaguers,

Sending a few words hoping they find you and everyone well. I'm fine and just finished my two weeks of night duty. We nurses are always glad when they are over. Went to our 10 o'clock services at the Chapel this morning and my girlfriend and I are going to the Lutheran Services tonight. Will close with a Happy Easter to all.

Sincerely,
Inez Bieber

છીછીછી

Camp Phillips, Kansas
April 18, 1944

Dear Violet and Leaguers,

I am very sorry I haven't written for sometime but I knew I was going to get moved so I waited till I arrived here at the new camp.

I received my Messenger in last nights mail and I enjoyed it very much. I got off my shift at 10 o'clock last night and sat up till almost midnight writing a few letters and reading the Messenger. Was surprised to hear that lots of my friends have been moved around to all parts of the world and states just like me.

This camp isn't much like the one I just came from. It isn't quite so nice. I have to cook with coal and that is a little more unpleasant after being used to gas stoves like at home. But I still can do it only it's a little more work!

I made a Pfc, and T/5 all within two days. So now I'm a T/5 Cpl. that is a second cooks rating and expect to get a 1st cooks rating before long. I have worked hard to do it so I figured I deserved it.

I had a little vacation from the 12th of March until the 21st. I was on my long waited for furlough and I really enjoyed it while I was home. Enjoyed seeing a lot of my friends at Ottawa Lake but was very sorry that I didn't get to see all the rest of the folks as it was hard for me to see them all in such a short time. I wanted to spend most of my time with my little daughter Jane Lee and Dorothy which I did.

The weather is not quite as warm as in Arkansas. It was like the middle of July when we left there everything was in bloom and the trees were all leafed out. Here it's something like back home. Cold and rainy ever since we have been here and we arrived last Friday, the 14th.

It's getting late and I got up at 3:00 this morning and I am getting pretty tired now. I wrote several letters tonight so I'll say "thank you all a lot for the Messenger" and I'm always glad to get it. I am sending my best regards to Rev. Mueller and Mrs. Mueller, all the members of Zion Lutheran Church, and all my friends in service in the Army

As ever,
Frank J. Klauda

≈≈≈≈

Up in the Yukon Territory
April 29, 1944

Dear folks,

Recently I had the privilege of making a sector supply trip to one of stations up the "Road"—Alcan Highway. It's quite fascinating to ride along the gravel bed in a tiny jeep with the mystifying trail unfolding and winding up and down the hills and mountains before you. After one has traveled ten miles you have seen as much in variety as having traveled the 1500 mile between Dawson Creek and Fairbanks.

Since it is not longer considered confidential I guess I can tell you a bit of our past winter. Our lowest temperature was 43 degrees below zero but with hardly any winds here it seemed no colder than 10 or 15 degrees above zero back home. Never was it necessary to wear more than cotton undershirts, woolen OD shirt, sweater, and regular field or flight jacket. The mildness of a cold temperature here is almost unbelievable. We had a nice Easter service here. Quite a number of us here took communion.

Love,
Olin Fischer

≈≈≈≈

Keesler Field, Miss.
April 25, 1944

Dear Leaguers,

I really enjoy reading the "Messenger" and I'm always looking forward to each issue. It's radiant beams flash forth. Whenever I'm reading the "Messenger" someone will ask, "What paper is that?" After some explanation and a chance to read it themselves come deep appreciative words and comments. We in the service are real thankful to receive it.

April showers have been plentiful here. The sky is cloudy now. Starting about 8:00 A.M. Easter morning, rain continued to fall until late in the evening. Early sunrise services for protestants on Easter morning was very inspiring to the many who attended the services in the outdoor theater. The service was conducted by several chaplains. Music was furnished by the band. There was a choir which was composed of WAC's and soldiers.

We had a swell Easter dinner. Turkey was included in the menu. Table clothes appeared for the first time since I have been here. I guess table clothes appear every holiday at this field.

Last Tuesday I went to Gulfport, Miss. Late in the afternoon I went to Mobile, Ala. A chance to get away from the usual surroundings makes life look much brighter. Enjoying the recreation and scenery offered by other localities is nice.

I have many letters to answer so I will have to close.

Sincerely,
Bernard Myers

అలలల

England
March 13, 1944

Dear Violet and Leaguers,

We have so much to be thankful for. Did you hear of the assassination of Kaj Munk, the clergyman of Denmark by the Nazis? Courageously he denounced some of his parishioners for aid to the Germans. Also Pastor Tori of Grua, Norway was arrested and is now in Kongsvingers Prison. Also, I noticed in my recent issue of the "Herald" our N.L.C.A. journal, the complete imprisonment now of Bishop Berggraw, loyal head of the church of Norway. Bishop Berggraw also is the author of the book "Land of Suspense" a story of the life of the people in northern areas of Norway. I feel deeply indebted to Norway to be the best soldier I can to help deliver her from the enemy. In 1843 her immigrants founded the great N.L.C.A. of today in Muskego, Wis. my own home state. We as true Christians must save her. I am glad God has allowed me a hand in the noble task that lies before us.

Once again, by God's grace, we are enjoying another beautiful Lenten season. Truly this year it means more to me than ever before. The National Lutheran Council sent me a Lenten devotion booklet, "The Savior of Mankind". It's daily messages are so beautiful. So daily the Lutheran Church reaches me through this medium. Also, my "herald" is a God send to me over here. Lutheranism doesn't exist here as far as I can determine. So I also place my literature in our Chaplain's office for my other buddies as it's so scarce and precious. I don't receive much outside of the weekly journal but I share it. Once in awhile and article of mine appears which arouses so little curiosity. I have one gone to press now.

Sincerely,
Vernon Packard

New Guinea
April 10, 1944

Dear folks,

I'm glad that I was able to attend the services on Good Friday night and also take communion as I was unable to attend them yesterday. We made out the payroll for April and yesterday afternoon one of the clerks here wanted to take his roll to the hospitals and get the men there to sign them. I had a few to get signed too and I had to see one of them about an allotment. It was about 30 miles to the hospitals and the roads weren't too good. It took us almost all afternoon in fact it was rather dark already by the time we got back. We had to go to about 4 different hospitals. The hospitals here are really some contrast from the one's that are in civilian life, but they are still as good as they can get them for this country over here. I got to see some white girls again as it had been better than a month since I had seen them. In fact I haven't seen but a couple of native women all the time we have been over here. They seem to stay in their villages and they are off limits to us. Speaking of the roads, you can't imagine the shape that they are in over here. I don't thing that there is a road back in the States that can compare to the best road that they have over here.

Your son,
"Pete" Leroy Fischer

HOME ON FURLOUGH

We were very happy to see the following home on furlough during the last month: Frank Schumaker, Donald Gilhouse, William DeNudt, Malcolm Gray, Clayton and William Fischer.

When we put the "May Messenger" together and got it ready for mailing we were glad that Frank Schumaker from Del Rio, Texas and Donald Gilhouse from Camp Carson, Colorado were with us that evening. After the work was completed Frank gave us a very interesting talk about the planes and his work in Texas. Frank looks fine and had a grand coat of tan and even talks a bit southern. We hope that we'll see him again real soon.

Donald Gilhouse is a Chaplain's assistant in Camp Carson, Colorado. Don talked about an hour on his many duties at camp. He loves his work and we're sure that the boys he works with are pleased to have him. He says that their work is never really finished as they have so many different things to do. "More than once", says Don, "I have given the blushing bride away at the Military Wedding in the Chapel". The Chaplain has a jeep which the assistant drives and keeps up and he never says "Take the jeep into town" it's always "Take the transportation into town". We all enjoyed Don's talk and hope too that he'll be back soon in our midst.

Don is a member of the Olivet Lutheran Church. William DeNudt and his wife were invited to our party but they were unable to come.

William DeNudt who has been stationed in the Aleutian Islands for the past two years was home for several days visiting his wife, folks, and friends here in Ottawa Lake. He looks fine and says that he's very glad to be home and back in the U.S.A. again. He's stationed at Fort Bliss, Texas and the closest town is El Paso and he writes that there are many colored people and Mexicans there.

Malcolm Gray came home from Camp Phillips, Kansas and really looks fine. He too has a nice coat of tan since he was on maneuvers in the south. Malcolm had waited a long time for his furlough and we're really happy he was able to come and we were able to see him.

George Dannecker visited his folks and sister and friends in Maybee. George is now in Texas. We're very glad he was home on furlough too.

Clayton Fischer and his wife, Eldora, came from Tyler, Texas and arrived here on May 28th. Clayton will go to Ft. Meade, Md. and be there June 10th. Both are looking fine. At the service on June 4th Clayton said a few words. He painted out three things that we at home can do for the people in the service: first, pray for them; second, write them often and third, be prepared to meet any crisis that may come. After the special service on D-day everyone gathered in the basement to see the moving pictures that Cy McKinney from Sylvania has of the boys in service from Sylvania and vicinity. He had about 100 boys in his collection and all of them were taken while the boys were home on furlough. It will be a very happy day when those boys come home and can see themselves and their buddies on the screen. Thanks, Cy for sharing your movies with us. After lunch was served we enjoyed group singing led by Fritz Fischer and Hermis Nieman with Rev. at the piano. The evening was climaxed with the "Lutheran League Friendship Circle" and singing of "Blest Be The Tie That Binds".

William "Bill" Fischer, son of Mr. Dan Fischer is home from San Diego, California for a few days. Bill looks fine and he will return to Oceanside, California.

❧❧❧

Dear Reverend,

Was glad to receive your V-mail dated April 30. A picture post card today of Zion Ev. Lutheran Church of Ottawa Lake, from Geraldine Schmidt which I was glad to receive after being away for two years this month.

The weather here has been quite cool. It wouldn't do to write about my line of duty. I am just a rolling stone now days. Have some days off which I spent riding in Jeeps seeing the pretty country scenery about me and also bike riding, camp shows and dancing at the Red Cross.

Am always glad to receive letters from the folks around the home town. And the Messenger too.

Yours truly,
M.E. Bieber

శ్రీశ్రీశ్రీ

Somewhere in Italy
May 18, 1944

Dear Violet and Leaguers,

I received the letter you wrote April 30 and sure was glad to hear from you. I want to thank you for Don's address. At present he is a good ways from me. I was in combat alongside the outfit he is in but that was before he joined them. Olin Koester sent me Edgar's address so now I have most of them again. I don't believe there is another organization that does as fine a job on the Messenger. I can't thank you and the staff enough for the work you are doing.

I got a letter from Pete yesterday and he says he is doing okay. I haven't heard from Joe in some time but Pete said he thought they might get to see each other some time. I just can't find time to write them all. I am feeling fine.

As ever,
Kenny Brodbeck

శ్రీశ్రీశ్రీ

Somewhere in Italy
May 11, 1944

Dear Violet and Leaguers,

Wednesday and all is well, I just received your copy of the Messenger. This is the first issue I have received overseas and I'll say it was very welcomed. I noticed that Lieutenant Inez Bieber and Kenny Brodbeck are over here. I wish I knew exactly where they were located as I sure would like to see and talk with them. I am with the 45th Division 5th Army on the Anzio beachhead, Italy. From the papers back home you probably know more of what is going on here than I could tell you.

At the moment I'm sitting in a dugout about a thousand yards from the Jerry lines. The valley here is in full bloom and with the surrounding mountains it makes a beautiful sight. Too bad there has to be a war to tear it up. I'm looking forward to receiving the next Messenger and news from home and friends in the service.

Sincerely,
Don LaPointe

ৰেৰেৰে

Somewhere in New Guinea
May 25, 1944

Fellow Leaguers & Readers of the Messenger,

I hope that you will forgive me for not writing sooner, but it is getting hard to find anything interesting to write about from here. It seems to be the same thing day after day so if I repeat something that I have already written in a previous letter I hope that you will overlook it.

I will try to make this letter shorter as I think that I am taking up too much room in the paper and no doubt I am cheating some of the others from getting their letters published.

Since I last wrote to you I have received both the March and April issues of the Messenger. I want to thank you for sending them to me as I really appreciate them. I don't enjoy reading any paper or group of letters as much as I do the Messenger. It is always good to hear from the other fellows and Inez and also you back home and what everyone is doing. So keep up the good work, as we really appreciate all that you are doing for us.

I received quite a number of Easter cards this year and want to take the opportunity now to thank all of you for sending them. I hope to be able to write each of you and individual letter thanking you, but until then I want to thank you now. It is really good to hear from you back there, even though it is only a card or a few lines in a letter.

As yet I haven't been fortunate enough to find anyone over here from back home, but I am still hoping to run across someone before too long. It surely was nice that Kenneth and Inez were able to visit each other over there in Italy.

Last Sunday I was unable to attend the church services as the weather wouldn't permit. It was another one of those rainy days and I mean that it really rained. The Lutheran Services are held in the afternoon and I always try to go to them. We have a new Lutheran Chaplain here in the Regiment, the first Lutheran Chaplain that we have had in the Regiment. Although we had two of them in the Division and they generally held the Services here in the Regiment for us. I haven't had the opportunity to attend the Services held by the new Chaplain as yet, but hope to hear him next Sunday.

I will close for this time, as I can't find anything more to write about. I'm feeling fine and hope this finds all of you the same. Again, thanks for the Messenger and I'm looking forward to receiving the May issue.

A Fellow Lutheran,
"Pete" Leroy C. Fischer
P.S. "Hello" to all.

ঌঌঌ

Ottawa Lake, Michigan
June 6, 1944

Greetings! The great and long-expected D-day will be history by the time you read this. We write on June 6th — D-day. In special prayer services this day we remember all our fighting men and women, that God may protect and guide both body and soul. Our prayers are furthermore for a speedy and just peace. An editorial writer says, "this invasion is not for land, riches, and power". If that is true, as we hope it is, then God be thanked that finally in the years of history, mankind, under God, has learned to use might with justice, that the mighty ones use their power to punish evil and wickedness. When the oppressed nations shall have been liberated, and when the post-war police force shall have been established, then it will become more and more evident that "not might is right, but right is might". More and more the world must learn to war no more. All peace-loving citizens of this planet, the good Earth, should seek to promote the force of ideal, rather than the ideal of force. Perhaps you will say that the above statements are but a play on words. Right! But they express truths just the same. Furthermore those truths will and must stand. They are God's laws. All the armies in the world can't change the fact that two and two are four. Neither can on man—or a hundred million men—oppose God's laws of living...and win the battle! God rules, and will rule men. Read Psalm 2.

Finally, you men and women in the service, who have gone out from Zion at Ottawa Lake, we salute you for your courage, for your stalwart faith that you manifest in your letters, for sacrifice for you country. May God be with you until we meet again. May we encourage you to faithfulness in the Lord Jesus Christ, you Savior. Nothing else matters when eternity confronts you! To have Christ in your heart and to believe in

Him firmly as your Redeemer means everything. And so—until we hear from you...

> Cheerio
> Your Pastor and Friend
> Marcus Mueller

ৡৡৡ

"PETE" FISCHER AND EDGAR STRABLE MEET IN NEW GUINEA

Again this month we have the happy news that two boys on our Messenger Honor Roll have been on foreign territory. In a letter to his folks on Aug. 7th Pete wrote: "I finally ran across Edgar over here. A couple of weeks ago I heard something about his outfit moving somewhere in our vicinity but really wasn't sure about it. I kept on the out-look and a few days ago I saw his outfit. I found out just where his company was and Sat. morning I got permission from the personnel officer to go and see him. I found his unit about noon and he was out on the job working. He is a mechanic and was quite busy. I went out where he was working and while he wasn't busy we talked things over. He got off work about 3 PM so we had quite a long talk Sat. night. I stayed over night with him and came back here yesterday afternoon. Surely was good to see him again and he is still the same old Ed. He is looking swell and really has a swell tan. The last time I saw Ed was in Nov. of 1942 when all of us fellows were home at the same time, he, Kenny Brodbeck and myself, remember? So of course we had something to talk over. He had been home on furlough last fall sometime so he knew more about what was going on back there than I did. We really had a swell visit and I helped him dig his foxhole"

Then this written on August 20: Edgar came over to see me Sunday night. He came after he was through work and stayed all night with me".

159

Elwin Beck has a birthday on Sept. 25 and he will be 20 years old. He is still down in the South Pacific and hopes that everybody is fine up in the old home town of Ottawa Lake. Happy Birthday, Elwin and may you celebrate many more here at home.

Melvin "Butch" Dauer has arrived in England and is fine. We hope that he has time to drop the Messenger a line after he is settled over there.

Mr. & Mrs. Arthur Shanly are stationed in Richmond, Virginia at this writing. Miss Winnifred Shanly accompanied them to Richmond and spent a week with them there.

ᛩᛩᛩ

Camp Robinson, Ark.
August 24, 1944

Dear Mom & Dad:
Here is another day in the army and we marched all day and tonight we had a parade. It was pretty about 8,000 was on the parade ground and in step. It makes you feel proud to be one of the many thousands of men in this army but I'd rather be home any day but I'll make the best of it.

We marched all day. They only give you so much time to learn a thing. They have each day planned, what to do and it's got to be done in that day and not the next day.

I'm looking forward to your letters Mom as I know you are writing.

I'd better close and get to sleep because we have a bid day ahead of us. God bless you all and keep you.

Your loving son,
Lee   (LeRoy Breire)

ᛩᛩᛩ

Merle Gust is somewhere in France. In a recent letter to Olfin Koester he wrote the following: "I got the Messenger today. I was cleaning my gun when I got the mail and I just left it until I read it through. By the way, I almost forgot to tell you that it was the June issue. I met a couple of guys from Adrian that are with me now. I didn't know them before but it's good to meet somebody close to home. Please notice that my address has changed".

⚘⚘⚘

Somewhere in Italy
August 22, 1944

Greetings:
 To folks in the States what I may have to write will be entirely new but to many of my buddies from home who are advancing before me what I have to say may express many like experiences in camp. I will attempt to describe a typical evening of a G.I. overseas.
 Very soon on arriving at a new location the fellows learn of the location of a theater area. After attending a movie once the fellows learn a few rules of the game and are governed accordingly. The site of the area is marked by a semi-stationary screen. The area may be flat or it may be a sloping area to afford natural elevation between rows of patrons.
 The stage performance may be schedules for 7:30 with a "news" broadcast at 8:30 and a movie at 9:00 o'clock. There does not seem to be any set schedule of evenings of state acts and so large numbers of the G.I.'s will go early each evening so that nothing will be missed. I said they go early. To assure one of a fair position one must plan to be in the area at least an hour before the performance will begin. In other works there is a good assembly there at 6:00 o'clock.

Now the fellows don't just go over there to sit and wait. They take cards to have their games. Some take writing paper and write letters while others pass the time in reading or visiting with buddies. Oh, Yes, and there a re also those fellows who are interested in improving their own financial condition and also provide a pastime for the other fellows by operating dice tables near the area. Of course, occasionally the MP's make a raid and business is temporally discontinues. Some of the fellows have made some very genuine tables and operate like a regular US gambling house. I don't believe that the gambling spirit will ever be taken from the veins of the American in spite of the fact that all must know that when ones' gain must that someone must loose and no G.I. soldier can afford to waste to loose his money.

The stage show is always a varied program. It may be a "crooner" contest among the enlisted men. It may only be a concert by a station band. Or the USO may give a program. I neglected to mention the seating facilities at the theater. The lounging plush seats are all for gotten. Even the officers have to be content with back less picnic benches. Each G.I. brings his own seat. In most cases it consists of his steel helmet or helmet liner upon which he places either a board or one of his G.I. blanket. In my case I do not like to make up my bed after returning from the theater so I do not use my blanket but instead I have a faithful board about six inches wide and 16 inches long. I find several uses for this board. Besides being a seat at the movie it serves the same use at the church service. Also it becomes the basis of a writing desk in my tent. During the day I have to hid the board in my bed to be sure to keep it.

Extreme silence and great interest exists during the nightly report of the news over the loud speaker. I mentioned that we have a movie each evening. They are generally a surprise for the titles often are never announced until the evening of the showing. The pictures are average. Occasionally the camp officials will present a training film before the main feature. Of course this meets with disgust because these films have generally been resented to the men several times and they are tired of seeing them. Sometimes also they have several "shorts" and one wonders if they ever will come the main feature.

The usual cry is "Down in Front". Now it would be unusual for a movie to run along smoothly. Just when it seems to hit a climax the thing will stop. This means that either the film is broken or a new reel must be put on. Of course, this gives the audience a change to rise, stretch, rest their backs and other portion of the body that may be tiring. As soon as the pictures come on you hear "Down in Front" and we resume the showing. One is sure to have at least 4 or 5 rests during a picture or maybe even more. About 11:00 o'clock we travel for our tents. Now best wishes to all in the Service and God bless and keep you.

> As Ever
> Clayton Fischer

৵৵৵

Italy
Aug 14, 1944

Dear Ethel (Komsteller):

Reviewed your two letters but haven't felt in much of a letter writing mood and we've been very busy on our ward with lot of sick patients with malaria but I enjoy taking care of those fellows and making them as comfortable as possible but with so many we often can't do as much as we'd like to do.

Now that I've told you how hard we work and how busy we are, wait till you hear this one. I'm spending a 5 day rest leave at this lovely hotel reserved for nurses and can really say I'm enjoying it beyond telling. My girl friend and I have rooms next to each other and we spend most of our time together.

She's lying on my bed now while I'm doing some letter writing. You'd like my girl friend Katie. She's very sweet with dark hair and be brown eyes – from Georgia and talks with a cute southern accent. We are almost half sisters as we've been together ever since we left Ft. Harrison a year ago.

I brought a story book and all my letter writing along to keep me occupied part of the time. Have 6 more letters to write then I will be caught up for the first time since I've been over seas but hope I have a couple waiting for me when we get back to camp.

We have a beauty shop in the first floor of our hotel so one of the first days we were here I got a permanent because when we are on duty it is hard to arrange appointments. I hold my breath when those Italians take their sheers and begin but it usually turns out to be fairly good looking. Even had a manicure for the first time in my life. I have lost a little weight this summer but sometimes it is so hot we just don't have much of an appetite.

We did some window-shopping but the extent of our buying was some stationery. Prices are terribly high and things I'd like to buy would be too difficult to carry around.

We go to the Red Cross almost every day because they serve delicious ice cream, cookies and coffee.

Last evening we five nurses went to the vespers services at t big church near by. Spent a half-day at the world famous St. Peters and saw many other interesting and worthwhile sights.

It was terrible shock to hear of Jess. Just answered your letters the other day so won't have a lot of things to write about but must be sure to let you know right away that I received your big box this afternoon and it was in perfect condition and the cookies are so good and the orangeade hits the spot. Some of these nights we'll have popcorn night and pop the corn but will drink orangeade and coffee while the cookies last. Many, Many thinks to you all! We've been several days without letters so I did enjoy all the Sylvania papers too.

It has been dreadfully hot here during the day and I really feel sorry for all these fellows with temps of 103-104 on days like this because we all feel miserable with normal temps.

Yesterday I had my day off duty but did nothing but rest and read and write a few letters. Bought some peaches and a melon at the fruit market. Peaches are 40 cents a kilo or 40 cents for 2 lbs. Should say 40 lire but it's the same difference. The peaches are really good and now the grape season is beginning.

It is dark later in the mornings and notice too our evenings are shorter. Guess it means fall is getting near but hope we'll all be able to plan on coming back to the States before winter. Would hate to spend another rainy winter here although the summer has been perfect.

Lots of Love,
Inez Bieber

ৰেৰেৰে

Somewhere in Italy
August 2, 1944

Dear Violet and all:

I must drop you a few lines this morning and say "Hello". This is my birthday and I am cpl. of the guard which happens to be a break for me as I get time to do a little writing. Thanks for the greeting card.

I saw Inez a few days ago and she felt pretty badly about her brother my sympathy. The first she knew it was when the Messenger reached her. I got the news the same way. It hit me like a club when I opened the envelope and it was on the cover. I am very much pleased to see the organ fund developing so well. This is a short note but hope it finds you all well. I am O.K.

Kenny Brodbeck

New Guinea
July 18, 1944

Dear Rev, & Readers of the Messenger:
Hello to all. Sorry that I haven't been able to write to you before, but we have been quite busy over here. I just finished writing to the folks, so though that I would try and drop you a few lines yet tonight. I will have to write this in a hurry, as I will have to get it done before it is time for lights to go out. We use candles for light, and they really come in handy.
First of all I received both the May and June issues of the Messenger, and was really glad to get them. I got the May issue about a week or ten days ago, and today I got the June issue. I haven't been able to read the June issue as yet, but maybe get to read some of it tonight if I get done writing in time. Surely was glad to get the May issue, as it was some time since I had gotten the April issue, and really missed it.
Again I want to thank all concerned with the Messenger, as I think that it is the best piece of work that could be published for all of us. It is always good to read all the letters from the other fellows from all the different parts of the works. It makes you feel as though you were right there talking with them, and brings home closer to you. Keep up the good work, and hope that the day will soon come when we can all come back home and talk things over rather then carry on a conversation through the mail. So let's Pray that the war horrors.
Well, we have moved again, and this time we really got into a muddy place. It is heavy clay here, and it always ticks to your shoes. And of course with these big shoes that we have it makes a fellow tired just to carry himself around. We have only been here a short time, but have the work tents fixed up fairly good, especially for being in New Guinea and in such a muddy place. We had to haul a lot of sand in from the beach. We are only a short distance inland, but always used to set up

right along the beach, and it was generally fairly cook, but it is plenty warm here.

This area that we are now in hasn't been taken from the japs so very long ago, but the front is a short distance ahead of us. It is fairly safe here, and hope that it continues to be. We are just ahead of the heavy artillery, and about every night around dark they fire a few round. They really make a lot of noise, and when the first shot goes off it really makes a fellow jump as he just isn't expecting it.

The area here used to be a Jap garden, and it had just nicely gotten started. They had watermelon, egg-plant, pumpkins, sweet potatoes, etc. planted here. I tasted one of the watermelons, but is wasn't ripe and didn't taste too good. They were just small.

I have seen some of the Japanese equipment that they captured here, and of course some of it they just had to leave. Some of their equipment really is in good shape, and some of it quite modern. They must use horses quite a bit, as we have found a number of horseshoes and shoeing tools. We haven't been able to find any of the horses.

Monday afternoon we had Lutheran Communion Services, and I was able to attend and to partake of the Lord's Supper. The service was held by Chaplain Poch, our Division Chaplain, as he generally holds the Lutheran Services. I really was glad that I had the opportunity to attend the Service, as it happened to be the last service that Chaplian Poch will hold here in the 5th Division. He is really a swell speaker and a swell man personally. We will all hate to see him leave us as he has been with us for a long time. Of course, I am glad to see that he is going to get a promotion. He is going to make full Colonel and to go to the higher headquarters. I also had the opportunity to meet the Chaplain, or rather the Chief of Chaplains of the 6th Army. He was at this Service and spoke a few words to us. He is a Protestant Chaplain, Chaplain Miller.

Well, I think that I have covered most everything for this time, so will draw this to a close.

Glad to hear from all of you, and hope that the day will soon come when I can come back there and see all of you. By that I mean, that all of us are able to come back and worship together again.

Good luck to all.

A fellow Lutheran
Pete" Leroy Fischer

❧❧❧

OTTAWA LAKE TWINS CITED IN PACIFIC

Army press releases from Washington told of an incident in Southwest Pacific in which Privates Forrest H. and Horace F Nearhood, Ottawa Lake, Michigan took part. They are members of an American Infantry unit which maintained a jungle road block on an undisclosed island.

Yanks, serving with American Infantry Division, were discovered during the night by Japanese and the enemy, moving up with machine guns, opened fire at dawn in an effort to cover their advance.

After a brief battle the enemy was driven back. It was still dark and impossible to count the enemy losses. The Japs carried away their dead and wounded in the withdrawal.

Privates Forrest and Horace Nearhood, 20 year-old twin sons of Mr. & Mrs. Robert Nearhood were inducted April 1, 1942 and until they received orders for overseas duty were at Fort Leonard Wood, Mo. They have been in the Pacific area a year.

❧❧❧

GARLD HOLMES IN SICK BAY
LEROY FISCHER IN HOSPITAL WITH TROPICAL DISEASE

Garld Holmes is in sick bay with blood-poisoning in his leg. We hope you are better.

Leroy Fischer has been in the hospital in New Guinea since Aug. 14. He writes thus: "I'm at the 128th Station Hospital now. We flew by plane for 7 hours making one stop-over to stay all night at another hospital. I must have lost about 20 lbs. or so. That cot surely got hard after laying on it for 26 days straight without being able to get up. I'll be in the hospital a couple of months yet so keep writing to the same address until I tell you different"

అలుఅలుఅలు

Italy
September17[th], 1944

Fellow Leaguers in the Service:

Now with over tow months of overseas service to my credit, I feel more qualified to discuss problems that are bound to confront us. Some of things are serious matters and we will all have them whether we be back at a rest camp after returning from line duty or if you are an inhabitant of a replacement center.

As long as the conflict continues with such splendid progress and losses are below expectations and at the same time replacements are continuing to be sent over, many of you still in the States may turn to traveling and set foot on foreign soil to be on hand if needed. Thus many will be confronted with the problems which I have noticed in my stay thus far.

The very first thing that I have observed is the use of certain undesirable words by nearly all of the men. I would be shocked if I should ever meet some of you speaking thusly and

I am sure that any of your folks would not be proud of you. You want to return a gentleman and anyone using this language comes far from the most liberal definition that can be given the word. Anyone speaking in this manner only displays the lack of other words in their vocabulary.

Another thing that will confront everyone is the problem of drinking. And very closely connected with it is the question of relations with the opposite six. Again I want to remind you that each one want to return a gentleman and you can not take a chance of diseasing your body and cause a blemish against your records.

There many be an opportunity for you to become slightly shiftless and have a tendency to do as little as you can get away with. Daily I see fellows who are laying a good foundation of work dodging for after this war. I can now see how the last war was said to be 'the making and breaking' of many a man. Many more times the number of that war are now under arms and I fear that when we return the problem will be proportionately serious. Few men will be able to change rapidly from a life of dodging work to a life of usefulness. What will you be like when you get home? It rests entirely
on your shoulders. I know that we will all return successful if we but constantly keep on guard.

Do not conclude that all is bad in our army life. Quite the contrary, for I would not give a lot of lifetime friends one makes while here. Also we are given many opportunities to see many important and interest8ing scenes in the world. Take advantage of all chances that are given you. It may never come to you again at such little cost.

As ever,
Clayton Fischer

Italy
September 4th, 1944

Dear Leaguers:

Should be able to write you before time for our evening services over at the Chapel begins. They are held each evening at 7:30 so I try to go at least a couple of times each week.

We have regular Lutheran services every Sunday morning. Our Chaplain is colored and from New Orleans. His sermons are excellent and there is an increase in attendance every Sunday since I've been going to this early service. At 10:00 o'clock the Chaplain from our outfit has the regular Protestant Service.

I received a letter and a card from Elg dated Aug. 5th and he is O.K. I was in hopes of seeing Clayton but haven't as yet. I've heard from him since he's been here though.

Glad to hear Pete is O.K. and I don't imagine things are so pleasant there. Was so very sorry to her Mr. Papenhagen was burned and died.

I spent a few days leave in Rome and enjoyed seeing some of the high points of interest. Appreciated just living in a lovely hotel room with all it's luxuries for a change from our tent.

Katherine Cornell is to be here Thursday so I hope to get to see her.

Last week one evening we made some peanut butter fudge and put enough in a box to pass around on our ward. It was fun making it and they enjoyed it.

Lots of Love,
Inez Bieber

Del Rio, Texas
September 21, 1944

Dear Violet & Leagures:

I'll bet you thought I never was going to write. I really am sorry because I've been thinking about doing it every day but you know how it is, always put it off until tomorrow maybe it will be cooler and soon weeks have passes and still no letter is written.

By the looks of things I'll have to come home again soon and see my new little nephew. Roy's new boy. I received the last Messenger the other day. The pictures in it of our folks certainly were good. I'll bet that paper is getting to be a lot of work for you people isn't it? It really is nice and I really appreciate you sending it to me. My work down here is just about the same as when I last saw you all.

Gee, I've been in the Army over three years. It sure doesn't seem that long but to think back over those three years I wouldn't want to go through them again but I guess I'm lucky after all still being in the States. I guess I'd better sign off for this time. It's chow time and I have to go to work at 10:30 tonight.

Your friend,
Frank Schumaker

❧❧❧

Northern Canada
Sept. 1, 1944

Dear Friends and fellow servicemen:

It's been quite sometime now since, for various reasons (all alibis as they are perhaps – the same "excuses" all you guys have used too – Hail:) I last wrote a letter to the Messenger.

The last week of July brought what has now proved a good fortune to me. At that time I was still at a small air base of the America to Russia line, near beautiful Yukon Lake. The water's edge was in fact but pitching distance from our back door. My orders transferred me to what is called an "isolated" post, although the term is ambiguous and needlessly alarming.

One sad feature in the deal I'll now mention. Having played short field for our softball team all season (we won 8, lost 4), it was my good fortune to be selected to the post team and with it the privilege of traveling to a centrally located post for the Regional Tournament. Things didn't work just too well though, for I was moved 4 days before the team made the trip.

To mention a bit of the softball season, mostly for Pete and Kenny Brodbeck's benefit, I will "brag" with no reserve modesty of my one home-run of the season. Don't ask me how that certain outfielder hurt his leg, and why the opposing team still played him. No, like George Washington – "I can't tell a lie" — and even though the fielder should have caught it, he didn't touch it, wasn't an error, and so I made a home-run.

A bit for a more serious thought now about the more interesting things of this country. Although by now I've lived among the mountains for a year they still hold a definite fascination for me. At my present location there are mountains on three sides of us, and the 8 miles distance between us seems as only a few hundred yards. About 400 feet below our station runs an important river of this area. These are a vital means of transportation to the trappers as they float their rafts of supplies in at fall time and hole-up their definitely isolated cabins for their winters' well.

Of my work I can say little, but that we are busy nearly all the time – mostly in maintenance of our unit.

There is this one thought that I wish to express before closing. The Red Cross, with its cigarettes and sundries, and the Department of Special Services care for us wonderfully. Our radio plays nightly, our new supply of the latest books, magazines, and newspapers arrive weekly. We want for very little and owe it all to the above organizations.

This winter when our temperatures hold at 30 to 40 degrees below it would seem we'd freeze but our army arctic-issue will keep us very comfortable. Our sleeping bags seem as stoves in themselves as we nearly roast in them at 40 degrees below.

So here's my invitation – if you, anyone, suddenly takes a notion for trapping, hunting, or prospecting just drop me a line and we'll arrange to meet here in the Yukon. However, trapper, prospector, or no – drop me a line anyway.

Bye for now. Here's hoping to see you all on a short furlough before Christmas.

As Ever,
"Oli" C. Olin Fischer

❧❧❧

France
September 4, 1944

Dear Violet and Leaguers:
Just a v-mail to let you know I am fine and Okay. I had a letter from Inez. She wrote that she received a letter from Clayton and though he was near by. Also that she saw Kenny B. again. I haven't heard from Stanley Kastel but I guess he's over here too. It will soon be two years overseas for me. The last camp show I was to was "China". I'm writing this in my pup tent. It is a nice day out today. Am sending my best regards to everyone. Hoping to see you all soon as the war news is going well.

Sincerely,
M. Elg Bieber

❧❧❧

EXCERPTS FROM EDGAR STRABLE'S LETTERS DURING
THE PAST MONTH
On an Island in the Southwest Pacific

Dear Mom:

We finally stopped moving long enough that I can now drop you a few lines. I'm fine and couldn't be better. This sure was a surprise that Pete Fischer and I finally get together and what a happy reunion that was. He stayed with me two days and a night.

I now have a nice foxhole just outside my tent. In fact Pete helped me dig it. It sure seems like a miracle to meet someone like that so far from home. I haven't seen Pete lately as we have been so busy and he moved again but I know where he is.

We have seen quite a bit of action lately. Those of the yellow race have been paying us unannounced visits. We had some air raids, Mom. I'll say its no fun to sit in your foxhole and sweat out each bomb wondering where the next one will land.

I finally got to see Pete again and I found him in the hospital. He was a very sick man but he is now well on the road to recovery and I hope he continues to gain.

We get the latest news by radio every evening. Seems good to get it over here. Well we moved again and now I'm somewhere in New Guinea.. I made Sgt. Again and am awarded the Bronze Star Medal for my work since Aug. 31.

Today was payday and the mail came through so I had a busy day. Pete has left and now I'm all-alone over here again. Sure was swell to see him though.

It gets awful hot here and it was about 140 today at noon. Say "hello" to everyone. I'll write more later.

> Your loving son,
> "Eddie" Edgar Strable

෮෮෮

September 1944
HOME ON LEAVE OR FURLOUGH

The following were home during the past month and it was so very good to see them and talk with them again.

Lt. Vernon W. Bauer, son of Mr. & Mrs. Charles Bauer of Toledo, OH returning to the U.S. and spent about 21 days with relative and friends. Vernon was overseas two years and stationed in N. Africa. He and his bride went to Miami, Florida where he reported for duty.

T/Sgt. LeRoy P. Gray, son of Mr. & Mrs. Charles Gray, Ann Arbor, Michigan is enjoying about 23 days with his relative and friends in Ann Arbor. He was stationed in the China-Burma-India theater for 29 months. He served as a member of the signal section of the Air Forces. In addition to the good conduct ribbon he was awarded the Asiatic-Pacific ribbon and the American defense service ribbon. At a little party at the home of Violet Fischer he told many interesting habits and customs of the natives in India. He too will report the duty at Miami, Florida. He brother Don, who will graduate with a Medical Unit in Texas next month, is expected home on a furlough after graduation.

Cpl. Edwin Crots was home on furlough from Camp Howzo, Texas.

Cpl. Kurt Drust spent a 21 day furlough with his parents and sister.

Pvt. Robert Hall was able to be home on a week-end pass a few weeks ago.

It was nice to see Pvt. Basil Harroun home for a few days. We want all of your fellows and Inez form church to add him in the circle of those serving Zion as he has a star on the Service Flag with the rest of your.

T/Sgt. Frank Klauda is home visiting his wife and daughter as the Messenger goes to press, Sept. 6th.

Chas. McConnell, son of Mrs. Thelma, McConnell, Sylvania, was home and was married in the M.E. Church in

Sylvania. More about the wedding on another page.

Arnold Nearhood who is in the Navy was home on a short leave.

Pvt. Kenneth Schmidt who has spent several days in a hospital in Vancouver, Washington spent a long furlough with his family in Lambertville.

Arthur Shanley and his wife were home during the past month before reporting to Virginia.

Pvt. Wayne Strouse, son of Mrs. Hattie Strouso was home and has returned now to New Mexico. He missed his sister, Fern who cam home from Cherry Point, N. Carolina only by a day or two. Fern looks grand and she's in the Marines.

Sgt. William Shoemaker arrived from Georgia to spend a 15 day furlough with his wife and daughter and other members of his family.

Messenger Honor Roll

CORNELIUS, JR. BLOOM so of Mr. & Mrs. Cornelius Bloom, Sr. Blissfield, Michigan was killed at the port in Italy on Dec. 2, 1943. He was in the merchant Marines.

JESS, JOHN BIEBER, son of Mr. & Mrs. Frank Bieber was killed in the South Pacific on June 20, 1944. He was in the Navy.

HAROLD, JASMUND, son of Mr. & Mrs. William Jasmund Route 10, W. Toledo, Ohio died in England on July 23, 1944 from a subdural hemorrhage as a result from a fall from a bicycle. He was in the Army in the Medical Corps. He was a member of the Olivet Lutheran Church, Sylvania, Ohio.

Ottawa Lake, Michigan

September 1944
TO OUR FRIENDS IN THE SERVICE:

The other waves bring in repeated communiqués of Allied succession the European front. The Nips, too, are more and more being hemmed in. The dragnet of the Allied armies are closing in. How dreadful and alarming must be the feelings in the hearts of our enemies! We can sympathize, but at the same time, we can stand with the Word of God and say "whatsoever a man soweth, that hall he also reap." That holds true for individuals, and it is a natural law also for nations. My God have mercy on the leaders of ungodly nations! They hurl themselves before the judgment throne of God with the blood of their fellow men on their hands.

Rewards for good and punishments for evil come as surely as do day and night, summer and winter. We may not always see in full detail such rewards and punishments. And yet the moral law of god exists and operates unfailingly among mankind.

As we write these lines we again commend you, our loved ones, to the care of Christ, the Good Shepherd. Please keep in mind that the Bible says "Heaven ad earth shall pass away, but my Word shall not pass away." Bibles and bullets are being produced in mass productions. Bibles proclaim life. Bullets preach death. Life and death are meaningless abstract terms when spoken of in a general way. but when we say Mr. A. is alive, or Mr. A is dead, then we become very specific with the words "life" and "death". And even then —they are still relative terms. When I am "alive", I mean I have "life". But that life is not mine. It was given to be by God Himself. And what is true of me, is true of every human being. The Word of God says so. GOD HATH MADE of one blood all the nations of the earth. So also "death" is a relative term. Death is the absence of life...more specifically it is that state or condition of the individual human being when he has been deprived of physical life.

As Christians we do not care merely to talk in a philosophical way about life and death, but we wish to give the Bible view on these things. So, our life is of God. Death results because of human sinfulness (general and specific sins). By "general", we mean inherited sinfulness. The wages of sin is death. Death is the gate-way through which all human beings must pass—sooner or later—to stand before their Maker, and their Judge Jesus Christ. The Bible does not speak of earthly life coming to an end in the sense that there is annihilation or oblivion. No! There is everlasting life (or existence) after physical death. Do we not confess that Bible truth is the creed..." I believe in the resurrection of the body and life everlasting"? Heaven? Hell? Yes, they too are real! And Christ Jesus is the Savior form sin and all who will permit themselves to be saved. The devil is the real foe and arch-enemy of Christ, of His Church, and of all Christians. Resist the devil with prayer and with the Word of God and he will flee from you. May God grant to all who read these lines an increase in faith in Jesus Christ. May the peace that comes when sins are forgiven by Christ be yours! Our continual prayer is that war may end and that millions more may turn to God in the crisis of this age. Keep up the courage lads and lasses, men and women. God will hear your prayers, for God is faithful!

Cheerio —
Your Pastor & Friend
Marcus Mueller

Somewhere in New Guinea

Dear Mom:

Once a year a day is set aside for Mother's Day. A day that is never forgotten. Even here in the army with ll the trials that one has to face and all the discomforts where it is even hard to remember what day of the week it is, Mother's Day stands out in front so far. It can't be forgotten.

When any trouble come up who do think of first? "Mother". When we go to take a bath, what do we think of? "Mother". Who used to make us scrub our neck and back of our ears? When we had a little hurt Mother was the first one we went to.

Now Mother although we are many miles apart all those little things make us remember you, Mother. So may you have very happy Mother's Day.

Your loving son,
Morgan Mehan

Camp Gordon, GA

August 1, 1944

Dear Violet and all,

I am awful sorry I haven't written sooner but have been just too busy to do so.

I receive the Messenger each month and enjoy it very much.

I was sorry to hear that Jess Bieber had been killed in action. May he rest in Peace. The war is over for him but for some others it is just beginning.

The weather has been rather wet down here all week. It looks as though it is going to rain right now.

How is everybody at home? In good health I hope. Give my regard to everybody.

I've been going to a church I though I might join it but I think I'll wait until I get hip and join the church there.

Well, I guess that's all for this time. Hope to hear from soon.

Yours,
Merle Harroun

જીજીજી

In a recent letter to Rev. Mueller and Rev. Marcus Rieke, Youth Director of our Luther League, Columbus, Ohio wrote the following:

"I couldn't help but drop a line to express my appreciation for the Zion Lutheran Messenger which comes to my desk so regularly. Almost in the same mail we received a special gift for $10 as a memorial for Jess John Bieber. We wish to express our sincere promotion of a Mighty Fortress".

Our sincere sympathy goes to the Maybee Luther Leaguers and the relative of Norman and Dorothy Hasley and Rolland Knabusch were killed in an auto accident on August 12 at Maybee, Michigan.

George Dannecker, son of Rev. & Mrs. Theo. Dannecker, Maybee, Michigan is stationed at Camp Howze, Texas.

Joe Steiner is still in San Antonio, Texas and he has been in the hospital but we hope that he is out at this writing.

Kenny Brodbeck's family have received recent letters from him. He's O.K. and he entered France on the second D-Day. He writes the people are nice there and he seems to enjoy it there.

꒰꒱꒰꒱꒰꒱

August 20, 1944

Dear Violet and the rest of the folks;

I haven't forgotten you folks but figured I'd be home on a furlough, but the orders changed and I won't get on till after Sept. 12th now.

Thanks alot for the Messenger. I really enjoying reading it. It gives me some news to read about from home. Beside the sell letters I get from all my friends from around Riga and Ottawa Lake.

I met a couple of boys from home at Camp Phillips. I met one of Gray boys who was stationed there. He came over one Sat. afternoon and we had a nice chat but I was workings and it was around chow time so I had to go to work. I wanted to go over to his company and I got shipped out. Now I'm in Forting Beuning, so I didn't get to seem anymore.

It has really been awfully warm here in Georgia since I have been here and lots of rain also. This is a pretty nice camp but there is not place to go. We are stationed six miles from the main post on that they call Sand Hill and its really sand. But there is no wind to blow the sand, except when it rains we get lots of sand under our barracks that the rain washed under there.

I just can't wait till this war ends so all of us boys can get back home to our loved ones and our friends again. It will be a little hard to get away from the army life but I think I 'd take that chance.

I've written several letters so its getting late and I have to get up at 3:30 a.m. so the boys can eat. Because if I don't get up and make breakfast someone will be hurting. It probably would be me mostly. So here is all the good luck and hope to see all of the boys back home soon. The way the news reads in the papers, I don't think it will be too long.

Yours as ever,
Frank Klauda

❧❧❧

Somewhere in France
Sept. 16, 1944

Dear Violet and Zion Leaguers:

I received my first edition of the Zion Messenger on foreign soil the other day. Many thanks for sending the news from Zion. I know a great many of you and so your paper has been very appealing to me.

How is everything going on the home front? I trust that everything worked out as planned for the Zion-Olivet melon feast in August. How well I remember similar occasions. May our earnest prayers bring a total victory soon.

My work as Chaplain Frey's assistant becomes more interesting each day. The attendance over here have increased by great numbers. We have many interested in choir work and wish we could sing for you some Sunday. Our trio will sing tomorrow. It took Chaplain Frey and our two Lutheran Chaplain nearly thirty minutes to administer Holy Communion at a Protestant Service aboard shop because of the great numbers.

Our present bivouac area is very impressive as far as scenic beauty goes. Hedgerows and orchards are all around us. We are slowly accustoming ourselves to the French way of living. Their language has most of us baffled at present. Many of the towns and villages in this area lay in ruin from enemy bombardment.

Time is short tonight and so I must end here. May I extend my greetings to everyone at this time. May His fullest blessing be with each one of you always.

Sincerely,
Don Gillhouse

August 26, 1944

Dear Violet and Leaguers:

Thanks for the address of Raymond Shanly. I don't think I know him but I know he will make a pleasant acquaintance. I don't know where he is located. It may be on the other end of the Island and out of our zone that we are permitted to visit but I will keep the address and we may meet in the near future. I wouldn't be surprised if we move nearer the front soon. Right now we are about as far from the action as the Generals.

It is Saturday night and I just finished chow. We are having a dance tonight and I intend to be there. We don't have much entertainment here.

Your brother Olin and myself are in the wrong spots. I understand that they have WAC's in some weather stations in the States. Imagine us doing women's work. He must be quite busy. We have more personnel in our Station. I received the August copy of the Messenger – thanks to Miss Schmidt. I was sorry to hear of one of your members becoming a casualty. It always seems worse when it is someone you know.

Sincerely,
Carl Schmidt

ๆๆๆ

Camp Carson, Colorado
July 28, 1944

Dear Mom & Dad:

Here I go again on a letter that should have been written several days ago, but it seems like I never get around to writing when I should.

Well, I guess my vacation is over for the present as the third platoon is taking their furloughs and won't be back until the first of August; so the rest of the boys are much different when they do get back because by that time I will be through with school and I suppose I'll have to go with them.

Well, we passed our M.T.P. tests with flying colors so now we are all ready to go across, but is doesn't look like they want us over there very bad as the sixteenth Corps is about to go and so they transferred us into the thirty-sixth Corps and as near as I can find out the thirty-sixth is strictly a non-combat outfit so now I don't know what the score is.

The 104th Inf. Division is in the 16th Corps and they are stationed here at Camp Carson so they are getting ready to leave and in the past they have been taking care of all the M.P. duties here in camp, at the stockade, at the German prison camp, and also at Colorado Springs, so yesterday we started drawing their duties at the stockade and they say when the 104th pulls out, we will take over all of it. I don't know what they are doing so who am I to try and tell them what to do?

You asked about our eats, well sometimes it is good and sometimes it is pretty bad but we do get all we want now and that's something we didn't have at Camp Roberts. I just came back from supper and we had roast lamb, mashed potatoes, corn on the cob, salad, bread and butter, bread pudding, and lemonade so I think that is a pretty good meal and it tasted real good too. We always have some kind of dessert, this noon we had apple pie and last night we had cake and yesterday we had pumpkin pie and Sunday it was ice cream. So you can see we do get nice things to eat, but no strawberry short cake, with or without cream.

You asked if I could get ice cream or cold drinks near her, yes we have our Post Exchange right here about a hundred yards from my barracks and you can buy all kinds of pop, ice cream, sodas, sundaes, candy, cigars, cigarettes, or most anything you want.' In fact, it would be very possible to live right here without ever going out of camp, and we have a nice Chapel right next to it and about a mile up the street is a nice theater where we can go to a show every night if we want to and it only costs us fifteen cents so that isn't bad.

Well, I can't think of much more to say so good luck and write when you can.

Your loving son,
Ellis Rosenbrock

❧❧❧

England
August 14, 1944

Dear Violet:

Received your welcome v-mail Birthday taken okay Thanks! I received several very nice birthday cards this year. It was my 2nd over here. Am busy now days trucking or hauling.

"L" Co. ranks first in the C.T.O. for black eyes we have several in the company. I also received a shot on the arm by the Med. Yesterday. We are having summer now. The farmers are busy harvesting the wheat and cats. Am quite busy now days with shese Jerries.

Received a V-mail from Inez the other day. She has been to see Rome. Went to the Cinema last eve and saw "Flowing Gold".

Am sending my best regards to the folks.

Yours Sincerely,
Pvt. Matthew E. Bieber

❧❧❧

France
July 24, 1944

Dear Violet:

Just a few lines to let you know that I received the Messenger yesterday and sure was glad to get it. I really enjoy it a lot for it's a good way to get home news.

I am no longer in England any more. I am now in France and it is much better then England. The people here are really happy to see us in their country. They will give you anything they got if they can.

Some of us had our washing done by them and they did not even want any pay for it. We had a hard time to make them take it. The weather here in France is much dryer then it was in England. We have only rain once since we came over. There is only on thing I don't like and that is I cannot speak French. For there is quite a few pretty girls over here. But is don't do me any good for I don't know what they say.

The large guns are fairly quiet tonight as I write this letter but I only hope that they are quiet for good before long so we can all get together again like old times.

Stanley Kastel

ৈৈৈ

August 15, 1944

Dear Violet:

Just a few lines to let you know that every thing is going fine here with me although combat life is not so easy. You should see how happy the people are when we take a town or city back for them. I have never been kissed so many times in one day in all my life as I have here on this push.

The French people are sure swell people and there is not anything they won't do for us if they can do it. France also has some very pretty homes and city's. Lots better then England has. They also drive on the right side of the road here, where in England it is on the left.

Well, I have to close for now but will write again.

Stanley Kastel

❧❧❧

Howard "Huck" Schmidt is still in Italy at this writing. He wrote recently that he is close to Robert Dietsch from Sylvania and hopes to see him. He's fine and will enjoy hearing from you kids back home.

William DeNudt and Bernice are still in Texas. On Sept. 14 they with friends enjoyed the weekend at the Carlsbad Caverns, New Mexico. Bernice is working on the Army Post at the hotel there.

Kenneth Korth is in the Southwest Pacific and writes that he receives the Messenger and is please to get it. He went to school with some of the boys that write letters to the Messenger Staff.

LeRoy Breier and Leon Harrwaldt are fine and still at Camp Robinson, Ark. Leon wrote home that he enjoyed a visit to Little Rock, Ark. recently.

Herbert Kodelman son of Mr. & Mrs. Ernest Kodleman of Riga, Mich. Is over in New Guinea. He wrote his cousin, Lois, the following: "I don't know if I've told you before or not but Louis Kremnetz from Ottawa Lake is in my Co. and we talk about home a lot. He lives near Whiteford Center. I always let him look at the paper that your church send me."

Congratulations to Sgt. And Mrs. Steve Cunnison who were married in Toledo on July 5th. Mrs. Cunnison is the former S/Sgt. Lorene Flegle. Lorene is still stationed at Fr. Meade,

Md. Also our Best Wished to Lorene's brother, <u>Algvin and Mrs. Flegle</u>, Topledo, Ohio with the arrival of a new son born on Sept. 2nd. Mr. Flegle with Mrs. Egbert have attended our Sunday School with their Boy Scout Troop from St. Mark's Lutheran Church, Toledo, Ohio several times.

Mrs. Breier expects to talk with her daughter, <u>Juanita</u>, by phone on Oct. 1. Juanita is in Washington, D.C. and likes her work very much.

ℲℲℲ

Nov. 1944

ZION HONOR ROLL!!!!!

Our cover page this month is beautiful by the pictures of those in Service from Zion. As you will notice two errors have been made namely; the names of Kurt Durst and Kenneth Brodbeck should be reversed. We are very sorry that John Wotring's picture doesn't appear but that the picture of Kenneth Brodbeck is above John's name. We're really sorry John, and we hope to have your picture in with the group of pictures next month. For those of you who do not know each of these young men and Inez we'd like to have you all know where they are stationed. JESS BIEBER was killed in action June 20,1944. KENNETH BRODBECK is in southern France; ANDY ERY is with the Atlantic Fleet; INEZ BIEBER is an army nurse and in Italy; KURT DURST is in Florida; MATHEW E. BIEBER is in Northern France; CLAYTON FISCHER is in Italy; WM. FISCHER is in the Hawaii Area; LEROY BREIER is at Camp Robinson, Ark.; CURTIS (OLIN) FISCHER is in Northern Canada; LEROY C. FISCHER is in New Guinea; JOHN FISHER is in Oregon; WILBUR FACKLAM is in California; GARLD HOLMES is with the Pacific Fleet; MERLE HARROUN is in England; LEON HARRWALDT is with LeROY BREIER at

Camp Robinson, Arkansas. VERNE JACOBS is in Alaska; FORREST and HORACE NEARHOOD is in the South Pacific; FRANK SCHUMAKER is in Texas and JOHN WOTRING with the Pacific Fleet.

Word has been received from the Marine Corps combat correspondents that Pfc. Russell Creque was in the invasion at Peleliu, Palau. He is a vetern of 16 months of service overseas. He is the son of Mr. & mrs. Leo Creque of Ottawa Lake. He left for the service on Dec. 8, 1942 and was at Camp Pendleton, Oceanside, California before going overseas.

In a recent letter from Kenny Brodbeck to his mother he wrote that he was writing in the home of a French family. He likes France better than Italy.

ৎৡৎৡৎৡ

Nov. 1944

IN MEMORIAM

Our sincere sympathy to Mrs. Nellie Vanderlaan Seeley whose husband, Pfc. Clayton Seeley died in France Sept. 25 of wounds received the same day. He enlisted in the Army April 23, 1941 and was sent to Pine Camp, Watertown, N.Y. for basic training and to Los Angeles, Calif. He received advanced training at Camp Bowie, Texas and was sent to England in Dec. 1943. Besides his wife he is survived by a daughter, Elsie, 3 years; one son Raymond, 8 months and his parents Mr. and Mrs. Roy Seeley of Holland Ohio; three brothers and two sisters. One of his brothers, Pfc. Edward is in the South Pacific with the 37th Division.

We command all sorrowing hearts to the Lord Jesus Christ, and to His Word: "Let not your heart be troubled. Ye believe in God; believe also in Me. In my Father's house are many mansions. I go to prepare a place for you....... that where I am, there ye may be also." John 14.

BOYS MEET IN NETHERLANDS EAST INDIES.

It makes us happy here at home whenever we hear of friends in Service meetion on foreign soil. It must have been a great day when Worthy White saw Dick Dusseau and the two of them a few days later called on Morgan Neham. I'll bet the main topic was home, their friends here at home and in Service and yes, I can imagine little Ottawa Lake rated a bit too!

THE LIGHTS ARE COMING ON AGAIN—By Aunt Nellie Root
The lights are coming on again
        In places where they were dim
Seems like the sunshine after rain
To see smiles return to faces thin.
To have the lights come on again
Is a blessing for all to see,
The blacked out places all lit up
To shine for V-I-C-T-O-R-Y.
When they all come on again
And one by one, each town is free'd
May God bless each heavy heart
And hive them the strength they need.
There will be a white Christmas too
And beautiful mornings galore
Which will give us all a wonderful feeling
To know the lights can shine once more.

Netherland's East Indies
  Oct. 19, 1944

Dear Mom:
I've received all of your mail and am glad to hear that one and all and everything is going along O.K. at home. We had today off. I had a lot to do but I went swimming instead.

191

We have a movie tonight then I'll have to try to get the work done.

I finally got some pictures of the natives. I am sending you a couple. They are very intelligent and this surprised me. Some of them visited us sometime ago and a group of the youngmen and boys sang "Pistol Packin' Mamma" in English and you could hear everyone from the smallest on up.

I haven't heard from Pete yet not since that first letter from the rear. If anyone asks about him tell them he will be O.K. in a short time.

I've celebrated my third birthday in the service. I didn't do much celebrating as we are awful busy and the work has to be done. Anyone who thinks this war is almost over ought to trade places with us just a few days and they would change their minds in a hurry. Say "Hello" to one and all. I'm O.K. and feeling great and take care of yourself.

> Bye now, Your loving son,
> Eddie (Edgar Strable)

∾∾∾∾

Somewhere in France
 Sept. 17, 1944
Dearest folks,

Just a line from France to let you know I am fine and hope this finds you all the same. Things are the same as you see them in the papers or in the shows. The weather here is hot in the day and cold at night. It is hard to get used to. There is not much I can write about from here but I will try and write more often. So long and God bless you.

> Yours loving son,
> Malcoln Gray

WOUNDED IN ACTION:

Word has been received by Mrs. Melvin Dauer and also Mrs. Margaret Elg that Lt. Melvin Dauer was wounded in Germany on Oct.6th. He is at the present in the hospital in England and in a recent letter he wrote that he would be getting a much needed long rest. Sorry that we did not have quite room enough for the letters of <u>Clayton Fischer, Kurt Durst,</u> and <u>Paul Freeland.</u> We will print them next month.

France Sept. 4, 1944
Dear sister and family, (Mrs Jim Pfeifer)

Just a few lines to let you know I am feeling fine and am sorry I haven't written sooner but I just couldn't get around to it. You knew anyway that I was in France as Shorty (brother Henry) wrote you. I saw him about 3 weeks ago but the next day we pulled out for the front. So now I don't know where he is but some day we probably will run into each other again. Maybe the next meeting will be in Germany. I had a letter from Earl Smith quite sometime ago. He was in the hospital at that time but I think he must be out by now and back to work.......We sure have been getting plenty of rain here lately and I sure don't like it. Say if you don't get any letters from me drop me a line anyway as I sure don't get much time to write. So long and good luck.

> Your brother;
> Eddie (Ed Cevora)

Cherry Point, N. Carolina
Oct. 23.

Hello everybody,
...I am just fine and back in that old harness again. Glad to hear Pete is better and if I know Pete he won't be in the hospital very long... At the present time Tyrone Powers is getting up a talent show for next week and it sure sounds good. Last Friday night I went to Atlantic Beach roller-skating but the floor isn't too good out there but I managed to stay on my feet. ...It sure is a swell day as it's real warm out today... Last week we had an awful storm (hurricane) here but no one got hurt. It tore up quite a few buildings though. Hello to everybody.

As ever,
Fern Strouse

❧❧❧

At the present time Elwood Brenke is in a hospital in England. He was wounded in France in July, nursed in a Red Cross tent for 20 days in France and again was sent out to the battle fields and the third day was seriously wounded and then they sent him to England. He has been awarded the Purple Heart and also the Oak Leaf Cluster. We hope that he is feeling much better.

❧❧❧

Ottawa Lake, Michigan
Dec. 12, 1944

MEET OVER IN NETHERLANDS EAST INDIES

Again we're happy to print that boys on our Messenger mailing list have seen buddies overseas. Harold Bunting in a recent letter to Mrs. John Wahl wrote that he had a suprise of his life on Nov. 5th. He saw the outfit that Worthy While is with. He stoped and inquired about him and they told him he was there so he went back the Sunday of Nov. 5th and meet him, Worthy took him to see Bob Creque and from there to meet Dick Dusseau and Morgan Mehan. He said they had a swell time together. And to think they were right there together on one island. Now they see each other quite often. This was the first time he meet anybody he knew since he was across and that was a year last August. He also writes that he misses Mrs. Wahl's cooking and he's very hungry for chicken and pie. He hasn't had any fresh meat for 7 months only beef bullion. He's fine and would like some popcorn.

We're also happy to note that John Wotring and Lester Knuth meet over in New Guinea. Sorry we haven't more information on this meeting at this time.

Geaoge Dannecker is in Southern France now. He wrote home that they went through a terrific storm and feed the fish. After leaving the boat they walked through 12 miles of red mud with their equipment and all. He wishes to give his regards to the Luther League and he hopes to write us soon so until then Best Wishes.

KURT DURST is now at Victorville, California only about 100 miles from Los Angeles. He went to Los Angeles for a week-end recently and stopped and stayed at the Lutheran Service Center there. From all accounts he has a very good time.

December 1944

You all no doubt have heard the fellows call the fellows in the Medical Branch in the army "Pill Roller", but after seeing them take care of the wounded and the wonderful care they gave me when I was in the hospital up here I think that they should be given all the credit that is due to them and don't think that they're not doing their part in this war. Words cannot express the wonderful work that they do, and to think that before the war a number of these boys were just common fellows with little knowledge in the medical line. In short what I want to say is that if you have a son, or brother, sweetheart, relative or friend in Service that takes sick or gets wounded I think that you can be rest assured that they are given the best care possible. I know that this can be said about the Medical care that is given in the combat area.

I'll just skip over the high spots of what has happened since I last wrote to you, as no doubt most of the interesting news you have already heard. I want to thank all of you for sending the nice cards and letters that you did while I was sick and don't think that for a minute that they aren't appreciated. Of course most of them I received after I had gotten better but still I knew that you were thinking of me and wanted it to reach me while in the hospital. I also want to thank those who write to me and don't think that I don't care to answer your letters but it is just that I have so many people to write to and it is generally sometime to get around to answer each and every letter. I want to thank Eloise Piehl nd Mildred Paselk for their interesting letters and appreciate the League drawing names to write to each month.

I have done some traveling since I have been over here as I had made three trips almost the entire length of the island. I went by plane when I went to the hospital down south but made it in two jumps. That is really a swell way to travel and plenty fast too. Those trips I couldn't enjoy too much as I was on a litter and couldn't see out. On the way coming back I traveled the first part of the trip by boat, and finished by plane. This boat trip was really enjoyable as it had some good meals, and it was really a treat to get fresh meat, fresh mashed potatoes, fresh vegetables, fresh butter, fresh cofee, fresh fruits, and etc. I think that I enjoyed those meals more than any that I have had since I had fresh foods. The food was fixed up swell and they weren't afraid to put it out. Naturally I managed to get my share and think that I even put on some weight. I managed to gain my weight back; in fact, I think that I weigh a little more than I did before I got sick.

The remainder of the trip I took by plane, as I mentioned before, and this is really the first trip that I enjoyed by air. We left early in the morning and it was rather cool and foggy up there. We traveled over some of the islands close by here and they look good from up there. It surely doesn't take long to travel a few hundred miles that way.

When I got back I had hopes of seeing Edgar Strable again but found out that his outfit is no longer here. Surely would like to have seen him again but maybe we can get together over here later on. I did manage to see a couple of fellows from around Sylvania while I was down south and it was good to see them and talk over olden times and things at home. They were Chink Lang and Don Ruietz. Well, another Thanksgiving is over and Christmas is coming soon. We enjoyed a turkey dinner again this year and also most of the trimmings. It was really a better meal than I thought that it would be, as it is hard to get fresh foods over here, as we don't have the necessary equipment to keep fresh foods. Even though we are still at war and going through some of the hardships and misfortunes that we do, we still can be thankful that we are still alive and in as good health as we are. Surely hope that we can worship together next Thanksgiving day and are able to be with our families to enjoy the wonderful meal that is cooked like no one else can cook it, that being your Mother's cooking. Thanksgiving night they had Church Services here at the theatre and I enjoyed the sermon very much. We have a new Chaplain here, at least he came after I went to the hospital and he is really a good speaker. He always has a good message for us.

Well I know that I have rambled on too much but once I get started I just can't seem to stop. As it is almost impossible to get Christmas cards over here this year. I hope that you will accept this means of wishing all of you a "MERRY CHRISTMAS" and "A HAPPY NEW YEAR". God's Blessings on all of you. Surely would like to be, with you to enjoy the holidays, both socially and spiritually.

"HELLO" to all, and "God Be With You Until We Meet Again."

A Fellow Leaguer and Friend,
Leroy "Pete" Fischer

P.S. Received the Sept. Messenger a couple of days ago and the Oct. issue today. Really glad to get them and appreciate you sending them to me. Keep up the good work and I know that it is enjoyed by all of us in the service.

❧❧❧

Italy
21 October 1944

Dear Leaguers:

I thought you might be interested in me relating the happenings on my day off. Of course, I have visited the neighboring towns on two different occasions and therefore I have little desire to go there again. I could visit other things of interest but I have delayed going there until I receive my camera so that I can take some pictures while there and I don't feel that I want to visit them over once.

On my last trip to town I had felt the need of higher tops on my GI shoes so I stopped at a local shoe shop and had a pair fixed that way. Of course, the operator was interested in his own profit. As a result only after a few weeks the sewing has started to come out. Therefore I have had to take steps to do some repair work for I once was told that a stitch in time saves nine.

As inspection of my sewing kit shows that all the thread seems to be No. 50 and even when used double is very little match to sewing leather. However, I found that it could be threaded thru a darning needle double and thus would give me 4 strands for sewing. I also recalled that most shoe thread was waxed to give it added strength. Now necessity is the mother of invention and so I decided that the nearest thing that we had to wax was our candles and so in true 'Daniel Boone' style I pulled the thread thru the wax deposited at the base of a burned candle. Timm will tell how successful I have been. It was fortunate that the holes were already present or I would have discovered some kind of awl in pure primitive style.

At most of the fellows have already experienced, living from a barrack bag is no fun. Things have a tendency to get mixed up. In fact, I have often thought of suggesting to the war dept. that they modify the bags so that they will have an opening at each end for invariably what you want is always at the bottom. Things were rather mixed up for me and so I thought it advisable to do a little job of repacking, particularly when most of my winter clothes were at the bottom.

There are always letters to be written so any idle time can be consumed at this job. I also noticed that my hair was getting long and so I decided to have it cut even tho I realized that this would make my head even cooler on these chilly mornings.

The GI field Barbershop is a little different than the shops back home. Among the things that you will first miss is mirrors generally available on every side. Also the button-controlled hydralic chair works a little differently. In fact, any adjustment of height is made by the angle at which the customer sits in the chair. The barber chairs are a crude facsimile of the regular chair less the leather overstuffed seat and have been constructed from the first available crates or wood on boxes.

I have been amused about a small article in the Yank recently in which a GI had to challenge a statement made by a civilian back home in which the civilian contended that a GI at $50 a month could save more than a civilian making $3000 a year. It's too bad for those poor civilians isn't it? Perhaps if the poor fellow would eat "C" rations regularly for at least two meals a day and live out in a tent he would be able to save a little more. If he does like that perhaps his draft board could help him.

In a recent article, sent from the States, in a daily newspaper of this theatre the appalling number of draft dodgers routed out by FBI was revealed. They should perhaps it will be possible to send some of those home who already have given their-share of time conflict.

I hope that all the fellows and Inez are feeling fine as well as everyone at home. May God Bless and Keep All until we can be united again.

As ever,
Clayton Fischer

ବ୍ୟବ୍ୟ

New Guinea
24 November 1944

Fellow Leaguers and Readers of the Messenger:
I just got rained out at the show, so thought that tonight would be a good time to drop you a few lines. I had intended to write to you all before but I suppose that Sis has put in parts of my letters to her and the folks so you heard from me in that way. Hope that you will forgive me but it seems as though I just got so far behind in my writing since I went to the hospital that I just can't seem to be able to get caught up.

I finally got back to the old outfit, and was really glad to be back with the fellows here. Most of the same fellows are still here and after being with them for about three years they seem to be somewhat like brothers to you and when you are away for a few months it seems good to get back agin. I have been back about a week now, and was away just a little over three months. Two months of this time I spent in the hospitals and the other was spent in various casual camps and traveling back.

I suppose that you all have tried to figure out just what for a disease I had but I think that most of your guesses were wrong. When I got back here they told me that I could write and mention what it was so to keep you from guessing any longer the disease that I had was "scrub typhus". It is one of the tropical diseases over some mite that is spread by the rats over here and there are plenty of them. I was only in this area a few days before I took sick and was taken to the hospital and had to stay there until the fever broke which took about a month.

Leroy "Pete Fischer"

જીજીજી

Norfolk, Va.
7 Nov.,1944

Dear folks:
Guess I'll take a few minutes off this a.m. to let you know of my new address. A few days ago we come up from Goldsboro, N.C. to Norfolk, Va. for some advanced training. Haven't had much time to write before since I get up at five everyday except Sunday and don't get home until 6:30 or 7 at nite. Then I should do some studying. It makes a good full day. Don't know where we'll go from here but maybe to China or India.

This is an advanced flying school where we get advanced aerial gunnery, ground strafing, dive bombing, skip bombing and smoke screen work. The easiest part is bomber escort work at 30,000 feet. We fly down to S. Carolina or Georgia meet the bomber group and fly information with them for while and then return home. At my next station, wherever it is, I should get a new airplane for myself a $120,000.00 fighter. Oh, boy!

The ones here are good but a brand new one is better. We sure throw them around the sky at high speeds. The fastest I have gone so far is about 450 mph. That's not too slow. The clouds and other airplanes really go past you in a hurry.

We fire real bullets around here. The other day a gun went off on the ground tearing shingles off a house 2 1/2 miles away. When you get loaded up with a lot of ammunition it takes a lot of gas to get off the ground. The runways are a few feet short of a mile in length but on days when there is no wind blowing you need all of it. When you land on the ground at 120 mph it takes only a short time to use up a mile of concrete runway.

We have a 2000 h.p. engine that works like a Packard. It sure picks up speed in a hurry. Then we do some high altitude flying— 30,000 feet. From this altitude we do some fancy flying— up, over and around. The fastest I have gone to date is about 450 mph.

Don't know when I'll be home again. This Air Force doesn't seem to be very free with their leaves for furloughs.

Your Son,
Art Shanley

&⁊⁊&

LEROY FISCHSER "PETE" is out of the hospital and back with his old outfit. He has written a long letter and it shall be printed in the next month's Messenger. Clayton is fine too and Eldora has been hearing a bit more regularly from him. He is still in Italy.

FRANK SCHUMAKER writes from Del Rio, Texas that he received the League Xmas box and wishes to thank them for it.

ROBERT WOTRING is now located on the West Coast. He likes San Diego very much. We hope to print his letter that was received in the next Messenger. Rolland, his brother, is in Chicago doing shore patrol duty until he receives further assignment.

We also have interesting letters from <u>INEZ BIEBER, CARL SCHMIDT</u> and <u>WILBUR FACKLAM</u> which we hope to have in the next Messenger. Aso one from <u>FRANK SCHUMACHER</u> and from an Luterhan Chaplain <u>C.E. SKOIEN</u> who administrated the Lord's Supper over in Italy at which time Inez Bieber attended.

త్య్య్

Luxemburg
Oct. 29,1944

Dear Sister and family,

I haven't seen Shorty since he is wounded. I would like to see him but we are busy every day and he is quite always from us. I had a letter from him the other day. He says he is getting along ok. They sure got good medical care in this war. I get those papers from the Ottawa Lake church and they sure are O.K.

Your brother,
Edward Cevora

త్య్య్

Oct. 28, 1944

Hello everybody;

Well, here it is another week gone by. The time certainly goes fast. It won't be long until Christmas is here. The weather is beginning to get cool here now. I think it is about like at home. We had quite a white frost last night. I have been receiving the Messenger and also the addresses of all the fellows from around there. It is quite interesting. I went to church to a different town today. It is a new town most of the buildings are quite modern. The church is beautiful. I never saw any as nice in the States. It seems funny to go in a church now after going in a tent or old building for so long. I am living in a tent now. There are six of us living in it. We have it fixed up quite nice have a door in it with windows it. You can have a tent fixed up quite comfortable if you try. I have a lot of letters to answer so will write later on.

Your son,
Raymond Berry

꙾꙾꙾

Somewhere in Germany
Nov. 1, 1944

Hi Olen (Koester)
I received your letter of July 25 and I was glad to get it oven if it was a little old. The news from home still sounds the same; home at 5:30 and to work at 7. I wish I could be doing that now. If we do get to bed we go there at six o'clock with guard all night with 2 hrs on and 2 hrs off to sleep. Very seldom do we get to sleep one night clear through.

I had a good laugh the other day. A black boy (American Indians as the Army calls them) stopped where we were at and said that he was lost. I told him that he was now at the front line. His face turned from black to white. After we told him where to go we told him to lay on the gas and not to let up until he came to the next town. The last we seen him was really going. He made it back to where it was safe but I'll bet he makes sure where he's going the next time he goes out. I sure hate to see this cold weather come. Us guys outside with no fire and sleeping on the ground. We'll have to shovel the snow away where we sleep or sleep on top of it.

An ole Pal,
Merle Gust

৵৵৵

Philippine Islands
Nov. 12, 1944

Dear Mom:
　　Well, here we are on dry land once again although the landing was a little rough we made it okay. Many natives welcomed us at the beach.
　　Souvenir hunting is great. We find many interesting things the Jap's left behind, picture books, tools, and many more things to numerous to mention. Life here is much different than any place we have been yet. Some people speak perfect English and are well schooled. This country is much different than any place I've been over here although it's strange and it's more like home. The people here have many ways like our own. Our food is as good as can be expected. We are getting enough to eat. Our rations consist of candy and leading brands of cigarettes. My mail hasn't caught up with me yet but I hope it will get here soon. I thought UI saw action before I will now amidst it was just a sample. We had it quite rough here for a while. I was in a foxhole nearly 48 hours. Some of the boys here found some very nice pineapples and large stalks of bananas but they are green now as it's out of season.
　　Everytime I write home I think of the cold weather and how I would like to see snow again. We can't tell the difference in the season here. Everything is green and mosquitoes the year around. We get payed in peso's one peso is worth $0.50. I must close say Hello to one and all and God Bless you All.

　　Edward Strable

France Nov. 7, 1944
Dear Rev. Muller,

I should be ashamed of myself for not writing sooner. I hope this finds you all well. I am feeling fine and for a change I'm not working in the rain today.

I received the Christmas package from the church and wish that you would extend my thanks to them for the fine box. Everyone in my squad had some cookies and wish to send their thanks. Of course all of the boys aren't so fortunate in getting Xmas packages so we share alike.

I was able to attend church services last Sunday the first in 2 months and really enjoyed the service. I have been working every Sunday and really miss the church services. I certainly wish I could be home to attend church. We all pray it will soon be over.

Sincerely, Kenneth Brodbeck

✿✿✿

ENTERS SERVICE.
LaVerne Schmidt left home on Monday, Dec. 4th to serve in the armed forces.

MEMORIAL SERVICES HELD
Memorial Services were held for Harold Jasmund, son of Mr. and Mrs. William Jasmund at Olivet Lutheran church on Dec. 10th at 2:30, Rev. Paul Getter, Pastor.
Mr. and Mrs. Jasmund gave a donation to the Messenger as a Memorial for Harold.
Gale Smith, Jr., who had seen Harold overseas is home on a 30 day furlough and attended the service.

DALE VIERS has been receiving the Messenger. He writes that he is fine and is now in the Phillipines. We believe that someone meet Dale in New Guinea but we didn't make a note of it right then so we're at a loss to tell you now. Will print in next month if we find out who it was.

RALPH REGER has arrived in India and we hope that he might see Jack Seitz and Franklin Kummerow who are stationed there.

ANDY ERY was in the invasion of Southern France and he is still in the Mediterranean when his folks heard from him two months ago. He has been getting the Messenger regulary and enjoys it. He has been a Machinist Mate second-class for over a year and hopes to make another rating soon.

We hope that the two patients, ELWOOD BRENKE and MELVIN DAUER, who are in the hospital in England are getting along O.K. In a recent letter to his mother Elwood said that he was hit by shrapnel shell back of his left ear, neck, left shoulder, back, hip, and hand. One piece hit his billfold and stayed in it. He had to have more surgery done but is getting along fine. Melvin is feeling better and is up some.

Germany
December 18, 1944

Dear Violet and Zion Luther Leaguers,

The November issue of the Messenger came last night. The make-up of your paper is excellent. I don't know of anyone who can enjoy reading the Messenger more than I. Your League should be highly congratulated for this project.

Things are going quite well for us here. My duties as assistant to Chaplain Frey are always a privilege as well as a pleasure. We have seen quite a bit of action already.

We hold services whenever the situation permits. You would enjoy seeing our present Chapel. It was a fairly large tavern until we changed the atmosphere recently. Our Altar is beautiful, complete with two blankets serving as a dossel. A well decorated Christmas tree stands on each side of the Altar. We have two pianos.

It was a lot of fun going to the forest and cutting our own Christmas trees. We found sufficient decorations in the homes we are occupying. Our battalion tree had to be camouflaged with a net. Believe it or not!

Our Public Address system is a great asset. We have a complete set of Christmas Carol recordings including Handel's "Messiah". We have had several Carol Vespers. Nearly everyone attends services over here and have proven that there are no atheists in fox holes. We had a service in an old castle two weeks ago. Was quite spooky, but served as a very impressive background. Could write a volume on similar happenings. More later. Extend my greetings to everyone. Goodnight.

Sincerely,
Don Gillhouse

❦❦❦

December 20, 1944

Dear Violet and all,

Just a few lines to wish you all a Merry Christmas and a Happy New Year. I still haven't seen Pete and I guess I won't. I don't think he will come to the P.I.'s. Worthy is here someplace I don't know just where but I hope to see him soon.

I am in the hospital now. We got mixed up with a few Japs and I got hurt. Not very serious but just the same it was sore and still is for that matter. It is healing very nicely so I will be leaving here in a few days.

Sure was planning on spending Christmas at home this year but they sure can change their minds. So I really can't say when I will be coming home but do hope it is soon.

I suppose you have read in the papers how nice a place that we are in. Well, it is a lot of bosh. If there are any nice places I have failed to find any of them. I really do believe it is worse here than in New Guinea. Every place you go is mud. You just can't find a place to get out of it. At least in New Guinea when we came out of the swamps it was always dry. If it did rain it never got muddy like it does here. The natives are much nicer here. Most of them talk very good English and dress quite nice. I imagine in peacetime they were quite stylish. The Japs have taken most all of their things that they could use and destroyed an awful lot of other stuff. Those little fellows sure are destructive. They certainly enjoy breaking things.

Well, I haven't much more to say. Hope you all are in the best of health and wishing you all the happiness in the world in the coming year.

So until next time.
Sincerely,
Morgan Mehan

৵৵৵

November 25, 1944

Dear Rev. Mueller:

I received the November issue of the Messenger when I reached San Diego. I noticed that it had been sent to Little Creek so I thought I would drop you a note giving you my latest address.

I have left Little Creek and am now on the West Coast. It's needless to say that I am glad to be away from Norfolk. I think most anyone in service will say the same thing once they are stationed in the surrounding area. Our trip was quite uneventful and things were the same every day. When we were underway there was a lot of sea sick fellows among the bunch. Most of them looked as though they wanted to die one moment and then the next moment afraid they actually would. I am one of the lucky few who weren't both red with sea sickness and I can sincerely say I am glad. They type of ships we are on are famous for their being plenty rough.

I made one Liberty in Panama. It happened to be their Independence Day and what a celebration. Most of the stores were closed except the bars and they were doing a rushing business. I thought later in the evening they were going to roll up the sidewalks. I took in a bull fight which in my estimation was a grade A flop, but the Panamanians really seemed to think it was big time.

I bought some nylon hose and perfume for gifts for Mother. You could buy most anything you wanted gasoline, tires, and most all foods. I thought about the folks back home and what they wouldn't do to get the precious rationed articles.

I am now on training cruising here. It's the third such cruise I've been on since last summer. I think we are going to use the army on some of our maneuvers in the very near future.

We all had hopes of getting a leave before we left the East Coast but all we received was a 64 hour Liberty. My mother came to Newport News and spent the three days with me. I haven't any idea we will get a leave from the West Coast.

I think San Diego is quite a nice city. It has a good many nice stores and places of entertainment. There are a great number of marines, sailors, and soldiers out here but the city is large enough to accommodate them.

I haven't heard from John since in September but he had the misfortune of getting hurt and so I am quite sure that accounts for it. Rolland is now in Chicago doing Shore Patrol Duty until he receives further assignment.

Well, I guess I haven't anything more to say this time except I sure do enjoy the Messenger and am sure all the Service people from Ottawa Lake and vicinity take a keen interest in it. Until later I guess this is it.

Yours sincerely,
Robert Wotring

એએએ

Fort George G. Meade, Md.
January 1, 1945

Dear Mom, Dad and all:

Here I am at Fort Meade. Leon isn't in my Company but is in the same Regt. I think we will get to stay together. I hope so.

I called Sis and we had a nice long talk together and it seemed so good to call her and talk to her.

Leon and I sat together all the way and enjoyed eating our lunches. Boy, those sandwiches were swell and I'm glad you made them for me.

Well, Mom and Dad I better close for now and don't worry about me because I'm alright and may God bless and keep you always.

Love,
Your loving son,
Lee (LeRoy Breier)

એએએ

December 6, 1944

Dear Violet and League members:

Just a few lines to let you know I am okay.

Received your Christmas package last evening which I am glad to receive. Many thanks!

We are having the same old routine of duty so I haven't a whole lot to write about. I spent last Sunday in Paris. I saw the Eiffel Tower again also the Arch of Triumphe which has all the names of the French Victories. You could walk up in the Arch before the war. The Tomb of the Unknown Soldier is there also. A gas light is burning there all the time. The F.F.I. Parade place of the Concorde which is near by the Seine River.

They have the underground or metro in London.

It was a rainy day so I hope to get another pass because there are many places of interest to see.

Yours truly,
Matthew E. Bieber

(Elg, thanks for the nice hanky you sent me from Paris - - Violet)

ೋೋೋ

November 4, 1944

Hello Violet and Leaguers,

I received the October issue of the Messenger and I found the letters all quite interesting, especially the one from Olie Fischer telling of his excitement in the far North. He must have moved quite a long distance when he moved. I hoped that when I got to Corsica I would locate Ray Shanly but have had no luck so far.

We don't have much excitement here. We haven't an E.M. Club for entertainment at night and we have our movies and church services in the open. Our mail service has been poor and we have had poorer rations. I have only left camp once on pass but I do intend to visit Napoleon's birthplace in a few days and take some pictures if I can hit a decent day for the trip. We have had a lot of rain and cold weather here and the old tent gets cold at night. It is Saturday afternoon and it has been quite nice here today. I worked from midnight until 8 this morning and I am on the same shift tonight. I am going to listen to the football game tonight if I can pick it up from the States. We get a lot of enjoyment out of our radio.

"Schmidty" Carl Schmidt

૭૭૭

Philippines Islands
December 19, 1944

Dear Mom:

I suppose you thought I had forgotten you but really I haven't as we have been very busy lately and I can't seem to find time to write any more.

I'm still on top and going strong and feeling great so don't worry, Mom. We are now on the beach again in our last area we were up to our knees in mud. Then we changed to beach sand in this area. What a wise move that was. Here we can't keep the sand out of anything but I'd like to live on sand the rest of my time over here and with pleasure.

We are fairly close to a nice sized town but it's off limits to us for more reasons than one. Maybe you can think of a couple of reasons. We have a nice movie tonight but it's raining cats and dogs. My Buddy Al went and took his raincoat. It's funny Mom I never thought I would stay at a movie out doors when it starts to rain but if they keep on showing it we just sit right there raincoat or not. We do countless things we never dreamt of doing.

Oh, yes, I have some news I came in for dinner this noon as I came out of the tent with my mess gear who should be standing there with hand shoved out but <u>KENNETH KORTH</u>. You could have knocked me over. He sure looks great. He left home the same time Harold did. He's in the same kind of an outfit Harold was in. We aren't very far apart. I expect we will see each other as much as we can before we split up, like Pete and I did. Mom, you can't imagine how it makes a guy feel to meet a Buddy. I consider myself lucky to meet Pete and now Ken.

Mail has been slow. It must have been sent some place else. I suppose when it does get here I'll have lots of mail to answer. I won't know where to start.

I haven't noticed any change in the climate since I've been overseas. In the Tropics weather is all the same, always hot.

Ken has been over there two years. He spent much of that time in Australia. This is as close to the front as he has ever been but he has a good job. He doesn't have to roll around in mud like I do to fix a truck.

Well, Mom, I'm tired tonight and I must clean my rifle yet. Hoping this finds you ok. Say "Hello" to everyone. We are a busy as ever. Not much time off. I'll try to write more often. I think of you always.

Your loving Son,
"Eddie" Edgar Strable

❧❧❧

India
December 26, 1944

Dear Violet and Leaguers:

Just a few words to let you folks know back home that I am fine and hope you all are the same.

I received the November Messenger about a month ago and sure do enjoy reading it. I read every page from front to back and it is just like reading a book. In fact it's as good as a book to me. I'm looking forward to getting the December issue in a few days. I can't complain about the Messenger not coming through. It takes anywhere from ten days to two weeks to reach me.

We are having some nice weather over here. Just like our fall back home. Sure glad to hear that the Luther League play turned out alright.

Sorry to hear that Kenny Brodbeck was killed in Italy.

Had a fairly nice Christmas and Christmas dinner was swell. Couldn't expect anything better: fried chicken, mashed potatoes, gravy, dressing, cranberry sauce, pears, corn, fruit cocktail, raisin bread, ice cream, tea, nuts, candy of all assortments.

I went to church Christmas morning. He was an Indian Catholic priest. He has also been in the States and at Cincinnati for several years.

Well, there isn't much more to say so I'll close for now and hoping you all had a Merry, Merry Christmas and a Happy New Year.

As ever a friend,
Martin Seitz

ଈଈଈ

Italy
December 28, 1944

Dear Violet,

First of all I want to thank you for the thoughtful package and V-mail you sent me.

Everything will come in so handy and I can't begin to tell you the fun we had opening all the individual wrapped gifts.

Hope you had a nice Christmas and all the other home folks.

We had a wonderful turkey dinner and also some Christmas parties. One afternoon we had about 150 Protestant Orphan children at our Red Cross for a Christmas program. They sang many carols in English and Italian and later Santa gave each one of them a small gift and they were served cocoa and cookies.

I'm fine and at present I'm on the night shift again but have only a few more nights to go.

A couple weeks before Christmas some other nurses and I enjoyed a five day leave at a small town called Sarrento. Also spent another day at the "Isle of Capri".

Mom sent me some crochet cotton and a hook so I'm having fun learning and feel quite proud that I've completed one doily already. Ruth sent me some embroidery work too, that I'm anxious to start.

I enjoyed the books you included in your package.

Many thanks again and Best Wishes to all.

    Sincerely,

    Inez Beiber

Netherlands East Indies
December 24, 1944

Dearest Folks,

Will drop you a few lines this morning before I go to church. Well, another Christmas season is here and we are planning a number of special services. I'm enclosing both a church bulletin and a program sheet of what we are having tonight. Of course there are a number of things we are doing without over here but we can still worship the same Lord and have Services similar to those we had back there.

The turkey has arrived already so I guess we are going to have it for supper today as they have no way to keep it cool and afraid it may spoil.

I don't think the choir is going to go over so good as we haven't been able to practice as much as we had planned. We are to have a practice this afternoon and hope all the fellows are able to attend.

I'm feeling fine. I was terribly sorry and really surprised to hear of the death of Kenneth. It just doesn't seem possible but anything is possible during a war. I'll never forget the good times he, the rest of them and I had when we were home in November 1942, in fact we took him to the Station in Toledo about 1:30 a.m. on a Sunday and I left the same morning about 4:30 a.m. or so. Surely hope the community never gets such bad news again.

Your loving son and brother,

"Pete" Leroy Fischer

]

Italy
October 29, 1944

Dear Violet and all,

Sunday afternoon – rainy and dreary outside. One of these days I'm glad to be on duty instead of having nothing to do. I've been averaging about three days on one ward and then higher ranks would decide to have me work on a different ward. Now I'm working on my old ward where I was just a year ago when we set up our hospital here. At present I'm working with psycho patients. The work is interesting although there is little actual nursing care for these fellows.

I didn't get your letter finished while I was on duty so am writing this evening. The power just went off so this is by candle light. Makes me remember a year ago when we first came here and we had very strict black out regulations and we even had to use candles on duty as we had no electricity.

We look forward to Tuesday and Friday evenings as we have our sing-song sessions or choir practices then and won't be long and we'll begin working on Christmas songs.

Sincerely,

Inez Bieber

~~~~

Olin Fisher is waiting to return to Northern Canada. He called home on December 23.

~~~~

OBITUARY – KENNETH BRODBECK

Kenneth Frederick Brodbeck, son of Mrs. Ida Brodbeck, and the late Wm. Brodbeck, was born in Ottawa Lake, Michigan, August 2, 1919. The holy sacrament of Baptism was administered by the Rev. Zeitner, August 17, 1919. Catechism instruction and confirmation was likewise under Rev. Zeitner. He was confirmed in the year of 1933 on June 4.

Kenneth was inducted into the U.S. Army on February 26, 1942. He served with an Engineer Combat Battalion. After more than a year and a half of military service on foreign soil his life came to a close on November 20, 1944. He was given a military burial in an American Military Cemetery in France with a Protestant Chaplain officiating.

Kenneth was an active member of Zion taking part in all its work.

He leaves his mother, Mrs. Ida Brodbeck, brothers, Henry, Arthur, Edward, and William; sisters, Mrs. Rinehart Fink, Mrs. Blanche Paselk, Mrs. Luella Piehl, Mrs. Ruth Sieler, Mrs. Elsie Dominique, and Mrs. Wilma Fetzer, also a host of other relatives and friends.

Let our whole comfort be in the brief words of Holy Scripture, "He that believeth and is baptized shall be saved." To us the living ones the Lord says, "I go to prepare a place for you." May we so live and trust at all times in Christ our Savior, that at His coming we shall be found ready and go to our heavenly abode.

Thank God for faith that wins o'er grief
For love of God that brings relief,
For hope that's anchored in the skies,
For life in Christ that never dies.
Amen

$101.50 were given in Memory of Kenneth by his relatives and friends and were given to the following places:

Toledo Orphan's and Old Folks Home, Williston Home of Mercy, Toledo Inner Mission, and the Organ Fund for the Church.

Mrs. Brodbeck has received the Purple Heart. She wishes to thank everyone that remembered her in her sorrow with cards and letters.

Fresno, California
January 31, 1945

Dear Violet,

Received your card today and much to my sorrow I see I have failed to write to you for the Messenger. You keep putting those things off until you forget. Though I have been busy and haven't been able to catch up on my correspondence. Everything here seems all right but being in the Army one never knows what to expect. We have been having some very delightful weather here the past week. I received the Messenger and was very surprised to hear about Kenny. I just can't get him out of my mind. I'm very sorry I haven't written before and I'll try to do better in the future.

As ever,

Wig Wilbur Facklam

January 1, 1945

Dear Violet and Leaguers,

Was very glad to have the "Messenger" of November which arrived the day before Christmas. It is proving very interesting and so are the front page photographs. I wondered whether I am the first Englishman to know about the Zion Luther League?

Before I go any further I cordially extend to you and all your friends my Best Wishes for the New Year and may many of you be united with parted loved ones before 1946.

Well, I hope Bernard Myers gave a good description of Palm Springs. I've heard and read of it quite a few times before. This land is full of wooden shoes and flat wet fields. It does nothing but rain or freeze. I dare say Merle Gust will tell you much the same thing.

I'm afraid this note is somewhat short as I've no more news to write for now. So Cheerio.

Your sincere friend,

Frank Broughton

Word has just been received by the parents of Robert Philabaum that he is a prisoner of War of the Germans. Captain Joe Bissonnette is home from Italy and returned there the last of February.

1945

Fort Benning, Georgia
January 19, 1945

Dear Violet and all:

I just received the Messenger and really was glad to get it. I sat down and read it from cover to cover and it really seems good to hear some of the news from back home and to read the nice letters all the boys write from overseas.

But was sorry to hear of some of the boys that had to give up their life over there.

I was home on my furlough from December 14 until December 26. I was very lucky to get to stay with my family until the morning of the 26th. I enjoyed every bit of it. Seen lots of my friends and had a nice visit with your dad, Christ, and Fritz. I would like to have seen everyone but it's impossible to do it in such a short time.

The weather here has been very changeable. It rains, sunshine, colder and it just doesn't seem to make up its mind how to stay. I stayed at the U.S.O. last night and woke up this morning and was it really coming down. I got a little wet trying to get over to the bus station to get back to camp. I work 24 hours and then am off 24 hours so I stayed in town. We had a few games of bingo and it's a nice place to pass away the time when off duty. I won three games.

Say, those pictures of the boys in the Messenger are really good, aren't they? It seems good to see the faces of most all of the Pal's I used to know.

I am sorry I haven't written before this but it keeps me busy answering mail. I've been getting all the way from four to seven letters a day and have been trying to keep caught up on answering. The first Sgt. calls me the "Lonely Heart Club Commando" because I get so many letters every day. But I just grin and say, "Well if you soldiers take time to write letters you might be able to join also." Mail is a soldier's morale builder. So folks keep the mail rolling and I'll try my best to answer.

It's 11:30 and I have to go to work at noon so I'll have to sign off. Thanks a lot to you and all the folks for the Messenger as it's a great morale builder to us boys in Service. I'll try to keep you in contact with my change of address as I expect to have in the near future. I'd like to send my best regards to everyone. And may Victory come soon.

Yours truly,

Frank Klauda

∞∞∞

With the 12th AAF – Raymond Shanly has been promoted to staff sergeant. He is in the crew chief of a 12th Air Force P-47 Thunderbolt.

His group has been awarded a Distinguished Unit Citation for outstanding performance in action against the enemy in the Mediterranean theater.

A graduate of Burnham High School, Sylvania, Raymond entered the service in January 1942. After training at Chanute Field, Illinois he attended the Bell Aircraft School at Buffalo graduating as a qualified crew chief on fighter aircraft in May 1942.

Overseas 25 months he has seen service in French Morocco, Algeria, Tunisia, Corsica, Sardinia and Italy, for which he wears four bronze campaign stars on his campaign ribbon. His unit is now dive-bombing and strafing enemy installations in the Po Valley. A brother, Lt. Arthur Shanly, is also in the Air Corps.

Harold Leininger is now reported safe
Pfc. Harold Leininger, son of Mr. & Mrs. Mathew Leininger, Flanders Road is reported safe. His parents are greatly relieved

to know that their son is alive and not a prisoner of war. He has already been awarded the Purple Heart, Bronze Star and Combat Infantryman's Badge for superior service. He is with the 2nd Division and has been in service for three years.

৵৵৵

December 12, 1944

Dear Leaguers and friends,

How are you all. Fine, I hope. I am taking a rest again in sick bay. My leg has been acting up again but I am feeling better. We have a fully equipped hospital aboard and the doctors really know their business, swell guys! The Chaplain and Doctor tell me what I need is a good breath of fresh air back in the States. The climate here is awful.

We got some mail today. Some of it was from August. There was a Messenger with it. I have been reading it and find there is some of the fellows from back home near me. Wish I had time to hunt them up but we never stay long enough in one place for that we have been pretty busy ever since we came down here. I have been in four invasions in seven months. That makes me nine in all.

We had a strange thing happen to us on the way to the Philippines. We were headed for Leyte. We had the assault wave. On the way our paravion picked up a mine. This is the first time in History for a ship of its type to have anything like that happen. We had to ball out of convoy till we got loose from it. Jap planes tried to come in on us. It sure kept us busy and boy, were we scared not knowing which was going to get us first, the mine or air raid. We made it ok. One of the fellows got a letter from the States saying there was quite a write-up in the papers about our ship. When we invaded Leyte Bay the Japs really had "welcome" wrote all over the air. They were out to

227

get our ships or die trying. Well, the most of them died. We got their ships.

Well, I guess I better stop. I'm sitting up now and it sure seems good to be out of bed. In another week I'll be back to work again. Will be glad as time goes so slow if you have nothing to do but think.

The best of luck to you all wherever you are and whatever you are doing. I hope the day is not so far away when we can all meet once more in that little church at Ottawa Lake. Christmas will be over before this letter reaches the paper so will wish you all a Happy New Year.

So long for now,

"Chub" Garld Holmes

Since Garld sent us this letter his folks have heard from him and he writes that he is feeling fine again. We're happy to know that Chub, and do take care of yourself!

December 17, 1944

Dear Mother and Dad,

Just a few lines to let you know that I am ok and feeling good. Well, how is everybody at home, good as ever I hope. How is Dad? Is he still working at the shop? He should see the way they use those jeeps here, they go anywhere. So tell him to keep making them by working every day. Well, mother, I hope you are feeling good this winter. Have you got a lot of chickens left yet, or did they sell good over the holidays? The other day I got a chicken and cleaned it and cooked it. It sure was good but tough as leather. I got some cabbage and some Jerry canned food. Boy, it sure looked good but it tasted very bad. There was a dog around. He ate some and I haven't seen him since. I am glad I did not eat any.

How is Nollie now. Is she still home yet, I hope so. How does she feel now? I hope she feels better now then she did when I was home. How is Billy? I hope his arm is getting better. Is he going to stay home? Has Dad got him a job at the Willys Overland yet?

I lost the razor that you gave me and everything that I had. I am using a German razor and soap but it isn't any good but I get by with it. I lost my writing paper. I still got my pens yet.

The way these towns look like the people just took off like a big bird. When we got here there wasn't over a half a dozen people left. We get enough cigarettes here and the chow is real good. I can't think of much else to write about. If I had some stamps I would send some things home.

Well, tell everybody around Ottawa Lake "Hello" for me. Will close for now so be good and take good care of yourself and good luck.

Bye now,
Your son,

John Vandelaan

ຂຂຂ

Mr. and Mrs. William Vanderlaan have received word that their son, John, has been wounded. Also Arthur Whitenburg, Sylvania, Ohio and Wilbur Kestel have been wounded and are hospitalized. We hope all you boys in the hospital are feeling much better and are getting along fine.

229

Italy

Dear Geraldine, (Schmidt)

Glad to hear from you and thanks very much for the medal. Think they are very nice. Enjoyed the Messenger and reading about all the weddings too.

Hope you have been well and everything going along smooth since the holiday rush is over. I've been sick in the hospital a couple weeks but feel fine now and will be happy to get back to work again.

The time passes fast for me for I spend my spare moments crocheting and I'm also hemstitching the ends of a small hand towel Ruth Paselk sent me and it's been more fun.

As always,

Inez Bieber

&&&

East Indies
December 18, 1944

Dear Leaguers:

It gratifies and gives me great pleasure to receive and read with attention the "Messenger". I must humbly apologize for my negligence to write sooner, opportunity at times does not present the occasion for correspondence due to unforeseen circumstances. I give me great pleasure to write this letter and express my sincerest appreciation for your consideration for the welfare of others, one is deeply touched when he reads of the work performed by the League.

I have been in the jungles thirteen months and this continuous grind certainly pries on one's mind and at times one feels greatly depressed. The intensity of the heat is difficult to bear but when I read the Messenger I feel inspired when I think that someone back home is behind me.

Thanking you for your kind consideration and interest at heart. May God bless you.

Sincerely,

Cpl. Harold L. Bunting

ல௸ல௸ல௸

December 25, 1944

Hello Everybody,

Well, I suppose about now you back home are just about through with your turkey and cranberries as there is five or six hours difference between here and there. It was just another day for us here only we had the turkey. It wasn't as good a dinner as Thanksgiving but maybe next Christmas we will eat at home. Well, I had a very nice thing given me for Christmas. Two days ago I was awarded the Bronze Star Medal and was very surprised and glad. The order read for meritorious service in direct support of combat operation. There has been four awarded in the Squadron so far. It is something you don't have to be ashamed to wear.

Tell Dorothy to send me a box from the store. It will taste good, anything at all. I still have only received one Christmas package so far but all the fellows are in the same boat. One thing she can send is some popcorn as some of the fellows had some sent and it tasted real good.

Well, I am going to bed and will write later.

Raymond Berry

Raymond writes that he is receiving the Messengers and like them a lot and wishes to thank the folks that make it possible.

ᆇᆇᆇ

Thursday, January 18, 1945

Dear Mom and Dad:

Hope this finds everybody with not too bad a cold but you have nothing on me as I have a little touch of a head cold myself.

I haven't written since the fourth Mom as I am very busy in the mess hall now. I wrote Dotty a letter last night and receive a very nice card from Mr. and Mrs. Lintner and she had the word "write" on the card so will you please tell her thanks for my card and I will try and write just as soon as I can possibly get a little spare time.

The weather has been pretty chilly up here in the mountains at night but hot in the day time. It rained a little tonight (just a cloud blew over). It sure seems funny to see snow on the mountain tops and so hot in the valleys.

It sounds as though you had a very nice Christmas Mom. I hope I'm home with you for the next one although I don't believe I am going to make it. I received a letter from Arlene and family and it sure sounds as though Russ, Jr. had a very nice Christmas too.

Well, Mom, I had better say good night for now as I still have to take a shower and it is 9:15 already.

Your son,

Dick (Richard Smith)

HERE AT ZION

✓ The first Lenten tea of the Ladies' Aid was held Feb 21st.

✓ The Brotherhood meets Tuesday, March 6th. Rev. Riehorn of the North Toledo Community House will show an education sound-film. Olivet brotherhood is invited.

✓ The Sunday School Teacher's met Tuesday, Feb 13th. They continued the ca\hapter of "Child Study", they also reviewed the book of Leviticus

✓ Lenten Services are held every Wednesday evening at 8:30 P.M. (Mich. Time)

✓ Mr. And Mrs. Roy Breier and family moved from our community. They have moved to Archbold, Ohio

✓ Holy communion was held Feb. 25th.

✓ Rev. Mueller spoke at a Lenten Tea at Epiphany Lutheran Church, Toledo, on Thursday evening, Feb. 22nd.

✓ The following ladies' from the Ladies' Aid helped at the Robinwood Hospital Hospital on Feb. 15.: mrs. Fred Fischer, Mrs. Fred Paselk, Mrs Roy Bungo, Mrs. Civila Olrich, Mrs. Paul Papenhagen, Mrs John Olrich, Mrs. Ida Brodbeck, and Mrs. Walter Komsteller.

✓ Our Sunday School offering on Feb 25th helped benefit the Educational Appeal.

✓ Rev. Mueller hopes to have a class of catechumens ready for confirmation on Palm Sunday.

✓ Inner Mission roll Call is Sunday, march 11th. Gerald Seegert is our chairman this year.

✓ Dian Jean Rittner, daughter of Mr. & Mrs. Alvin Rittner was baptized Sunday, Feb. 25th in Zion by the Rev. marcus Mueller. Sponsors were: Edward Brodbeck, Mrs. Kenneth Koestar, and Mrs. Melvin Gors.

✓ Local Pastoral Conference met Tuesday, Feb 27 at Zion Lutheran Church in Summerfield. The pastors celebrated Holy Communion.

✓ The Red Cross War Fund again asks for our support.

✓   The other Lenten Ten of the Ladies' Aid will be on march 14th at 2P.M.. The speaker will be the Rev. Otto Dagefoeade, of Toledo, Ohio.

✓   The church council met after the church service on Feb. 25th.

✓   The Aid met Thursday, March 1st.

୬୬୬

ZION LUTHER LEAGUE

It seems that Wilbert Fink has a hard time trying to decide whether his steady girlfriend is to be Betty or Irene Bexten.

Who was the boy we heard got stuck in Paselk's yard when he went after Mildred? It seems like everything happens there. A bunch of the kids also had to push their car to get it started before they could get any further. What will happen next?

Who is Janet Jacobs dream man? We heard he goes to Burham too.

The League enjoyed a box social on Feb. 7th. Blissfield was the only guest League present. Many games were enjoyed by everyone. About 50 were present. The boxes were auctioned off by Leo Bexten and Wilbert Fink. The League took in $16.50, which they sent to the "Mighty Fortress".

We are glad to see Junior Sanderson out with us again.

Juanita Breier is home for a month's vacation from Washington, D.C.

The annual League meeting was held on Feb. 22nd. They voted to have an Easter Sunrise Service again this year. We hope everyone in the congregation and all the readers of our Messenger in Ottawa Lake and vicinity will make a special effort to worship with us at this Service. Please watch the church bulletins and Sentinel for the time this will start.

The League Choir has begun again. They will sing on March 4th and also on Easter Sunday.

At the League Meeting each Leaguer wrote a card for someone in Service. Hope you boys and Inez enjoy them. We really enjoyed writing them to you.

HELPERS: (FEBRUARY ISSUE)

Many thanks to the following for helping with the messenger: Rev. Mueller, Mrs. Henry Brodbeck, Mildred Paselk, Mr. And Mrs. Christ Fischer, Lona and Fritz Fischer, Violet Fischer, Irene and Betty Bexten, Thelma Nearhood, Mrs. William Shoemaker, Mrs. Milton Trombly and Lelah, Helen Struth, Hermain Nieman, and Mrs. Ivan Holt.

We're happy to announce that <u>Mr. and Mrs. John Houseman</u> of Britton, Mich. Are the happy parents of a son, David Lee, born on Feb. 12th. His birthday is the same as his parent's wedding anniversary so they can celebrate together. Mrs. John Houseman is the former Kathryn Briggs.

Our Congratulations and Best Wishes to <u>Cpl. And Mrs. Bernard Anger</u> on the birth of a son born Feb. 13th in Lincoln, Nebraska. He has been named Albert Lee

<u>Howard Miller</u> from Whiteford Center, Mich. Has landed in France. He wrote home that the trip was O.K. over and he seemed to enjoy it.

<u>Elwood Brenke</u> is back in France again. We wish him Good Luck.

R E M E M B E R?
2 Years Ago

✓   The first issue of the Zion Lutheran Messager was printed and 150 copies made of that issue.
✓   "Geraldine "Gerrie" Schmidt is recuperating from a goiter operation.

✓ Eugene "Fritz Fischer is minus his tonsils, Olin Fischer had his removed in Bowling Green where he was attending college.

✓ Zion Luther Leaguers entertained the Leaguers from Summerfield, Dundee, and Maybee for a belated Valentine Party.

✓ The Brodbeck twins, Wilma and Bill were surprised on their 21st birthdays.

✓ The League of Ottawa Lake was invited to a box social at N. Blissfield. Riga Lewague entertained our League March 2nd.

✓ Lucille Schmidt slipped on the ice but no bones were broken.

✓ Mrs. Mueller was in the Robinwood Hospital

✓ Mr. And Mrs. Richard Rymill has named their daughter Judith Ruth.

✓ The Brotherhood has furnished the service flag in the church with the Staff and tassels.

✓ Kurt Durst spent a couple of weeks in the South.

✓ Paul Whitte was visiting in the Halter Home. Paul is a Sailor.

THIS IS WHERE YOU BOYS WERE TWO YEARS AGO

- ➤ M.E. Biever- North Ireland
- ➤ Andrew Ery-Out to Sea
- ➤ John Wotring- Out to Sea
- ➤ Henry Lunds- Norfolk, Va.
- ➤ Inez Bieberj- Joined Army Nurse Corp
- ➤ Frank Strable – Del Rio, Texas
- ➤ Edgar Strable- Lincoln, Nebraska

- ➢ Verne Jacobs – Ft. Riley, Kansas
- ➢ William Bernholts – Camp Forrest, Tenn.
- ➢ Will Denudt – Alaska
- ➢ Kenny Brodbeck – Mass.
- ➢ Eugen Hart – Texas
- ➢ Franklin Kummerow – Camp McCoy, Wis.
- ➢ John Fisher – Camp Chaffee, Ark.
- ➢ Wilbur Facklam – Miami Beach, Fla.
- ➢ Corp. Leroy Fischer – Calif desert
- ➢ Noble Woodyard – Africa
- ➢ Garld Holmes – Out to sea
- ➢ William Shoemaker – Alliance, Nebraska
- ➢ Jesse Bieber – Great Lakes, Ill.
- ➢ Clayton Seeley – California

1 Year Ago

✓ Our league entertained Riga, Liberty Corners, and Summerfield Feb. 25th.

✓ Mr. And Mrs. Frank Strahl sold their farm and moved near Chicago.

✓ A son was born to Mr. And Mrs. Rolland Osborn.

✓ Madeline Logan is betrothed to John W. McMahon (Midshipman).

✓ David Mueller was staying with his grandparents in Columbus.

✓ Betty Hammon was honored with a birthday dinner.

THIS IS WHERE YOU BOYS WERE A YEAR AGO THIS MONTH

- ➢ M.E. Bieger – England
- ➢ Harold Bunting – In the Pacific
- ➢ Merle Harroun – Camp Gordon, Ga.
- ➢ Inez Bieber – Italy
- ➢ Leon Harrwaldt – President of L. League

- Elwin Beck – The far North
- Kurt Durst – Tampa, Florida
- "Pete" Fischer – New Guinea
- Lester Knuth – New Guinea
- Stanley Kastel – On U.S. East coast
- Edwin Schieb – Camp Park, Calif.
- Vernon Packard – England
- Frank Klauda – Camp Chafee, Ark.
- Horace Nearhood – South Pacific
- Rolland Wotring – home on Furlough
- Bernard Myers – Kessler Field, Texas
- Wilbur Facklam – Lincoln, Nebraska
- Henry Lunde – Norfolk, Va.
- Vernon Root – Camp Livingston, Texas
- Lorene Flegle – Ft. Meade, Md.
- John Wotring – On Furlough
- Arthur Shanly – Canada
- Clayton Fischer – Camp Fannin, Texas
- William DeNudt – Alaska
- Kenneth Brodbeck – Italy
- Dan Mueller – Clewiston, Florida
- Howard Hotchkiss – Great Lakes, Ill.
- Russell Creque – South Pacific
- Howard Schmidt – N. Africa
- Kenneth Schmidt – California
- William Fischer – San Diego, Calif.
- Arthur Loomer – Ryan Field, Calif.

Francis Creque enjoyed a 30 day furlough.
Memorial Services were held for Cornelius Blome, Jr.

"FROM A PRIVATE TO A SAHGENT"
By Thelma Nearhood

I wish I was a wittle egg
As wotten as could be
I'd sit myself upon a limb
Away up in a tree
And when some bonehead Sahgent
Would start to shout a at me
I'd frow my wotten little self
And splatter he with me.

❧❧❧

Word has been recived by Mrs. Floyd Gray, Sr. that her son Floyd Gray, Jr. has arrived safely in France.

❧❧❧

Please notice
In case you send your Messenger overseas please cut the bottom half with the addresses off. This address list may be sent separately and I know the boys would like to have this list

❧❧❧

Brother-In-Laws meet in South Pacific
We are happy to hear that two sailors met and had a grand visit. Carl Ernst, Jr. son of Mr. And Mrs. Carl Ernst, Ann Arbor, Michigan and his brother-in-law Don Tickner, also of Ann Arbor, Michigan exchanged visits on each others boats at some harbor in the South Pacific. It had been about 2 ½ years since they saw each other.

❧❧❧

239

Italy, Jan. 27, 1945

Dear folks,

We really have a nice mess hall now. We bought some plates, cups, bowls and so all we have to do now at mealtime is go in the mess hall and sit down at the table. You no sooner get sat down than a good looking Italian girl comes along and puts a plate with meat and butter on it in front of you and the rest of the meal is in bowls on the table so it is really O.K. It sure tastes different eating off of plates and so we only have to wash our knife, fork, and spoon.

I had a day off the other day and went to Pisa. I visited the Leaning Tower again and took some pictures.

Yes, we hear quite a few radio programs that are broadcasted from the States. A fellow a couple of rooms from me has a radio and I go there sometimes and listen to it.

Talking about the weather we are really having it over here. You have heard about sunny Italy, well, I am seeing it now. We still have a little fire in our room at nite but the days are just like spring is back there. The sun shines every day and the nites quite cool. You ought to move over here and you would not have to bother about buying coal. The people here just go out and pick up a little wood and burn that. I don't think that they get over a day's supply at a time.
Of course they don't burn wood like we do back there. What we burn in a week would last these people a month.

I receive d the box of cookies that you sent the last of Nov. a couple days ago. They sure are good. Thanks a lot for them. I haven't been doing much lately although I did visit Pisa and took some pictures of the Leaning Tower the other day.

Tell the people "hello" and write when you can.

"Spud" Raymond Shanly

Philippine Islands,
16 February 1945

Dear Folks:

I'll be able to write more at night when we can use lights. Right now it is only about 7PM and it is almost dark already.

Yesterday we made a big move and saw and passed through quite a number of towns. I was surprised that most of the main roads are in as good as shape as they are. Quite a few of them are cement and few tar-bound. Some of the towns that we passed looked as though they might have been pretty nice during peacetime and quite modern. Some of them had some nice buildings and I would liked to have been able to have taken pictures of some of them. Some of the towns were torn up quite a bit and burnt but some of them were hardly touched. It seems as though the larger towns are damaged the worst. I suppose that is because the Japs picked them out to stay in as they like the best buildings that they could get.

We passed by quite a few rice fields in the way coming here and some of them were being worked now and were flooded. They also raise quite a bit of sugar can her.

We really have a nice place here as we are in a large building that used to be a schoolhouse. We have a nice set-up and there seems to be plenty of room. It is the best place that we have had so far. The last place that we were in wasn't bad either as it was a family house., The Japs had occupied the house not too long before we moved into it.

We are just out of a town a short distance and along a nice cement road. It is nice and clean here and is quite cool. The buildings are built high off the ground. I guess that it really rains when it does rain here so they have to keep things off the ground.

I'm feeling fine. Tell everybody "Hello' and write when they can and I'll try to answer as soon as I can.

Your Loving Son,
"Pete" Leroy C. Fischer

Feb. 11, 1945

Dear Rev. Mueller,

Salutations in the name of our amiable Lord. May this letter find you and your congregation happy in Him who gives life eternal to all who ask for it thru Christ. May each of us learn to lean on His everlasting arms.

With thankful heart, I received the Messenger. There is a book entitled:"Streams in the Desert" that is held in high repute for its spiritual blessing when the Christian is thirsty and weary but it cannot compare with the Lutheran Messenger when someone is thirsty for the home town hews and from the men overseas. So it is with grateful heart that I write you and your co-workers my humble, but sincere thanks for sending me the Messenger. May god bless each one of you for the wonderful edition of news that is compiled to make up the Messenger that each of us from Ottawa Lake enjoy so much.

Today being Sunday I have attended church at the new Chapel that was recently constructed on this island. I enjoyed the sermon very much but it wasn't like the sermon the pastor at home preaches. The Chaplains have a heavy load tho, and they need our earnest prayers.

My, the weather is wonderful in this part of the Pacific. It doesn't rain very often and the sun shines almost every day. I should be thankful for this lovely weather. The scenery out here is beautiful, especially the rainbows that appear. Our unit is situated in a large valley. A mountain is on one side of us and the sea is on the other. These large beautiful rainbows come out of the clouds and their ends are on our side of the mountain. I never looked at the bottom of the rainbow but I suppose the pot of gold is there. The beauty of these rainbows just can't be described. They must be seen to really appreciate their beauty.

Swimming, Basketball and volleyball are the main sports. We can go swimming whenever we are off duty. The salt water doesn't taste too good but it isn't bad if you don't swallow too much of it.

Well, it is time for duty so I'll quit for now. May God richly bless each of you in you fine work.

Love Because of Calvary,
Edwin Schieb

Dear Violet and Leaguers:

I've received the Messenger for a long time no and I really enjoy reading it and want to thank you and all the rust for sending it.

We are having our summer over here now and that means plenty of heat and rain too. So far I've been pretty lucky not to be sick or any thing but I will take home for mine any time

Another mate and I have made a wood lathe and made a few thins out of th beautiful teakwood here. The only draw back is to find spare time.

Sincerely,
Alvin C. Miller

Somewhere in Belgium,
3 Feb. 1945

Dear Violet and Leaguers,

How is everyone back in Michigan? I am O.K. and now out of the hospital and back in an outfit. I wanted to give you my change of address for the Messenger. It has been very cold over here and snow has been over knee deep although it rained yesterday and the snow is about all gone. How is the weather around home? Is Clayton still in Italy; Oli in N. Canada; and Pete in New Guinea? I received a letter from Matthew Bieber while I was still in the hospital Well, it kind of looks now as though this lousy war over here would finally end soon the way the Russians are storming on to Berlin. I hope so as does everyone else who has been in combat. Hope everyone is well and tell them I said "Hello".

       Sincerely,
       Melvin "Butch" Dauer

ᘓᘓᘓ

A few lines come from Jo Kamp who is now station at Santa Barbara, Calif. With the Marines. She's fine and writes, "I'd certainly miss the Messenger if I didn't get it. Been in Calif not quite a month but am not too enthused with the weather.

John Vanderlaan is in England now and in the Hospital. We hope you have a speedy recovery and get out of the hospital soon.

These few lines from Frank Klauda while he was still at Ft. Benning,Ga. "Just a few lines that I haven't forgot anyone in Ottawa Lake and hope everyone feels as good as I do. I am spending a 3-day pass at the U.S.O. in Columbus, Ga. And am writing letters and cards. Thanks for the Messenger every month and wish everyone a happy Valentine's Day." Recently we received a card from Frank with a New York A.P.O.

ᘓᘓᘓ

In Belgium,
Feb 2, 1945
Dear Violet and Leaguers:
Quite some time has elapsed since you all last heard from me thru the channels of Zion's Messenger. In as much as I

have both the ambition and inspiration to drop you a message tonite I may as well start the ink to flowing.

A few days ago I read an article "Street Scene" in our official overseas Service paper "Stars and Stripes". In it an American Soldier describes a scene he saw in an occupied town in Germany. Here in he described an old woman pulling her cart of personal belongings, a young girl, and school boy eagerly watching the U.S. Soldiers. In it he accuses these three elements of German society for the present World upheaval. He severely reprimands the smiles of the children when the German Army scored its victories over Europe. This biased opinion coming from an American Soldier, a Comrade in Arms, moved me deeply.

In the first place, the soldier was totally uninformed as to World History and Politics since 1918. Had he been informed he would have known how Nazism connived to get in the saddle and finally forced itself upon the unwilling Pres. And legislature of the Weimar Republic. He would have known the persecutions inflicted upon Christian Germans, and of course later on others. Then a few moments consideration in trying to find satisfactory answers to the following questions: (1) What chances would helpless children have to quiet an armed rebellion? Yet he said....."its's all your fault for not stopping it." Even American children in a free country couldn't do such a thing. (2) What understanding do children have of the significance of political movements? Few adults really do, even in U.S.A. where we are taught a variety of classes in school. Then I'd like to ask him, how much more would German children, who were taught one thing, "obey and keep silent", understand? It's a pity our schools, churches, and social institutions have failed to instill into the minds of the public true facts. Then such misunderstanding as this soldier possesses, which has developed in him, an unwarranted hatred of countless innocent victims of the enemy's political and war machines. Tragic, this man, in the grim business of war isn't even in possession of knowledge as to who constitutes the true enemy he's fighting.

Concerning his reprimand for the children's smiles over Victories, I'd say this on their behalf. Just consider human nature for a moment. What true patriotic children wouldn't smile when the army of their country is going good? Even our children back home are happy in such instances. They being immature physically and mentally didn't know or realize the significance of it all. They just knew their "heroes" were doing all right and not suffering. Children the world over idolize soldiers. Even here children who have brothers or fathers in the German Army still are friendly with us. To them we're soldiers just like their brothers and fathers. When I read an item like this I think it's high time the churches emphasize a little more "Love" preaching. The tyrant wants us to stoop to his low ways of hate and contempt. While so doing, it would also make him happy indeed to see us overlook him as the real foe, and pin the blame on the same ones he also dislikes and distrusts, so they'll suffer even more as a result of these actins.

Sincerely
Vernon Packard

Somewhere in Luxemburg,
Feb 13, 1945

Dear Violet and Leaguers,

I finally found time to write you a letter and I would like to thank the church for the Christmas box they sent me. I appreciated it very much.

I received the Dec. Messenger and enjoyed it very much. I might be near some of the boys but now knowing their outfit I can't contact them.

I am in the Third Army under General Patton. We've been fighting up in the Bulge.

I've been in combat about a month. The country over here is pretty but I know a place that's more beautiful then this. The towns are pretty smashed up from bombing and shelling. How is everybody at home?

I received the National Lutheran Council medal and I have it on my dog tag chain. Well, I must sign off for this time. Hope to hear from you all soon. God bless you and all.

Your friend
Merle Harroun

๛๛๛

Feb. 9, 1945

Dear Violet and Leaguers,

Sorry not to have written before but have been quite busy as you undoubtedly know. The situation doesn't look too bad at present but things happen fast out here so I haven't any comments on that topic.

I've rec'd many "Messengers" and needless to say have enjoyed them tremendously. I was sorry to read the news of the deaths of some of my acquaintances but everyone suffers the consequences of war in some form I'm sure.

Ottawa Lake is apparently well represented on all the far corners of the earth by the appearance of some of the boys' return addresses. Oh yes, my brother–in–law, Russ Creque and I had a few hours together a couple of weeks ago. We discussed the times we used to have back there previous to our enlisting in the Marine Corps, which included many of you. In conclusion I'll thank you again for the several issues of the "Messenger" that I've rec'd.

Sincerely,
Harold Pollock, Jr.

๛๛๛

Greetings Leaguers and friends,

Time is passing rapidly and soon spring will be here. To some the winter has been long, especially those in the States who I understand witnessed a real old-fashioned one with plenty of snow. This now will complete my second green winter. Many of you have not had an opportunity to make a snowball for a greater number than that. To all of us it will be a great day when we can go for a sleigh-ride or hay-ride back in Michigan or that vicinity.

Because of relative position latitude we cannot help but contrast things as they are here. I am sure that those of our number who spent a winter in Italy were likewise surprised.

One would not expect the grass to be green in January or February. On every slope and in every valley you can see fields of green plants growing. It would appear that the civilians must make greens their principal food. You can see women and girls as well as older folks out hoeing in the fields.

Most of the power on the farm is by oxen. The field crops now growing for the animals besides hay are apparently wheat, rye, or oats.

The other day I notice them shearing a flock of sheep.

My earnest hope is that each of you now in the service wherever you may be doing your part to encircle the enemies are enjoying as good health as can be had in circumstances and may God speed the day when we may all meet again if He so wills.

As ever,
Clayton Fischer

❧❧❧

Alaska, Jan 30, 1945

Dear Mom,

Just a few lines to say hello and things are going fine with me. We were going on a hike Sunday but it was too icy so we spent the day in town. The weather is bad up here. It seems all it does is rain. We have a lot of ice but not much snow. It is just below freezing. How is Dad? I hope he isn't working too hard or to many long hours. I will write to him soon. I don't get much time to write with my work and going to church on Sunday. I will close with love.

Harple Gray

જાજાજા

Eastern U.S.,
Jan 29, 1945

Dear Mom,
Well, a couple more days have passed and time to write again. I still haven't received any mail. Our mail hasn't caught up with us yet. I hope it comes soon. It sure is lonesome here without any mail. I hope this finds you all well at home as for me I have a slight cold but not serious. I will have to close for now, as I can't write much from here. Write as often as you can and I will try and answer

Your loving son,
Floyd Gray, Jr.

જાજાજા

Dear Violet and Leaguers,
Just a few lines to let you know I am fine and hoping you all are the same. We are having a mild Feb. so far. Yes, I am hoping to spend a few days in Paris again soon. I haven't had the chance to attend church service for quite sometime. Received the December Messenger and church papers also the Medal which I was pleased to get.

We now have a liberty run into the Red Cross nearby here. They have some good shows at the Cinema. "Going My Way" and Irish Eyes are Smiling."

Cheerio,
Matthew E. Bieber

৵৵৵

Italy, Feb 15, 1945

Dear Violet and Leaguers:

Gee, you folks sure had your share of snow this winter. I guess my folks had plenty of it to shovel as they complained about the trouble that they had with snow drifting in our long lane. I hope by now that your cold weather has passed. Those sleigh rides were no doubt a lot of fun. I used to take my father's horses and take a crowd riding like that but we haven't had sleighing weather for few years and of course the last three winters I have been away from home. Yep, 27 months overseas already and still going strong.

I must tell you a little bit about conditions at our new location. Things are a lot nicer than we have been accustomed to that I don't know what to tell about first. We arrived in Italy at A Southern Port and drove our vehicles to our present location. We made poor progress due to the hilly roads and the heavy loads on the trucks. It gave us time to take in all the scenery. We drove over some of the battle sites and also witnessed the results of the bombings. We passed through Rome and other pretty cities and seen some of the better-developed rural sections.

We arrived here and found that we could set up our weather station in the village near the airfield. It was the first time that we were able to do this. We got permission to rent rooms for living quarters and that meant goodbyes to the tents. The same four of us that usually shared a tent are now comfortably set up in a nice big room of a home about two blocks from our office. We have heat and lights and the bathroom and the lady does our laundry. We have our radio and phonograph for entertainment. We are near the water and look forward to swimming and fishing this summer.

I was fortunate to be able to vist Pisa the other day and we took time but to visit the tower and take a few pictures. I hope that the pictures are good. We climbed to the top and had a nice view of the city. The River Arno divides the City into two equal parts. We even rang the bells in the top of the tower.

I have been getting good service on my Messengers. Guess that's all for tonight.

Love,
Carl Schmidt

❧❧❧

Dear Rev. Mueller:

I received your church paper and was very glad to receive it. It keeps us busy with something to read. I also get a church paper from Olivet, Rev. Getter and Grace up in Springfield, Ohio where Rev. Anderson is pastor. I'm very glad to receive them.

I shipped from Kessler Field Sunday Feb. 4, 1945 at 9:30 P.M. and got here on Tuesday, Feb 6th at 4 A.M.

Texas is sure a hot state when you have to stand out in it but today it is trying to rain.

I am going through processing again and am ready to ship out Monday but don't know where as yet.

As ever,
Lester Gillhouse
(Lester is Don's brother. Don is in Germany and assistant to a Lutheran Chaplain)

❧❧❧

Jan 1, 1945

Dear friends,

I received and enjoyed the very fine Xmas package and many thanks to all for your thoughtfulness. We had a nice Xmas considering everything. One thing I missed was attending services and of course not being with my friends at home. Even tho we were on the line a hot dinner was sent up to us consisting of turkey, dressing, potatoes, cranberries, fruit, mince meant, bread, butter and coffee. We got our first snow last nite starting the New Year out in white.

I have been receiving the Messenger regular and now look forward to reading it each month. My sympathy to the Brodbeck family on the loss Kenneth. He was a good soldier, a swell kid and our friend. His mother can very proud of him.

I enjoy the full weather we're having here and really feel swell. Have seen a few deer in the woods so I may even get to do a little hunting. Thanks again for everything and best wishes for a happy new year to everyone.

Sincerely,
Don LaPointe

❧❧❧

Hi Violet and Leaguers,

It's raining here today and very dark out. I don't believe the sun has shown over 6 hours all winter. How is the weather in Michigan? The name of this Valley is "Take it easy, Valley"/ Hope this finds everyone at home well.

Sincerely,
John Fisher

❧❧❧

252

Dec. 7 1944

Dear Howard and Doris: (Never)

Boy, how the time flies. Here it is December already. I always think its June or July. Things are still going on. I have been getting your letters and sure am glad to get them. I got another issue of the church "Messenger". I like it very much. It seems like the place must have grown. I don't remember anybody it mentions but I guess it's been a long time since I've been around there. It must be a lot of work getting those out.. It's the finest thing I've seen yet on news from home. I hope they keep it up. Anything like that sure makes a fellow feel closer to home. Mom says she gets it too and thinks it's swell. Sure have been busy Lately. I'll be writing you.

Love,
Bill (Wm. Schultz) – Toledo Oh

Dear friends

It has been some time since I have written a letter to you and I am really ashamed of it but we have really been working. It has been seven days a week and 24 hours a day but I like it that way as the time passes much faster.

I hope you had a nice Xmas and that the New Year will bring all of us together again.

It is too bad about Kenny Brodbeck. I sure was surprised when Esther wrote and told me about it. Esther's brother Fritz was also wounded in France. I don't know how bad but said he was coming along O.K. now. Will close this time and may God bless and keep up all till we meet again.

Franklin Kummerow

In a short note from Lillian Dannecker, written Feb 6th she writes that the last they heard from her brother George was Jan. 7. He then wrote that he is a messenger form Battalion to Company. This is quite a responsible joy and also dangerous at times. George is in Sourthern France. Lillian was on the sick list but is better. Glad to hear it, Lillian.

Mrs. Edna Korth writes that she hasn't' received any news of late from her son Kenneth so he must be pretty busy. We hope that he and Edgar Strable see each other often.

The following news comes from Edward Seeley and his wife, Mrs. Martha Allen Seeley: Martha received a letter from Edward the first part of Feb. and that was the first letter since Dec. 25th. He is in the Philippine Area and is in a hospital because of burns. His whole face and his right side received burns. He is getting along as well as can be expected. He sent home some Japanese money (one peso, 10 pesos, and 50 centavos). He will be spending another birthday overseas as his birthday is March 15th.

The letter Feb, 17th Martha writes us, "Edward wrote that he had good visit with the Nearhood boys. He has to have a shot every three hours in his right arm. They had to give him a blood transfusion. He has been in service 4 years Feb. 1st and has been overseas 3 years in May. He is still in a hospital and in New Guinea. His right arm is just getting so he can use it again but it is a long ways from being healed up." We hope that you are feeling better Edward and get home soon.

Feb 2, 1945

Dear Violet,

It has been quite some time since I have written so I decided to take a bit of time out for a few lines before going to work tonight. I received your card while still in Oklahoma but didn't have time to answer. The picture of old Main St. in Sylvania sure looked good too.

I'm down in Cape Cod at a small air station now waiting for a new carrier to be completed. We don't know when we will go aboard but have a good idea that it will be soon

We are about 60 miles south of Boston so I spent a 72-hour Liberty there last week. This is very pretty country but very cold too. We wear fur lined flight uniforms and 5 buckle artics so I manage to keep warm.

I'm working in an engineering crew doing overhaul jobs on hell divers. At the present time our bombers are on a test hop to Florida so we're working on Fighters temporarily. This is very good duty but as soon as our squadron is formed we will be plenty busy.

I imagine that our ship will be ready just in time for the final push on Tokio. I hope that I have a box seat on that raid.

I may be able to get a leave just before shoving off, at least I hope so.

I was really sorry to hear about Kenny getting killed. It sure makes things tough at home when thngs like that happen.

Many of ther other boys seem to be getting Purple Hearts too.

Well, it 's nearly 5 o'clock and I have to muster in the hanger at 5:15 so I'll have to close. Say hello to everyone for me will you?

> As ever,
> Howard Hotchkiss

જ∾જ∾જ∾

Feb 17, 1945,
Somewhere in Germany

Dear Rev. Mueller
I finally got some time to write you a letter. Over here you don't have much time for yourself.

At the present I'm in Germany. I've been in England and all the way through France. I'll try to give you an idea what this country is like. All of us boys thought he countryside of England was the prettiest of all. Everything is clean even along the railroad. Some of the farmers were plowing and the grass is getting green and the hills and woods set in so nice. Sure was a pretty picture but I don't think much of their cities. France is beaten up in some parts and Germany is a pretty country if they only had peace. They also have a lot of hills and woods and all the farmers live together in towns about the size of Ottawa Lake and all the houses are made of brick. We're having a lot of rain. I wish I could say more but there is a lot I can't say.

I'm not with Leon anymore the last time I saw him was a half hour before we got off the boat. I sure wish were together. We had a swell trip over. We saw many sea fish. They had church about every other day on the boat which Leon and I went to but over here they haven't had a church service since I've been here. I miss them.

One thing, which made me very happy, was one night they said I had a letter and when I opened it here it was a birthday card from the Luther League. It was the first mail I got over here and I haven't received any since. I want to thank the League for all their cards and papers and showing me a good time when I was home, I like to thank the Ladies' Aid for all their fine boxes they sent me. They certainly were swell.

We boys get our smokes and shaving things and candy bars free. I don't think I've spent a dollar since I left the States.

Since I've been over here they made me a bazooka man that's a gun that's about four feet high and shot from the shoulder and is shot at tanks, trucks, and pill boxes. Most of us fellows are getting the expert infantry metal, which pays ten dollars more a month.

Rev. I've said about all I can think of for now. Tell everyone I said "Hello" and anyone who wishes to write I would appreciate it very much for that's the only thing that keeps us boys going and write whenever you can..

Truly yours,
LeRoy Breier

ക്ക

Feb. 2, 1945

Dear Violet,

It has been quite some time since I have written so I decided to take a bit of time out for a few lines before going to work tonight. I received your card while still in Oklahoma but didn't have time to answer. The picture of old Main St. in Sylvania sure looked good too.

I'm down in Cape Cod at a small air station now waiting for a new carrier to be completed. We don't know when we will go aboard but have a good idea that it will be soon.

We are about 60 miles south of Boston so I spent a 72 hours Liberty there last week. This is very pretty country but very cold too. We wear fur lined flight uniforms and 5 buckle artics so I manage to keep warm.

We are working in an engineering crew doing overhaul jobs on hell divers. At the present time our bombers are on a test hop to Florida so we're working on Fighters temporarily. This is very good duty but as soon as our squadron is formed we will be plenty busy.

I imagine that our ship will be ready just in time for the final push on Tokie. I hope that I have a box seat on that raid.

I may be able to get a leave just before shoving off, at least I hope so.

I was really sorry to hear about Kenny getting killed. It sure makes things tough at home when things like that happen.

Many of the other boys seem to be getting Purple Hearts too.

Well, it's nearly 5 o'clock and I have to master in the hander at 5:15 so I'll have to close. Say hello to everyone for me will you?

As ever,
Howard Hotchkiss

❧❧❧

Feb. 18, 1945
Burma

Dear Violet:
Well, here it is Sunday evening and not much to do so I figured it was about time to write a bit for the Messenger.
Two of the boys just came back from hunting but didn't get anything. They did see a deer and as they got ready to fire, the gun jammed. There they were steak stranded. Two others came back with a little fawn weighing about 30-40 lbs. They call them barking deer here.
How are all the folks all back home? I'm fine and hope everyone is the same.
Today we didn't work so I decided after getting up at 9 a.m. to wash clothes down at the creek. I took a five gallon can down and some gas so I could boil them. After a little rinse job. The G.I.'s are clean. Ironing is something of the past. We are working on pole line construction work which is rough and touch. The line is through jungle and heavy brush. Found out through the Messenger that Frank Kummerow is here in Burma and I'm hoping to meet him some day. Well, that's about all for now so I'll close with the best of luck to everyone.
A friend,
Marty Seitzie (Martin Seitz)

❧❧❧

Somewhere in Germany

Dear Rev. Mueller:

I finally got some time to write you a letter. Over here you don't have much time for yourself.

At the present I'm in Germany. I've been in England and all the way through France. I'll try to give you an idea what this country is like. All of us boys though the countryside of England was the prettiest of all. Everything is clean even along the railroad. Some of the farmers were plowing and the grass is getting green and the hills and woods set in so nice. Sure was a pretty picture but I don't think much of their cities. France is beaten up in some parts and Germany is a pretty country if they only had peace. They also have a lot of hills and woods and all the farmers live together in towns about the size of Ottawa Lake and all the houses are made of brick. We're having a lot of rain. I wish I could say more but there is a lot I can't say.

I'm not with Leon anymore the last time I saw him was half hour before we got off the boat. I sure wish we were together. We had a swell trip over. We saw many sea fish. They had church about every other day on the boat which Leon and I went to but over here they haven't had a church service since I've been here. I miss them.

One thing which made me very happy was one night they said I had a letter and when I opened it here it was a birthday card from the Luther League. It was the first mail I got over here and I haven't received any since. I want to thank the League for all their cards and papers and showing me a good time then I was home. I'd like to thank the Ladies Aid for all their fine boxes they sent me. They certainly were swell.

We boys get our smokes and shaving things and candy bars free. I don't think I've spent a dollar since I left the states.

Since I've been over here they made me a bazoota man that's a gun that's about four feet high and shot from the shoulder and is shot at tanks, trucks, and pill boxes. Most of us fellows are getting the expert infantry metal which pays ten dollars more a month.

Rev. I've said about all I can think of for now. Tell everyone I said "Hello" and anyone who wishes to write I would appreciate it very much for that is the only thing that keeps us boys going and write whenever you can.

Truly yours,
LeRoy Breir

లంలంలం

Word had been received by Mrs. Arthur Shanly that her husband Art has arrived in England.

Mrs. Don Dennis Temperance, Michigan has received word from her husband that he has arrived in France.

Lester Gillhouse is now in Liberal, Kansas having arrived there about Feb. 25th.

Howard Miller from Whiteford Center, Mich. Has landed in France. He wrote home that the trip was O.K. over and he seemed to enjoy it.

Elwood Brenke is back in France again. We wish him Good Luck.

లంలంలం

Feb. 19, 1945
In Germany

Dear Violet and Zion Leaguers:
Greetings from this fast shrinking land of our bitter enemy. Your most interesting and much appreciated V-Mail dated 29 January came last evening. It was indeed a pleasure hearing from you. The January issue of the Messenger is before me also. I am able to follow the activities of Zion Church very closely through this publication and also the Sylvania Sentinel.

Our work, in His glorious Name, becomes more interesting as each day passes hurriedly. The past weeks have been extremely busy for us and it seems that we shall never catch up. Most of last week was devoted to official correspondence besides assisting Chaplain Frey with fifteen services. Five were held a week ago Sunday and each with a fifteen minute sermon.

We work with the Battalion Aid Station as the Infantry advances. Chaplain talks with every casualty that comes through and offers prayer for those requesting meditation.

Taverns continue to be the most logical and suitable building for worship, and the place that shows less evidence of shell fire, in the villages we occupy. Our last Chapel prior to moving to this village was the tavern down on the corner. With a little adjusting, it soon became a House of Worship. The floor was littered with straw, plaster, broken glass, a dead rabbit and chicken. Glass doors from the kitchen cabinets looted in homes replaced the broken window panes. A partially destroyed auditorium provided our chairs, two stoves and speaker's stand as a pulpit. Our beautiful green pleated dossel was made from the stage curtains. A piano (made in Berlin) was moved from a nearby home. The local greenhouse afforded our tubbed scrubbery for each side of the Altar; our fern banked windows and the flowers on the Altar. The typical barroom pictures were removed and appropriate religious pictures hung in their place. We have our own Altar hanging. This gives you a rough idea of how a tavern received a clean face. Looting is our chief pleasure and pastime as you can see.

Two nurses from one of our hospitals sang a duet three weeks ago. It was really something different and the fellows appreciated their presence.

Services yesterday were held in a schoolhouse two hundred and fifty yards from the Germans. Just wish you could of sat in on this service. It does something to a person to hear front line G.I.'s singing Hymns of praise and thanksgiving as one large group. Another service was held in the basement of a factory.

I imagine you are observing the Lenten Season with midweek services. That has been true here so far. One can never tell from one hour to the next when a service has to be canceled.

Movies are sponsored and shown through this office whenever the Battalion goes in reserve. They are a great morale builder. The Red Cross Clubmobile comes regularly with their delicious coffee and donuts.

It seems so strange to us here to read and hear about a good old fashion winter in Michigan and Ohio this year and we have had nearly a month of Spring weather here. The days have been exceptionally warm for Feb. The only kick-back is the over abundance of mud and water which don't seem to help the situation much either.

Our present office is in the basement of a three story building. The flickering candles don't afford much light to type, but that is the best we have and so get by.

Would it be possible for you to send both Inez and Elg Bieber's addresses in the near future? I have lost their addresses and would like to write to them?

It is nearly time for evening chow and so will close for this time. We receive two hot meals a day and one of "C": and "K" rations. Please extend my greetings to all and my your have a Blessed Lenten Season and a joyous Easter.

Sincerely,

Don Gillhouse

৵৵৵

In Belgium
Feb. 13, 1945

Dear Violet and leaguers:

I finally found time to write you a letter and I would like to thank the church for the Christmas box they sent me. I appreciated it very much.

I received the Dec. Messenger and enjoyed it very much. I might be near some of the boys but not knowing their outfit I can't contact them.

I am in the Third Army under General Patton. We've been fighting up in the Bulge. I've been in combat about a month. The country over here is pretty but I know a place that's more beautiful then this. The towns are pretty smashed up from bombing and shelling. How is everybody at home?

I received the National Lutheran Council medal and I have it on my dog tag chain. Well, I must sign off for this time. Hope to hear from you all soon. God Bless you and all.

Your friend,
Merle Harroun

 formula

Dear Violet and leaguers;

Sorry not to have written before but have been quite busy as you undoubtedly know. The situation doesn't look too bad at present but things happen fast out here so I haven't any comments on that topic.

I've received many "Messengers" and needless to say have enjoyed them tremendously. I was sorry to read the news of the deaths of some of my acquaintances but everyone suffers the consequences of war in some form I'm sure.

Ottawa Lake is apparently well represented on all the far corners of the earth by the appearance of some of the boy's address. Oh yes, my brother-in-law, Russ Creque and I had a few hours together a couple of weeks ago. We discussed the times we used to have back there previous to our enlisting in the Marine Corps, which included many of you. In conclusion I'll thank you again for the several issues of the "Messenger" that I've received.

Sincerely,
Harold Pollock, Jr.

ରେରେରେ

February 18, 1845
Greetings Leaguers and friends:

Time is passing rapidly and soon spring will be here. To some the winter has been long, especially those in the States who I understand witnessed a real old-fashioned one with plenty of snow. This now will complete my second great winter. Many of you have not had an opportunity to make a snow ball for a greater number than that. To all of us it will be a great day when we can go for a sleigh-ride or hay-ride back in Michigan or that vicinity.

Because of a relative position latitude we can not help but contrast things as they are here. I am sure that those of our number who spent a winter in Italy were likewise surprised.

One would not expect the grass to be green in January or February. On every slope and in every valley you can see fields of green plants growing. It would appear that the civilians must make greens their principal food. You can see women and girls as well as older folds out hoeing in the fields.

Most of the power on the farm is by oxen. The field crops now growing for the animals besides hay are apparently wheat, rye, or oats.

The other day I noticed them shearing a flock of sheep.

My earnest hope is that each of you now in the service wherever you may be doing your part to encircle the enemies are enjoying as good health as can be had in circumstances and may God speed the day when we may all meet again if He so wills.

As ever,
Clayton Fischer

❧❧❧

Jan. 30, 1945

Dear Mom:
Just a few lines to say hello and things are going fine with me. We were going on a hike Sunday but is was too icy so we spent the day in town. The weather is bad up here. It seems all it does is rain. We have a lot of ice but not much snow. It is just below freezing. How is Dad? I hope he isn't working too hard or to many long hours. I will write to him soon. I don't get much time to write with my work and going to church on Sunday. I will close with love.

Harple Gray

❧❧❧

Eastern U.S.
Jan. 29, 1945

Dear Mom:
Well, a couple more day have passed and time to write again. I still haven't received any mail. Our mail hasn't caught up with us yet. I hope it comes soon. It sure is lonesome here without any mail. I hope this finds you all well at home as for me I have a slight cold but not serious. I will have to close for now as I can't write much from here. Write as often as you can and I will try and answer.

You loving son,
Floyd Gray, Jr.

❦❦❦

Dear Violet and Leaguers:

Just a few lines to let you know I am fine and hoping you all are the same. We are having a mild Feb. so far. Yes, I am hoping to spend a few days in Paris again soon. I haven't had the chance to attend church service for quite sometime. Received the December Messenger and church papers also the Medal which I was pleased to get.

We now have a liberty run into the Red Cross nearby here. They have some good shows at the Cinema. "Going My Way" and "Irish Eyes are Smiling."

Cheerio,
Matthew E. Bieber

❦❦❦

Dear Violet and Leaguers:

I've received the Messenger for a long time now and I really enjoy reading it and want to thank you and all the rest for sending it.

We are having our summer over here now and that means plenty of heat and rain too. So far I've been pretty lucky not to be sick and any thing but I will take home for mine any time.

Another mate and I have made a wood lathe and made a few things out of the beautiful teakwood here. The only draw back is to find spare time.

Sincerely,
Alvin C. Miller

❦❦❦

Feb. 3, 1945

Dear Violet and Leaguers:

How is everyone back in Michigan? I am O.K. and now out of the hospital and back in an outfit. I wanted to give you my change of address for the Messenger. It has been very cold over here and snow has been over knee deep although it rained yesterday and the snow is about all gone. How is the weather around home? Is Clayton still in Italy? Olie in N. Canada: and Pete in New Guinea: I received a letter from Matthew Bieber while I was still in the hospital. Well, it kind of looks now as though this lousy war over here would finally end soon the way the Russians are storming on to Berlin. I sure hope so as does everyone else who has been in combat. Hope everyone is well and tell them I said "Hello".

Sincerely,
Melvin "Butch" Dauer

ટ્ટ&ટ્ટ&ટ્ટ&

A few lines come from Jo Kamp who is now stationed at Santa Barbara, Calif. With the Marines. She's fine and writes, "I'd certainly miss the Messenger if I didn't get it. Been in Calif. Not quite a month but am not too enthused with the weather."

John Vanderlaan is in England now and in the Hospital. We hope you have a speedy recovery and get out of the hospital soon.

These few lines from Frank Klauda while he was still at Ft. Benning, Ga. "Just a few lines that I haven't forgot anyone in Ottawa Lake and hope everyone feels as good as I do. I am spending a 3 day pass at the U.S.O. in Columbus, Ga. and am writing letters and cards. Thanks for the Messenger every month and wish everyone a happy Valentine's Day. Recently we received a card from Frank with a New York A.P.O.

BROTHER-IN-LAWS MEET IN SOUTH PACIFIC

We are happy to hear that two sailors meet and had a grand visit. Carl Ernst, Jr. son of Mr. And Mrs. Carl Ernst, Ann Arbor, Michigan and his brother-in-law Don Tickner, also of Ann Arbor, Michigan exchanged visits on each others boats at some harbor in the South Pacific. It had been about 2 ½ years since they saw each other.

☫☫☫

Jan. 27, 1945
Dear Folks:

We really have a nice mess hall now. We bought some plates, cups, bowls, and so all we have to do now at meal time is go in the mess hall and sit down at the table. We no sooner get sat down than a good looking Italian girl comes along and puts a plate with meat and butter on it in front of you and the rest of the meal is in bowls on the table so it is really O.K. It sure tastes different eating off of plates and so we only have to wash our knife, fork, and spoon.

I had a day off the other day and went to Pisa. I visited the Leaning Tower again and took some pictures.

Yes, we hear quite a few radio programs that are broadcasted from the States. A fellow a couple of rooms from me has a radio and I go there sometimes and listen to it.

Feb. 7, 1945

Talking about the weather we are really having it over here. You have heard about sunny Italy, well, I am seeing it now. We still have a little fire in our room at nite but the days are just like spring is back there. The sun shines every day and then nites are quite cool. You ought to move over here and you wouldn't have to bother about buying coal. The people here just go out and pick up a little wood and burn that. I don't think that they get over a day's supply at a time. Of course they don't burn wood like we do back there. What we burn in a week would last these people a month.

I received the box of cookies that you sent the last of Nov. a couple days ago. They sure are good. Thanks a lot for them. I haven't been doing much lately although I did visit Pisa and took some pictures of the Leaning Tower the other day.

Tell the people "hello" and write when you can.

"Spud" Raymond Shanly

❧❧❧

Philipines Islands
16 February, 1945

Dear Folks:

I'll be able to write more at night when we can use lights. Right now it is only about 7 PM but it is almost dark already.

Yesterday we made a big move and saw and passed through quite a number of towns. I was surprised that most of the main roads are in as good a shape as they are. Quite a few of them are cement and a few tar-bound. Some of the towns that we passed through looked as though they might have been pretty nice during peace time and quite modern. Some of them had some nice buildings and I would liked to have been able to have taken pictures of some of them. Some of the towns were torn up quite a bit and burnt but some of them were hardly touched. It seems as though the larger towns are damaged the worst. I suppose that is because the Japs picked them out to stay in as they like the best buildings that they could get.

We passed by quite a few rice fields on the way coming here and some of them were being worked now and were flooded. They also raise quite a bit of sugar cane here.

We really have a nice place here as we are in a large building that used to be a school house. We have a nice set-up and there seems to be plenty of room. It is the best place that we have had so far. The last place that we were in wasn't bad either as it was a family house. The japs had occupied the house not too long before we moved into it.

10

We are just out of a town a short distance and along a nice cement road. It is nice and clean here and is quite cool. The buildings are built high off the ground. I guess that is really rains when it does rain here so they have to keep things off the ground.

I'm feeling fine. Tell everybody "Hello" and write when they can and I'll try to answer as soon as I can.

Your Loving Son,
"Pete Leroy C. Fischer

જાજાજા

Medford, Oregon
Feb. 12, 1945

Hi Violet and Leaguers,

It's raining here today and very dark out. I don't believe the sun has shown over 6 hours all winter. How is the weather in Michigan? The name of this Valley is "Take it easy, Valley". Hope this finds everyone at home well.

Sincerely,
John Fisher

જાજાજા

Dec. 7, 1944

Dear Howard and Doris:

Boy, how the time flies. Her it is December already. I always think it's June or July. Things are still going on. I have been getting your letters and sure am glad to get them. I got another issue of the church "Messenger". I like it very much. It seems like the place must have grown. I don't remember any body it mentions but I guess it's been a long time since I've been around there. It must be a lot of work getting those out. It's the finest thing I've seen yet on news from home. I hope they keep it up. Anything like that sure makes a fellow feel closer to home. Mom says she gets it too and thinks it's swell. Sure have been busy lately. I'll be writing you.
Love,
Bill (Wm Schultz) – Toledo, OH

℮℮℮

March 1945

TO OUR LOVED ONES IN THE SERVICE:

In the Name of our Lord Jesus, Greetings! The hold Lenten season gives us an opportunity, yea, obligates us to speak concerning the suffering of the Lord.

In John 18:1-13 we have the story of Jesus in the Garden of Gethsemane. Christ was waiting for "Zero hour". His hour was near at hand. And so, he agonizes in prayer, "Father if it be possible let this cup pass from me. Yet, not my will, but thine be done." Three times he prayed thus. His prayer was answered by the strengthening and comforting appearance of an angel. He was better prepared to go "over the top" for us. His death (in our stead) on the cross was only about twelve hours hence.

Jesus in the Garden urged his disciples to Watch and Pray. They were sleepy and sleeping when the press of the moment should have caused them to be sober, vigilant, alert, wide awake. "Eternal vigilance is the price of liberty!" In the church, too, there must be watchfulness. Indifference in the disciples leads to moral and spiritual decay, if not outright denial of Christ. Witness the later act of Peter! Guard with your life the integrity of your Christian faith! Watch and pray! Hear and learn the Word of God and according to the institution of the Lord Jesus. Remember it is the Word of God and your faith in the Word, together with the eating and drinking of the consecrated elements, that bring you individually the assurance of forgiveness of sins, renewed spiritual life, and life eternal. "There is therefore now no condemnation to them which are in Christ Jesus." Rom. 8:1

Jesus in the Garden resolutely goes forth to meet his enemies. He could have evaded or avoided the Cross. He could have "come down from the cross," but for your sakes and mine, he despised the shame and ENDURED THE CROSS. What a Friend we have in Jesus! His enemies sought Him out in order to kill Him. He becomes the Judge unto condemnation of all those who remain the enemies of the Cross. He comes the great Reconciler with God unto all who seek Him as their Savior. "Seek and ye shall find!" Lord, have mercy on me.

When Jesus in the Garden says to his foes "Whom seek ye? He makes them confess the object of their evil search. God grant that we search the Lord as our Savior.

Jesus in the Garden defends his followers. "If you seek Me, let these go their way." God still promises protection. Read Ps. 91: Ps. 23: Romans 8: John 10:27-29. He furthermore keeps evil doers from harming his followers. While death comes sooner or later to all of us in one way or another *the wages of sin is death—and we have all sinned and come short of the glory of God) God in His infinite mercy has for the sake of the bitter death of Christ and His glorious Resurrection on Easter, caused a lively hope of resurrection and life eternal to spring up in our bosom.

Jesus in the Garden is fervently defended by Peter, even by the sword. He cuts off the ear of Malchus. Jesus does not defend such action. Neither does the Church go to war with sticks and staves and weapons. They that take the sword shall perish with the sword!

It is still the first and last business of the Church to bring the Gospel to forgiveness in Christ, to shed abroad the light of the Word of God, to be a voice unto peach and righteousness, justice and mercy in this war-darkened world. God be thanked for our noble chaplains who carry the Cross of the living Jesus to the areas marked with death and destruction and despair. Christ doesn't need our feeble help for his safety. But each one of us needs badly the defense which Christ, the Rock of Ages, alone can afford. Fox-holes and flak-vests, parachutes and life-belts, plasma and sulfa, all are equally without avail when the call comes to "go the way of all the earth."

> When ends life's transient dream,
> When death's cold sullen stream
> Shall o'ver me roll;
> Blest Savior, then in love,
> Fear and distrust remove;
> O bear me safe above, a ransomed soul.

Jesus in the Garden, finally shows his readiness to drink the cup of suffering. The cords of the Cross are found in one word, John 3:16, "God so loved the world..." He drank the bitter dregs of the cup of suffering, He was obedient even unto death, that, being rooted in Christ, we might say "My cup runneth over" (with joy and gladness), goodness and mercy shall follow me all the days of my life, and I will dwell in the house of the Lord forever." Read Isaiah 53; John 14. A Blessed Easter to all!

> Cheerio,
> Your Pastor and Friend,
> Rev. Marcus Mueller

RECEIVED PURPLE HEART

Mrs. Clayton Seeley received the Purple Heart recently. Her husband, Clayton, was killed in action over in France. On Feb. 28th a Memorial Service was held at Zion. He is survived by his wife, Hellie and two children Elsie and Raymond Stanley, his father, mother, brothers and sisters and many friends. His brother, Edward, is with the 37th Division overseas in the Philippine area at the present time.

RETURN FROM OVERSEAS

Three of the men on our Messenger mailing list are back in the states after being in combat zones and working hard. Martin Schniepp is at his home in Riga returning from the South Pacific. Howard "Huck" Schmidt is in Percy Jones Hospital, Battle Creek, Michigan recuperating and resting. He returned from Italy. He spent the weekend of Feb. 25th at his home in Lambertville with his family and friends. Jim Clegg, son of Mr. & Mrs. Charles Clegg, Whiteford Center is home on a furlough from France. This is the first time he has seen his little daughter. We hope you enjoy your stay at home, all of you boys.

LEFT FOR SERVICE

Two more names have been added to our Messenger list. Rolland Schmidt, son of Mr. & Mrs. Leon Schmidt and Jesse Creque, son of Mr. & Mrs. Leo Creque left for service on Feb. 16th. A star will be placed in Zion's Service Flag for Rolland and he was given his Testament and Prayer Book at the service on Wednesday evening, Feb. 14th. Both of the boys were sent to Fort Sheridan, Ill. Jess is with the Para-troopers and we haven't definite word where they will be sent for training.

MEN OVERSEAS

Again we're happy to print that friends met over in the South Pacific this time it was Russell Creque and Harold Pollock, Jr. and the Nearhood twins and Edward Seeley has a visit together. Also Bernard Myers was in Los Angeles and saw Kenny Schmidt.

 люлю

Palm Sunday,
25 March 1945

Leaguers and friends:
On this, the first of Holy Week, 1945, men from congregation are worshipping if possible at the four corners of the earth. Last week I could not help but notice that our Western Front was in the vicinity of Worms, the place at which the founder of our Church appeared before the Diet in 1521. Perhaps some of our own pals are now in that very vicinity. Also it could very easily be possible for some of our number to be within the peal of the St. Peters church of Vatican City during this Holy Week while in certain sections of the Mediterranean Theatre.

At this Blesses Season, I am sure that I speak for all in the Service from our Church and community, when I say that we are thinking particularly of the immediate family is of those from our group who have already given their all for freedom. It has been their supreme sacrifice. This season we look upon another supreme sacrifice, yes, a sacrifice so that those who die for freedom or otherwise might again have life, the most abundant life. May the radiance of the glorious Easter-morn Savior remove all sorrow from their hearts and may they find comfort in His "Fear Not" even as do we away from home in the Service and also find it difficult to put in words the assurance received in His manifold promises to be with us and comfort us.

With Easter Blessings,
Clayton Fischer

ക്കക

March 18, 1945

Dear Mom:

I haven't much time tonight so this may be short.

How are things at home? Sure hope this finds you all well and getting along nicely.

This end of it is still on top and going strong. I manage to get rid of my cold and I feel much better.

We are living at the shop now, we have our tent just behind it. We go back and forth to the company area to eat, something just had to be done, they were stealing us blind, such at tools, tire equipment and even parts.

One of the mechanics build a washing machine out of a gas drum in his spare time (well, we all had a hand in it). We run a small tractor for an air compressor for the tire shop so we hooked it up to that.

My clothes come out as clean as ever, only some white pieces have tattle tale gray. Rinse might take that out but our corner store don't handle it. It's clean anyway.

This place certainly has fruit around. We have about 5 stalks of bananas and some pineapple hanging outside of the tent. The bananas are small but good. If we run out all we have to do is go out into the jungle and get some more. We have a Tarantula spider. It stays in the bananas. We don't kill him as he keeps the ants away. We all know he's there so are on the look out for him when we get bananas to eat.

We have three dogs, a monkey, and a couple of parrots. When we let Joe, the monkey loose he plays with the dogs. Some of the boys have seen monkeys three feet tall. We brought Joe from another Island and he's not that big.

When we first got here one of the boys went through a house and found an organ. It had Jap writing all over it. If it didn't belong to them they used it. It needs a little fixing and then it'll be OK.

Mail has been slow for sometime but when it comes I'll get it all at one time. I must close now as it's getting late. I'm, OK. Say "Hello" to all. We are so busy I haven't much time to write as least not as often as I'd like to. Please don't worry.

> Your loving son,
> Ed (Edgar Strable)

و‌و‌و

Dear folks:

And now for the big, big item which I don't think I've written of as yet. Did I ever tell you about the time we bagged the big buck moose when I was up in the Yukon? That's what I can truthfully say now. About Feb. 26 while we were still staying down at camp nights we were on our way back as we swung around a corner one of the boys spotted the moose. Both the boys have hunting licenses so one jumped out and let fly three times. We were up to the spot in no time and about 15 yds. Off the road back among some little evergreens lay the moose front feet folded under him like a cow resting in pasture. It took us about 2 hrs. to skin him. We butchered off the quarters and brought them up to the station. We distributed the quarters to three different stations and gave the fourth to an Indian fellow and his wife at camp.

You should see our recent menagerie — we call them "coal black twins". "Dina", short for "dynamite" is our recently acquired bear dog. Her arch enemy is "Tommy" a sleek, neat young cat. So far "Dina" isn't too sharp on Emily's book on "bathroom manners" but perhaps a few well-timed taps will teach her the straight and narrow – to the open door, even if it is cold outside.

Olin (Curtis) Fischer

సాసాసా

Dear Leaguers & all:
Well, it had been quite some time since I have written you. I have been getting the messenger regularly and sure appreciate it.

I haven't had much time to write lately as we have been having to fight the snow up here. It really has been terrible. It beats any snow I every saw in Michigan or elsewhere in Alaska.

An ordinary Jeep can't travel the roads at all. The snow plows work both day and night, but to no avail, for the next day or so it is worse.

There isn't anything to tell about this country, so will close for now. Looking forward for the March issue of the Messenger. Keep up the good work.

Verne Jacobs

సాసాసా

March 6, 1945

Dear Violet and Leaguers:
Just a few lines to let you know I am well and OK, but a long way from home. After two and a half years I finally got overseas.

The weather over here is cold and chilly yet but I have hopes it will warm up soon. We have a nice place to sleep though. It is a barn and there is plenty of straw on the floor. With that and a good bedroll I make out swell. The people over here are very odd, and their farm tools are Ancient and old. All of their farm wagons are two wheeled and they drive horses in front of each other, but enough of that for now.

I received the Messenger today and was very glad to get it. It sure is a treat to read about the boys I used to know. Well, I guess I had better sign off now for it is getting dark, and we don't have any lights.

As Ever,
Floyd Gray Jr.

ⁿⁿⁿ

PENINSULAR BASE HEADQUARTERS, ITALY:

Second Lt. Inez M. Bieber of Ottawa Lake, Michigan is a nurse with the 182ⁿᵈ Station Hospital which for sixteen months has been a vital part of this Base Section, the important supply and services organization for the Fifth Army. The Hospital's achievements since January 25, 1943, when it was activated, have been numeral and valuable, warranting special commendation by the Commanding General of the Corps Expeditionnaire Francais, which was enthusiastically endorsed by the Commanding Generals of the Fifth Army and of this Base Section at the time.

The Hospital was formed at Camp Breckinridge, Kentucky, of personnel largely from Ohio, Indiana, Illinois, West Virginia, and Kentucky. It's commander through has been Lieutenant Colonel Harry H. Jenkins of Knoxville, Tenn. After eight months of training, the unit went overseas in August 1943, and aboard ship made friend with the Japanese-American 100ᵗʰ Battalion, shipmates who later earned undying fame in Italy and many of them passed through the Hospital as combat wounded. While on ship, the Hospital personnel seemed to find a regard for one another, as attested by four shipboard romances which have since culminated in overseas marriages. Personnel also assisted the transport surgeon with medical and dental treatments and with one appendectomy.

Overseas service began with the landing at Oran, Algiers, on Sept. 2, 1943. Personnel and equipment were assembled, checked and rechecked in such good time that the unit was able to report itself ready for operation a month in advance of its scheduled date. Only the nurses' baggage was missing, and this took some four months before turning up in time for Christmas at the Hospital's permanent home.

The intended location for the 182nd was not known but once equipped and ready, sailing orders again came through. Prior to leaving the States, and even before the Allied invasion of Italy, a pool had been formed to guess the unit's destination and this was won by the Hospital's Chaplain on arrival in Naples, Italy, where he immediately turned his winnings over to a party for all. The unit arrived at Naples on October 10, 1943, though landing was delayed until the beaches were cleared of mines. Then operation of the Hospital was held up while all members went to work repairing the proposed site. Finally, through invention and application, the working Hospital was brought into being exactly eleven miles from the German rear units. (A station hospital be definition operated from fifty to two hundred and fifty miles behind the lines.)

The site selected was a former Fair Grounds whose architecture and landscaping are reminiscent of the New York World's Fair. However, this Fair was short lived, and by the time the Americans arrived, Allied bombings had left great craters in the areas, with roofless buildings, pitted walls and broken glass in profusion. Some spots had been gutted by fire while elsewhere walls had given way. Electricity and water sources had been destroyed by the retreating enemy. More unexpected work appeared for the staff to perform.

"Destruction" squads moved through the buildings, cleaning out until only bare walls remained. Nurses folled in work clothes with brooms, buckets, and even wheelbarrows to take over the housekeeping. Carpenters, plumbers, masons, and electricians were produced from the enlisted ranks. Tools and machines were found in disrepair but soon readied and operating. All lumber from crates was put to use. By October 17th, the Hospital's 500 beds were prepared to receive the first combat patients.

Initiation into combat operations came in the very first week, from an unexpected direction. Enemy planes made their first of many night raids in and around Naples and, though the 182nd Station Hospital received no direct hits, two soldiers and one officer suffered injuries entitling them to the Purple Heart while one of the nurses was officially cited for her meritorious behavior in staying with her patients who were too seriously injured to be evacuated.

Form that time forward, the Hospital has been a life-saving adjunct of all activities on the Italian peninsula, consistently exerting itself in the service of Allied operations. At one time the patient capacity was expanded to a total of 2,300 men, the largest census of any hospital in the Mediterranean Theater of Operations.

The unit may be called now a truly United Nations Hospital. At one interval it had 1,000 beds used by French, Goumiers, Sengaglese, and Arabs of the Corps Expeditiionnaire Francais. It has provided medical care for British troops and for Italian or German prisoners. Right now considerable numbers of Braziliens are receiving attention from the Hospital.

The hospitalization program is now equalized between internal medical types of cases and surgical cases. In addition, the Base Section Allergy Center for treating hay fever and other allerigic diseases is part of the Hospital. It has performed research into sandfly fever and infectious hepatitis, both of which have seriously impaired the health of troops in Italy. The Hospital buildings and ground are agreeably attractive to the patient as well as wholly sanitary. The wards gleam with new coats of paint; an Olympic-size swimming pool was available through the swimming season to patients and staff; officers, nurses and men of the staff are now billetted in well-winterized tents while all patients are housed in sanitary building. The record, of which each member of staff is proud, speak for itself.

Sent to the Editor of the Messenger direct from the Public Relations Office in Italy. We congratulate Inez on her good work over there.

❧❧❧

Sunday evening in Burma
March 5, 1945

Dear Aunt, Uncle, and Cousins: (Mr. & Mrs. Lorentz Seitz)
  Here I am again, the soldier of Burma. How is everybody: I am O.K. and hope all of you are fine. Heard that Betty is in Florida and how does she like it? I can just imagine that she likes it a lot because I did. They have nice places for soldiers there and the hotels were nice we stayed in. I wonder if they still keep them in hotels, or stationed in army camps.
  Today was Sunday and I didn't do much except wash clothes, cleaned my rifle and by that time it was two o'clock and then we had dinner and went for a walk to the village to take pictures and looked around. I watched the Burmese dye clothes and you would never guess how it's done. They get some bark from a certain tree and boil it in water by the times it's through boiling the water is black as coal and so on for all diffent colors.
  Just getting back from my pal's tent. Went over to get a cup of coffee and instead played checkers, won one game and the other came to a tie and neither one gave up. The reason I went to get a cup of coffee was because we have two meals a day on Sunday, breakfast at nine and dinner at two. Then by

night we get so hungry and don't know what to do with ourselves. In the army you can't go to the kitchen anytime you please but we always ask the cooks and they give it to us if they have it.

We are still working on pole line construction work every day and it's getting tiresome at times. It is tough and rough.

You know the fountain pen that you gave me when I entered service it's doing all the writing for me and it works good. It's never refused once and I wouldn't sell it for anything.

Well, I'll close with the best of luck and God Bless you all.

> Your nephew and cousin,
> Mart (Martin Seitz)

❧❧❧

Word has been received by Mrs. Mildred Nieman Shoemaker that her husband, William Shoemaker has arrived safely and is stationed somewhere in India. He writes that in the Bengal Air Depot and it is 110° in the shade. He was very happy when one of his buddies that he had known while stationed at Alliance, Nebraska dropped in on him for a chat. Our Best Wished Bill and we hope you see more fellow over there that you know.

Mr. and Mrs. Arthur Loomer have moved from Harlemgen, Texas to Kingman, Arizona. Ursle has a position at the post. We hope you like Arizona.

Word has been received by Mrs. James Grundy that her husband is now somewhere in France after being in Belgium and Germany. He writes that he is O.K.

We're sorry to hear that Charles Fetzer, son of Mr. and Mrs. Fred Fetzer, Riga, Mich. Has been wounded in the

European theater and we wish him a speedy recovery. Also "GET-WELL WISHES" go to Arthur Whitenburg who is recuperating in France.

From the Mariana Islands come news from Norman Eberlin who is as assistant to an Army Chaplain. He writes: "We are very fortunate out here. The days are warm, in fact hot, and the nights are cool so we do get sleep. I have enclosed a couple of our church bulletins. We think they are pretty nice and it will give you a brief ideas of our schedule here. At times it becomes pretty full and there is not much time for movies or letter writing. Now that we have finished work on the Chapel maybe things will straighten up a bit.

By the way how is your paper coming? I have been waiting for a copy of it but I guess it is like a number of other things sitting somewhere waiting to be shipped out. It is good to see such papers and read about people you know and various incidents happening to them. I got a letter from Larry Metzger and he is now in Hawaii and seems to be enjoying it."

L.t Bieber is the daughter of Frank J. Bieber of Ottawa Lake, Michigan, and obtained her training at the St. Vincent's School of Nursing in Toledo, Ohio, graduating in 1942. Prior to entering the Army Nurse Corps in March 1943 she served as a graduate nurse with the Bixby Hospital at Adrian, Michigan. Lt. Bieber came overseas in August 1943 and has served with the 182nd Station Hospital in North Africa and in Italy.

Kamba, New Guinea
Nov. 30, 1944
American Christians, listen to my words:

Yes, now the time is like this, we are in the midst of a big war. This fight has been going on here for 3 years. Five bombs were dropped on Kamba village killing men, women and children. At present we are fairly well but our houses, coconut palms, betel nut trees, pots, pans, bowls, and everything else of our belongings were destroyed. With machine gun fire they mutilated our houses and they also shot into the jungle and so we were sore afraid. Our large Church at Kamba in which we worshipped was destroyed and so was the one at Nobonob also the Mission station and other things in the surrounding country. Therefore we hid in the jungle and lived there.

When the Australian soldiers came they got us out of the bush and now we are again living in our village. During the time of the fighting there was much sickness in all the villages, and during this time many men, women and children died. Thus we existed.

The time when you were fighting the war also came to our country and on our ground of New Guinea. It puzzled and distressed us, our thoughts were multiple.

When are Japan, America and Australia going to stop fighting, so that we may again live in peace in our villages? This is all we have to say. We are thinking of you a lot and wondering what will happen.

These few words are all we have to say.

We are,
The Kamba Christians

March 4, 1945

Dear Geraldine, (Schmidt)
Just a few lines to let you know I am fine and hoping you're the same. I received your welcome V-Mail and League Valentine also church paper all okay and wish to thank you for your work.

Today is Sunday have been busy with week. I was washing and shaving after dinner when I received work the Chaplain was on his way. We had church service on the sunny side3 of the nice little old church.

It was the first service I was able to attend for several months. The red cross brought us some coffee and donuts later. They serve us some oranges now days.

I plan to wash my fatigues this evening before it get too dark.

As ever,
Matthew E. Bieber

ঌঌঌ

LIEUT. MELVIN DAUER KILLED IN ACTION

Once again we have to print in our Messenger the sad news that another comrade on our mailing list has given their life for the cause. We, who knew and loved Melvin, can recall many happy memories of school days together and we'll always remember him as "Butch".

He lost his life in Germany on Feb. 24. He was wounded last Oct. 6 in Germany and was hospitalized in England until Jan. 4. He was sent back into action on Jan. 23 and was with a mortar and machine gun unit as platoon commander when he made the supreme sacrifice. He enlisted in the Army Oct. 26, 1944 and received his basic training at Fort Wayne, Mich. He then was transferred to Fort Custer and in July of 1937 he was assigned to duty at Howe Military School in Howe, Ind. It was while he was at the academy that he married Francile Baer of Sturgis. He was commissioned a second lieutenant and served at Howe Military School for four and a half years or until 1941 when he was assigned to the military staff of the R.O.T.C. unit at the University of Dayton, Ohio. His promotion to the rank of first Lieut. came in Nov. 1942 while he was stationed in

Dayton. During his assignment he was sent to Ft. Benning Ga. For a refresher course then returned to his duties in Dayton. In March 1944 he was sent to Fort Harrision, Ind where he was in charge of a training unit of enlisted men. Last May he was sent to Camp Blanding for further duty and from that point he received his overseas orders. He was born in Haskins, OH. March 9, 1913. He spent his boyhood and youth on his parents' farm in Yankee Road and attended Seeley School and graduated from Burnham High in 1931.

He leaves his widow, Francile and daughter, Janet Marie, 4 yrs., Sturgis, Mich. Parent-in-laws Mrs. And Mrs. C.J. Baer, Sturgis, his mother, Mars. Margaret Dauer Elg and brothers, Edward, Maumee, OH and Ted and sister Mrs. Matilda Frenke, both of Detroit.

In a letter from the Chaplain to his wife he wrote the follows: "He was killed in the vicinity of Julich, Germany crossing the Roer River. His Company was crossing the Roer River and preparing to jump off for the Hambach Forest. He was buried with military honors under the rites of the faith which he professes."

Our sympathy to the morning family.

MISSING IN ACTION

LeRoy Breier son of Mr. and Mrs. Roy Breier, has been reported missing since March 1st in Germany. His parents received the word on March 19th. He was with the 94th Division of the 3rd. Army and served as a bazooka man in his Company. No further word has been received at this writing, May 13th., but we hope his parents hear from him soon.

CONGRATULATIONS

Two little soldiers have arrived at the homes of Cpl. Arnold Kummerow and Sgt. Thomas Read. The little boy born on March 25th to the Kummerow's has been named Arnold Albert, Jr. The son born to Sgt. And Mrs. Tom Read on March 19th has been named Thomas Roy Read.

Lt. and Mrs. Arthur Shanly are the happy parents of a little duaghter born in Flower Hospital, Toledo on April 30th. She has been named martha Pell. Her daddy is overseas in Europe.

A little son was born to Mr. and Mrs. Elwin Tabbert on April 18th in the Toledo Hospital.

అఅఅ

Springfield, Missouri
May 4, 1945

Dear Rev. Mueller and all:
Received your very nice box of candy and things today. Also your nice card. The things sure are good and I wish to thank you very much for it.

We are having some very nice weather down here in Missouri. The sun was shinning all day today. It gets pretty warm here during the day but it cools off some at night. So it makes good sleeping at night.

This is very nice hospital. The grass is so nice and green, bushed and shrubs are full of flowers. The hospital grounds are beautiful. We spend most of our time laying out on the ground in the sun.

I have been laying around now since March 1st. and it sure is getting tiresome.

I am very lucky. There is a lot of the boys here that have to lay in bed all the time. The only time I had to stay in bed was for 3 days after my first operation. That was when I was still in France but since then I have been up and walking around.

I still need one more operation. They are going to put a silver plate in my forehead where the bone has to be removed.

The doctors told me that they would not operate until I get back from a furlough because there are so many fellows ahead of me that needs operations so I expect to leave for home most any day now.

I must close for now but hope this letter finds you all feeling fine. For I am once again feeling fine and thanks very much for the box. Will try to see you all when I get home.

Yours truly,
Charles Fetzer

෴

Campe Maxey, Texas

Hi Mom:
Well, we finally got settled down. We started Saturday noon from Camp Sheridan, and we landed this morning in Camp Maxey. Some life that get you out of bed and have chow. We get up at 5:45 get dressed and wash and make our bed in 20 minutes. Boy, do you have to hurry and the bed can't have any wrinkles. If it has you have to make it over. It is warm and the wheat is turning ripe. We sure had a fine train ride. We hit a cow on the way. How is things coming at home. I hope fine. I have been pretty busy lately. Have 15 to 17 weeks training and then have 15 days home. Write soon.

Your son,
Clifford Papenhagen

෴

Dear Mom:

Not much news from this side of the world. It's the same old thing day in and day out but we do accomplish a lot though. The weather has been fairly cool the last few days and does it make a guy feel great after roasting most of the time, a cool breeze off of the ocean is great. I got the Messenger today and want to finish reading it.

In todays news I read where Pete moved up again. I haven't heard from him in a long time now but he has his hands full and maybe he will write soon. I feel that we may move up again before very long we have stayed about the limit. Some more outfits arrived that can finish the jobs we started.

You know Mom, if a guy forgets the hazards of war for a few moments and looks around these Islands have their beautiful scenery too. A sunrise on the jungle with everything green, the morning sun on the mountains in the back ground, palm trees swaying in the Ocean breeze you got to admit it's beautify but under conditions such as they are I wouldn't want any of them. If I get back to Ohio I'm not going to leave it, never!

Not much change over here, we are still very busy. Oh, yes, we have been enjoying fresh meats, steak, port chops and the like. It's luxury to us after eating dehydrated foods for so long. I guess we are getting accustomed to it now. I'm not gaining any weight but I notice some of the fellows are doing O.K. at it. It's getting late so I must bring this to a close. Hope this finds you all well, say "Hello" to the gang. I'm fine so far.

Yours,
(Ed) Edgar Strable

ʒʒʒ

Feb. 27, 1945
Somewhere in Germany

Dear Mom, Dad and all:

Mom, I got ten more letters this morning and it sure makes me feel good. You said you hadn't any mail from me yet. I write every change I get but sometimes I can't write. About a week ago we had our first change to go to church since I have been here. They had it in a German Church and he had a very nice sermon and the church was full. I also took Holy Communion, It wasn't like home but is meant the same things.

How's everything with you Dad? Take care of your self. I guess I better close for now and my God bless and keep you always.

Love and kisses from your loving son,
LeRoy Breier

෴෴෴

March 28, 1945

Hello:

Just received three Messengers and several Christmas cards. A little late but very welcomed nevertheless. Want to take this opportunity to say thank you to all the people who remembered me at Christmas time.

I see that several of the boys are out in this part of the world. Still haven't seen any of them except John Wotring. I sure was surprised that day when I looked up and there he was just like that. A little heavier than I remembered him but the same old John. We sure had a nice long talk and made arrangements to meet the next day. But the navy had different plans for us and he went his way and I went mine.

We have had a pretty interesting time this trip out. Have been away from the States for 16 months with never a dull moment.

A short time ago we had the honor of being the flagship for General McArthur on the Lingayen invasion. He spent several days aboard and when he left he gave each member of the crew an autographed picture in appreciation for the way the ship was handled during the operation. You have to give the old boy credit. He was right in there taking the chances with the rest of us.

Then we had our first opportunity to see our Paratroopers in action when they landed on Corrigedor. We really had a ringside seat for that show as we were using our guns to furnish the artillery support for them. The sight of them landing is one I will never forget.

I am hoping for a chance to come home soon as I have had overseas duty every since ware was declared. I'm not complaining though because the experiences I have had make up for the lonesomeness that comes from being away from home and loved ones. And I have seen just about every type of Naval action there is. So far I have made a collection of six different campaign bars. With eleven stars in them (each star represents either a major sea battle or amphibious operation). I took part in two of the largest naval engagements in American history, the battle of Savo Island (where the Boise made herself famous by sinking 6 Japanese warships) and the other the battle of Suriago Stratis.

When I write this it sor of sounds at though I ambgragging. It's not that at all but I have been on the Boise since it went in commission almost 7 years ago and I am pretty proud of her record.

I kept track for one month and counted 105 air raids that we had. So you can see we have been a very lucky shop and I thank God that so far I have come through unscratched.

Well, I see I am running out of time and space so I will close for this time.

As Always,
(Les) Lester Lnuth

292

April 2, 1945 France

Dear Violet and Leaguers:
    I received my first Messenger last night since I have been here in France and it really makes a person feel good to hear about the good old Ottawa Lake and to read all the interesting letters the boys write. So far, I seem to like France but I know of a place I" like to be better and that" back in Ottawa Lake. There isn't any place that compares to home
    I've started to receive my letters again that's been trying to catch up with me. I received 25 letters within 36 hours but I wouldn't mind if I had that many more on the way. That's what builds up our morals and it's mail from good old U.S.A. I am getting where I can talk a little French now. It helps to make it more interesting when you go to these little villages The French people really like us American soldiers. There is just enough room to thank all of you folks for the Messenger and to send all my regards to boys in service and their families back home. May God bless everyone on till Victory.

       Yours truly,
       Frank Klauga

❧❧❧

Percy Jone Hospital
April 12, 1945

Dear Gerrie: (Schmidt)
    I received the medal you sent me from the Lutheran Council and I wish to thank you for it. I sure enjoy reading the Messenger and to see the pictures of all the fellows from around home. I met John Schieb while I was down on Biak. He was

wounded on Luzon. We came back to the States together. He is right across the room from em. It is sure great being back in the States. I only wish I that my brother and all the fellows were back home too. I am sure sorry to hear that Kenneth Brodbeck and Leon Harrwaldt have been killed in action and LeRoy Breier missing. I saw some beautiful places while I was overseas and some not so beautiful but I will take the good old US any day. I have about run out of things to say so I will thank you again for the medal and for the many cards you sent me. Also thanks to the Messenger Staff for the box I received.

Sincerely,
Horace Nearhood

☙☙☙

April 10, 1945

Dear Mr & Mrs. George Schmidt:

Yes, I have finally gotten around to write to you and than you for the Christmas package that I received from you a couple of weeks ago. I have been wanting to write to you for sometime but it just seems that our time is limited and I just haven't much time to write letters. The package came in good shape and want to than you for everything. Our packages have been coming to us since the middle of December and I think I have more on the way unless they were lost. Just last Sunday I received one from Mr. & Mrs. Kummerow from Detroit but quite a bit of it had spoiled as it had been on the way since October. Since we have been here the mail service has really been irregular as the first 3 weeks that we were here we didn't get any mail at all and had a lot of old mail on the way for us that took as long as 2 months to reach us. Received the nice Easter Card that you sent and thanks a lot for it. Even though we are some distance from home these cards and letters make a fellow feel closer to home. Glad to hear that Huck is back in the States and close to home.

I have only been away from home for two years, that is it has been 2 years since I had the last furlough. We have been overseas a little over 18 months and in a couple of months I will have 4 years in service already. From the looks of things I think that is will be sometime yet before I'll be back there and a long time before I am able to be home for good.

Everything has been going fairly well here since we landed here on "S" Day the 9th of Jan. but have been in combat every since. I don't know whey they are keeping out outfit in combat so long but they have been on the go every since we landed. We have traveled over quite a bit of this island and have seen some fairly nice country but at present the boys are fighting in the mountains although we are a few miles back a little from the foot-hills.

As Ever,
"Pete" Leroy Fischer

April 11, 1945

Dear Gerrie Schmidt:

Since I last wrote to you I have received several cards also a birthday card that was sent in behalf of the League members. I want to thank you and have you relay the thanks to the rest of the Leaguers. Surely hope that before too long I'll, as well as the rest of the fellows, will be able to come back there and join you in your meeting and parties. I have been receiving the church bulletins quite regular. I got a letter from Paul Zeitner also the February issue of their paper.

A fellow leaguer,
"Pete" Leroy Fischer

Dear Violet and Leaguers:

Many thanks for sending Inez and Elg Bieber's addresses. I will write to them in the very near future.

The war is moving quite fast here and as a result we are seeing Germany. The retreating enemy keeps us on the move most of the time. The miles eastward in the last tine days have been many.

Germany has proven a very beautiful and interesting country. This section especially is very mountainous and spotted by pine forests here and there. The little villages in the valleys house the farmers who till and soil around the town. It is much different than the custom of living on the individual farms as in the States. It is hard for me to get used to all the barnyards in the villages.

Most of the churches here were built as Catholic many centuries ago and rededicated after the Reformation. This is especially true in this section. We used a Lutheran Church on Good Friday built in 1134 A.D. and still in good condition. The stone aisles showed much wear. It was a small church but had two balconies going around nearly three sides of the building.

We moved into town about the size of Sylvania last Sat. nite. It had a small Cathedral in which we worshipped, His glorious name, on Easter. The church was well filled as the bell rant at 8 o'clock and the huge pipe organ began playing, "Christ is Risen Today". Holy communion was administered after the service in the spacious sanctuary. A white marble, life size statue of Luther stood on the left of the high altar.

I was able to tour the famous Dom (Cathedral) in Cologne three weeks ago. It was a structure I shall never forget.

The weather continues to be ideal here. The old say, "April showers bring May flowers". Is very true as it has rained daily since Monday the 2nd. March was a month of sunshine and as gentle as a lamb.

There is much more to write about but time is short as are the hours for sleeping as will close for this time. Please extend my greetings to your family and to Zion L. League. Your Messengers have been coming through promptly and many thanks.

Sincerely In His Name,
Don Gillhouse (Ass't to the Chaplain)

⇗⇗⇗

Italy, March 25, 1945

Dear Folks:

Will write you a few lines tonight to let you know that I am still alive and kicking around. I have been to a couple of shows and we have dances twice a week so we have someplace to go about every night. It sure is different than it was last year at this time. I received your birthday card that you sent me. You sure had it timed all right as I received it on the 22nd. It sure is well over here. Everything is green and the trees are in blossom and it is very pretty. I had a day off the other day and a couple of fellows and I hitched hiked around the country a little and it was nice. By what Carl Schmidt wrote in the March Messenger he must be near where I am and so I will try and find out. If he is I will look him up. Vernue Seegert is probably in a different outfit then I am. I hope Art will get a chance to fly here as I would like to see him and I can't go there, at least not right now.

Time sure goes fast here. It seems that the first of the month was only a couple of days ago and here it is the middle of the month. I was out to dinner and supper on Easter. That sure is a big day over here for the Italians. I like to receive letters but don't do any writing myself. We have a building of our own and it's pretty nice. We have the inside all fixed up so it looks pretty good.

I received the letter with the pictures in and they sure are good. Everything looks the same as when I was there and maybe I will be there one of these years. At least I am looking forward to it.

Tell the people "Hello" and write when you can and I will try to do better from now on.

Your son,
"Spud" Raymond Shanley

ം∾∾

Dear Gerrie: (Schmidt)

Thanks for your letter and pretty card. I'm fine and hope you folks are all well. We like it here in Northern Italy and we have a very nice building for our hospital. We are also living in a building instead of tents.

We were given a weeks vacation to spend in Florence and I did enjoy this so much. I've always had a desire to visit this city so I made a special effort to see all I could of the interesting places while I was there. Many of the famous works of art and great paintings have been removed to safety during the war but hope they can be returned soon so we will be able to see these also. The war news is very exciting and everyone's morale is tops. Hope to see you all before too long.

Sincerely,
Inez Bieber

ം∾∾

April, 1945
Hi Everyone:

It's been a few months now since I've dropped in a line so I'll try to catch up on the latest.

First of all I'd like to change Websters definition of the word "Desert". He states it as a dry hot place. We are located on the desert to date we have had one snowstorm of 3 inches and several snow flurries. 50 miles away at San Bernardino it never snows and is warmer than it is here.

Yesterday I had my first view of San Francisco. I was above the city in a Liberator. The city looked really beautiful with the Bay Bridge, Treasure Island, and the Golden Gate Bridge. Oakland across the bay looked very nice too. The tow cities are located on the bay and behind are the mountains. Southern California has loads of nice mountains at times we had to go 16,000 feet to get over the snow capped peaks. The temperature there was five above zero.

Yep, it's spring again. We're just starting to wear our summer uniforms when it doesn't get too cold at night. The oranges are about all picked and the grape vices yards of which there are several thousand acres are just beginning to bud and sprout. I guess I said in my last letter I would put in a few lines on Hollywood. Well, here's my opinion in a nutshell. There are more blondes there than any place else I've seen. Evidentially proxide isn't too hard to get. Red heads are becoming popular too. They make some mixture out of eggs for red hair. Complete formula with all directions for five dollars girls! Just tear off the tops of two Fords and mail them with five dollars to cover handling and postage and complete instructions will be sent to you. If you are not completely satisfied try and get your money back, I'm taking a law course now!

The Hollywood girls are really beautiful, in the movies, or at a distance of more than 50 feet. They have a few cute gals but I think they hide them when we hit town. I can't imagine why, can you?

The USO and other services there are really tops. They don't bother closing, open 24 hours a day. The Lutheran Service Center there feeds you, gives you a place to sleep and all. In the morning when you get up you get your eggs fixed just like you want them.

In the line of entertainment there are loads of things to do all free. There are all the broadcasts, shows, and stage plays, and even the night clubs. Then of course there's the Hollywood Canteen. Between it and the New York Stage Door Canteen, I'll take the Newark one. The New York one is fixed modern with neat decorations and dance floor while in Hollywood it is fixed all barn type with wagon wheels and lanterns on the ceiling and rustic beams and posts.

Well my dear friends, that is it. I gave you the graces of Hollywood and all it's contents. As for me I'm a Pasadena kid. Personally I like the place.

> Bye for now,
> Kurt Durst

ৎৡ৹ৡ৹ৡ৹

April 12, 1945

Dear Violet and all:

No excuses! I'm too tired. Not physically but just mentally. For some reason or other I'm getting in a mood where it is a job to write a letter. I guess one reason is that we have a lot of entertainment here at Wright Field. I haven't done much all day. The fact that I didn't have a job more or less preyed on my mind and I couldn't write. Yesterday I was assigned to Quartermaster's Warehouse here. Now I'm at ease and I can write. I have an address again even though I don't have a bed to sleep in. Again I pass out of the Casual status and become a member of an organization. Really and truly I do believe I've been in more organizations than most fellows in the Army. Why? I don't know unless I just don't fit in. Ha! Ha!

I received my Easter card from Gerry this past week and thanks a lot for it. I do believe that was the only card I received.

I also got the two cards written to me by members of the League and again I wish to thank them for those cards.

It seems so odd to write to you so close by. All my army career has been spent so far from home and now to be so close. I sure was lucky to be sent here to Wright Field. I was so glad that I could again spend the Easter Season at home. I hope by next year we all can spend Easter at home. So until nest time.

As Ever,
Wilbur Facklam

France, April 8, 1945
Dear leaguers:

Many thanks for the nice Easter greeting cards. I just finished my night duty for one week with the same old routine of grind. Saw a good show this week, "A Tree Grows in Brooklyn". We had a party at my Company last evening. Had our band and a dance so I enjoyed the evening very much. I wish also to express my sympathy after knowing of the sand news of Melvin and Leon.

Cheerio,
Matthew E. Bieber

Italy, March 31, 1945

Dear Geraldine, (Schmidt)

Want to thank you for the very pretty Easter greeting and I do hope you all had a very nice Easter. I have been fine and tonight I begin another term of nigh duty but will stay up in the morning to attend the Easter Services.

I was very sorry to hear about Leon's death and pray that victory will come soon. We are not too busy at present and the weather has been just grand. Best regards to you and all the other leaguers. I am very grateful for the church papers and the Messengers you send me so promptly. Thanks much!

Sincerely,
Inez Bieber

ঔঔঔ

Italy,
April 10, 1945

Dear wife and son:
    Recently I had an opportunity to visit Rome. It will be very difficult to adequately express what I was able to see in a very short time. I thought that perhaps the best way to cover the most important spots in a limited time was to take a tour sponsored by the American Red Cross. If possible I may be able to buy a booklet of the Historic scenes of Rome and send it to you. In the meantime I will try to write you what I was able to observe and what was told us by our very superb guide who formerly had been an agent for the American Express Co. It was hard to remember the many things he had to say and I may be incorrect in some cases. I might also sy that I was able to take many roll of film of some of the scenes I hope they turn out good. Before starting on the tour the group were gathered in a theater and given a short illustrated slide lecture of the points that we were to cover. From the theater we climbed on busses. Perhaps I should have not said climbed for this may give you an idea that is was a convoy of government trucks usually used for all types of army transportation. Instead it was a large bus used at one time by civilians and while it was not as modern as a 1944 Greyhound but busses of this style may have been seen in our cities in the 30's.

The first place of interest to be viewed on the tour was the Baths of Caracalla. Of course, only the massive ruined walls remained of what once was a beautiful building covering 34 acres and was ble to accommodate over 1600 people. This was only one of several public baths of the city. We were then told of why they had such large public places of this of this type. It must be remembered that Rome during the second and third centuries, was the home of soldiers. Therefore, while they were not out fighting for the Empire they had to be controlled by being entertained. Now the Romans were very temperamental as to their baths. A bath consumed a long time for it was made up of many degrees of temperature of the water and containing many massages with creams. Naturally such an establishment employed countless number of slaves. These baths also were expanded to provide other forms of entertainment. To have a private library of a hundred books at that time was a possession of only the wealthiest of families. Therefore the baths had reading rooms with handwritten scrolls for those who wished to spend their leisure time in reading. Likewise there were other forms of games and entertainment provided by the rulers for the people but actually at the expense of the government. The important factor was to keep the populous content.

We then traveled along the famous Appian Way, the most important of ancient Roman roads connecting Rome with Naples and other ancient cities in the southern port of the empire. One of the outstanding facts of this highway was that after passing the place of Que Vadis Church, the place where Christ is alleged to have appeared to St. Peter when he was preparing to return east after the burning of Rome, the road was perfectly straight. The original road had been laid with stone blocks about 4 or 5 feet square have been replaced by the more modern paving stones about 6 inches square but some of the old blocks can still be seen along the side of the road. With the advent of Christianity more attention was given to the burying of the dead rather than cremating. Therefore members of the royal families and the wealthier people would build massive stone tombs along the Appian Way. Some were richly decorated to such an extent that guards were placed around it to keep the precious metals from being stolen. Of course, all that remains today is occasionally a crude ruins of what once was a grand cemetery extending about 40 miles along the main highway of the world. Extravations even during the last half century are revealing new facts of who may have been buried there. The most preserved of these tombs is the ones shown on the manila which I am sending is a souvenir from St. Sabastian.

Our first chance to disembark from the bus was at the Catacombs of St. Sebastian. To fully appreciate everything at the Catacombs I should have been a well informed Catholic. We were taken down through the tunneled sections by a monk and he explained everything to us but he spoke in a somewhat broken English so that is was hard to understand him. From time to time he would point out a scared place with inscription on stones relating to something of St. Peter and St. Paul. To more fully understand it I wish I knew more of its history. However, purely as a work of art it stood the elements for centuries. Perhaps some day we can learn more about his place but this will have to suffice for now.

Perhaps I should have mentioned that we passed thru the city wall at the Gate of St. Sebastian when we went to the Catacombs. As we returned in we stopped at the outside of the Wall and gate to view it there. I hope that the snapshots that I took there turn out all right.

Your husband,
Clayton Fischer

Stryker, Ohio April 19, 1945

Dear Geraldine Schmidt,

Mr. Breier and I want to thank you and the Luther League for your thoughtfulness of our boys in service. It takes much thought and time to prepare the serve and I know it must be well pleasing to God and it encourages our boys who are far form home.

We had planned so much on attending the service but due to other circumstances we were unable to be there. We want you to know all your efforts are appreciated. In firm Faith I know God is with Leroy and we put our trust in his living care for our boy.

Respectfully,
Mr. And Mrs. Roy Breier

ও ও ও

Burma,
March 30, 1945

Dear Violet and Leaguers,

Just a few lines to let you know that I am fine and hoping you are the same. Who do you suppose I met on the telephone last night about seven? Franklin Kummorow, he was talking on the telephone and I was listening in and someone wanted him to spell his name. By that time, I said, "Is this frank from Ottawa Lake?" "Yes, he said, "so I told him my name and was he and I surprised meeting on a telephone in the jungles of Burma. So after the boys got back from the movies I took a vehicle and went to see him. It was about 10 miles from our camp but by the time I got there he was just going to bed but he said to wake him up when I got there. We talked over the times we had in good old Ottawa Lake and army life. He is enroute to unknown destination which is where I'm going in the future and I'm hoping we can get together there. Frank looks good and healthy, the same Frank. He has been stationed twenty miles from where I was for the last four months and didn't know it.

I am working every day in the hot sun but not breaking my back of course, just manage to do my share. The weather is swell, every day a nice cool breeze and plenty of sunshine.

Well, that's about all I have to say for now so I'll close for now and God bless you all hoping this letter finds you in the best of health.

Love,
Martin Seitz

Our VE Day—Our service on May 8th was attended by about 150. The pastor based his address on 1 Chron. 29:10-15. Subject "we acknowledge God to be the Ruler and King of All." In the talk the pastor called for a confession of faith in God with redoubled emphasis and reconsecration. Also, it was urged that we be everlasting thankful for preserved freedom, that we be carefully on guard against false prophets, that we pray for grace and power from God to live the Christ-like life as a citizen of the U.S.A. as a church Member and as a world citizen.

Somewhere in Germany

Dear Mom, Dad and all:

Mom, I got ten more letters this morning and it sure makes me feel good. You said you hadn't any mail from me yet. I write every chance I get but sometimes I can't write. About a week ago we had our first chance to go to church since I have been here. They had it in a German Church and he had a very nice sermon and the church was full. I also took Holy Communion. It wasn't like home but it meant the same thing

How's everything with you Dad? Take care of yourself. I guess I better close for now and may God bless and keep you always.

Love kisses from your loving son,
LeRoy Breier

❧❧❧

Meet in Burma

Martin Seitz called on Franklin Kummerow over in Burma on March 29th. Martin tells us all about it in his letter. Be sure and read it.

SERVICE IN HONOR OF THOSE THAT ENTERED SERVICE FROM ZION AND COMMUNITY

This service was held April 15 by the Zion Luther League under the direction of Miss Geraldine Schmidt, Service Secretary for Zion. The program consisted of the following: Rev. Mueller played the organ Prelude; procession of the American flag and the Christian flag carried by Pfc. Verne Jacobs and Pfc. Horrace Nearhood followed by Pvt. Howard Schmidt and Howard Hotchkiss, USN home on furlough. Pledge to the flags by the congregation. Duet, "The Holy City", Herman Nieman and Eugene Fischer. Hymn by the congregation, "Onward Christian Soldiers". Then the playlet: The Spirits of Freedom. Those taking part in this were Nyles Sanderson, Jr., Eugene Fischer, Lois Kodeman, Maxine Schaddler, Melva Sieler, Joann Jacobs and Verne Jacobs and Horace Nearhood. The Leaguers sang, "God Bless Our Men". Next was the distribution of certificates by Rev. Mueller followed by silent prayer, the benediction and the doxology.

We were very pleased to see a nice crowd out for this service and many of you on our mailing list so we hope to have another service in a few months again. Watch for further announcement.

Zion has a total of 27 stars on its service flag. Three boys have given their lives and one is reported missing in action.

෧෧෧

Mrs. Nellie Crots has received the Purple Heart, Her son; Edwin Crots was wounded over in Germany. He writes he is feeling fine and still in one piece.

෧෧෧

Ottawa Lake, Mich
June, 1945

To Our Loved Ones in the Service:

Greetings from Ottawa Lake, Michigan! Not so long ago I read a columnist who said that we here at home ought to be writing you letters thanking you for making VE-Day possible. The statement was very much in order, and we do hereby certainly thank our men and women in the service for the way they have, and are still, serving their country. Nor are we unmindful of those who have made the supreme sacrifice.

On VE-Day, as mentioned in the last Messenger, we had a special church service in the evening. It was in that service that we voiced as one man our common thankfulness to God that organized hostilities had ceased in Europe. And now we look forward to VJ-Day. Wouldto God that it might be tomorrow—yes, even today! So much blood letting! Such despair, anguish, cruelty, persecution! We are indeed aware of what Jesus meant when he said that in the latter days there would be wars and rumors of wars. But let us not forget either that Jesus stated in the same connection that when all these things happen that we should be watchful unto prayer.

As human beings, creatures of a living and of an almighty God, we are not destined to go through life as if going on a sentimental journey. One thing we learn from the march of death in our day is that we—none of us—have here on this earth no abiding city. In view of our swift passage from time into eternity, what manner of men ought we to be?

Prayer is good and fine, but make sure it is Christian prayer spoken in the blessed Name of Jesus Christ, who alone is the world's Savior. Or are you among those who say "I had a little Talk with the Lord Today" and think that smoothes things over? Do you know what your personal salvation for all eternity—aside from all our or any other V-Days—really costs? Look to Calvary. Behold the crucified Lord Jesus, nailed to the tree, because God is Love, because your soul in God's sight has such an extremely great value.

Therefore, if you have the Lord Jesus Christ in your heart as your personal Savior; if you abide in Him in true faith; if you follow your duty as conscience makes it plain; if you hope for salvation in non other than Jesus—nothing, NOTHING, can hurt or harm you for eternity.

Concerning the vicissitudes, trials, and tribulations of this life St. Paul says that to the believer "all things work together for good to those that love God."

You in the service will therefore gladly avail yourselves of the services of the chaplain, and daily present yourselves before God in prayer. Our prayers for your steadfastness of faith are regularly being offered in our homes and in our church.

It will be a great and glad day when we can shake hands again. May the merciful and almighty God continue to protect you and always keep you in His grace.

Cherrio
Your Pastor and friend
Marcus Mueller

ળળળ

Dear Wife and Son: (Continued from last month)

Our next stop was at the ancient Coliseum. Here we were allowed to examine more closely the remaining walls of what was once the site of outstanding games and contests. A good portion of the main walls have crumbled and steps have been taken in recent years to prevent further crumbling. We were told of how the original stadium as constructed with an artificial lake in the center. This has since been changed by installing walls in the center to support the floor. We were pointed out the Emperor's Pillars and the bronze cross which has been erected to
commemorate the many Christians who were persecuted and also the Gate of Death through which those were taken if the audience turned 'thumbs down' when their life was at stake. Stones from the ruins of this building as well as from the Baths and other buildings were used in building St. Peter's and other places.

Our next stop was the pantheon, the magnificent temple to the pagan Gods. Its proportions were so exacting that it is hard to realize its massiveness. The many pillars in the patio are of solid marble 45 feet high and weigh about 80 tons each. It is outstanding to remember the fact that over 2000 years ago they had been transported by land and water several hundred miles. Then they were fitted together with such precision in spite of crude tools of the time. The building now has been used as a mausoleum of the kings of Italy and great men of art such as Raphael. The beauty of the marble has not been effected by the elements and the marble floor is so graded and furnished with underground sewers to drain away the water that may fall through the open dome having a circumference of 142 feet. Needless to say the statues to the pagan Gods have been removed but the vacant inches where they have been still remain.

We also passed the Memorial to King Victor Emanuel II. Its correct proportion also hides its massiveness. For example it is hard to believe that before the belly of the bronze horse in a statue there was sealed its size was shown to be large enough for 8 men to be seated and fed at a table. We also were pointed out the square where the populous gathered to hear Mussolini make his many speeches and the balcony from which he spoke. Newsreels shown us in the States gave us a slightly exaggerated slant on this place and some had grounds for disappointment.

In route across the Tiber River the bus was stopped on the bridge so that we could view the Castel S. Angelo, which was once considered a fortress for Vatican City.

One could write and spend a long time in the Vatican and it would have far more significance to a Catholic. The entire unit consists of some thirty odd acres. The semi-circular colonnade in massive and columns have been made from other buildings. The dome tower of St. Peter's extends over 400 feet in the air and the domes has a base of a circumference of 138 feet.

Time at St. Peter's was limited. We were pointed out the Triumphal Door which is only unsealed each 25 years for pilgrimages to enter. It next will be opened on Dec. 25, 1949 and will be resealed on the eve of Dec. 24, 1950. Being opened each 25 years is theoretically to make it possible for someone from each generation to perform this sacred act.

Many things of the exacting proportions of the magnificent art were pointed out to us. Beneath the altar rests the tomb of St. Peter. There is also a bronze triumphant are nearly a hundred feet high near the altar. Words can not describe the splendor of the mosaic art. This work is so exacting that if a man continued on the job for over two hours a day he would loose his best ability to use the correct color. Therefore many man-hours were used in each masterpiece. At the age of 75 DeAngelo started and planned the magnificent dome and when he passed away at 92 he had completed all plans in detail so that others could complete the great work. The dome actually is made up of two domes, one being of the shape of a cone and the other elliptic, the one being inside of the open and fastened together so that one will support the other.

A visit to the Papal City would not be complete with an audience with the Holy Father. It seemed to be an awe stricken assembly gathered on the third floor in a sacredly decorated room. The room was filled with service men and women of every country of our Allied Nations as well as a few native civilians. The colorful garb of the Swiss guards took one back to the stories of knighthood and should take any visitor's eye. After some waiting the Pope appeared and after addressing us with greetings in no doubt what was the basic tongues performed the ritual of blessing the group.

As I mentioned before our visits were limited and with some study one could profitably spend weeks in the city but I was thankful that I was able to cover as much as I did. After all I am not over here principally on a sightseeing tour. Perhaps the most important places that I did not visit would be the Roman Forum. Who knows, I may have an opportunity to return to the city at some future date.

Now to change the theme a little, I passed through the shopping district and in curiosity noticed some of the price tags placed on pieces of merchandise. You thought coats were expensive back there. Look at what things sell for where the average weekly wage of a man if $15 to $25. A man's shirt which could be considered as cheesecloth was $25 or the weekly income of a very good man while a regular shirt was selling for or at least priced at $35 to $40. Next I noticed a pair of dress trousers marked $83.50. A pair of regular sox for any man costs $3.00 while the neckties which would cost $4 or $1.50 at home could not take it with them here for less then $4.50.

Now for a few items for women. If a sinorita wanted to sport a leather purse she would have had to worked her fingers to the bone, had a good bank roll, or some other means for a good one would run $300.00. Of course, she might be content with an artificial leather one but even that would cause her to part with $45.00. I doubt if she would boast as many different shoes at the same time as the American girl for sandals cost from $25 to $40 a pair. In display windows they had a crumpled piece of goods which I took to be a dress with a tag of $1500 on it. At one place we saw fur coats displayed but no price tags were showing. You can be assured that a fur coat was a rare purchase.

I have been keeping my eyes open in hopes of getting something for Tommy. I saw a rag elephant about 8 inches long but a tag by it stating they wanted $3.00 for it. There was a wheelbarrow there which they wanted $4.50 for. It was made of wood and if I were able to pack it so that it would not be broken in shipping I am sure that he could break it in a few days now at his present age for it was built so poorly.

I guess that covers my visit in Rome which you can be assured I enjoyed very much.

> With Love
> Your husband
> Clayton F. Fischer

May 28, 1945

Dear Leaguers and friends:

Day after day seems to slip by quickly and quietly. Days add up to weeks, weeks into months – and still one has not accomplished much that should have been done.

Among these unaccomplished privileges has been my letter writing for the Messenger. However, this month I shall write a short letter, despite our monthly records which are needing almost our every spare minute these last few days of the month to be corrected and sent on their way by the deadline.

There is really very little to write of as far as happenings at our little "berg" in Northern British Columbia.

Our snow finally melted away the middle of the month. This being a newly established station, it is set in virgin ground, our area having been bull-dozed out during the winter. How that our snow has left our area appears in terrible condition—large branches, twigs couple inch-deep of pine needles, and more large stones and boulders than Silica could hope to produce—well, almost anyway!

The pine needle bed made a heaven for mosquitoes. As our temperatures warmed the mosquitoes did too, and decided to make a few reconnaissance flights around our place. Yes, they were definitely the incentive that drove us to rid our area of all the rubble that hid them.

Oh yes, we have our rooms pretty well "dolled-up" now. During the month Violet and some very efficient helpers made and sent us curtains for all our windows. We're in the process of painting the station office now and soon it should look pretty sharp.

"Dina", our little bear dog, and "Chum", a dog recently acquired from an Indian family named "Johnson:", combine their efforts to warn us of prowling bears. Last night we fired on one from our mess hall but was a bit dark to get an effective shot. However, he hasn't returned—yet!

Before saying goodbye for this time I want to add my thanks and appreciation to those who have so generously contributed their time and efforts in producing the little newspaper, the Messenger. My thanks also to those individuals who have had the persistence in writing us all, despite occasionally un-answered letters.

Thanks again to all of you. Let's us hope to all meet again soon.

As ever,
(Oil) Curtis D. Fischer

Feb. 28, 1945
Dear Violet and Leaguers:

Many thanks for the "Messenger" of the New Year issue and am glad to know you all are okay as it leaves me. I have not left the hospital and am in a Convalescent Depot in France and enjoying myself immensely.

This is a good place plenty of entertainment, physical training and discussions and on Sunday mornings we get up at 8:30am.

Very sorry to hear of the death of Kenneth Brodbeck when I noticed myself was one of the most consistent and interesting writers.

We've been having a few sports here the other day a football match took place between English and Scots personnel which was called a Depot International. It was a rattling good game and I for one was so interested as to forget all other matters completely. We do not play a very great deal of American type of football tho' the Rugby Association as it is called has a fairly large following tho' not half as large as soccer in which feet and head are only used except by the goalkeeper.

With this I will close. So cheerio and all the best. God bless you all.

Your friend, Frank Broughton

Liberal, Kansas
June 20, 1945
Dear Rev. Mueller:

I received your most welcome Messenger the first part of this week and sure glad to receive it.

The weather here has been just about the same as it was when I was home but today it is too hot to do anything. The evenings are pretty chilly. Today is gas mask day. We have to have ours on our body in the afternoon and then at 2 to 3 we have them on our face. They spray tear gas all over this area.

A week ago last Saturday we had the privilege of hearing Johnny Long and his orchestra. It was very good music to hear. This was the biggest ever that ever hit Liberal Army Air Field. The place was just packed. Johnny also was on the air over a blue network station at 8:30 till 9:00.

I am still at work from four until midnight this week yet but Sunday I change from midnight till 8 in the morning. This is if for now.

Cherrio,
Lester Gillhouse

❦❦❦

June 16, 1945

Dear Uncle Chris and all:

I am sorry I didn't get around to writing before but they really kept us busy on our basic training. We were only supposed to get 35 days of basic but they cut out pilot, navigator, and bombardier training all together. They don't need many gunners so they kept us on basic training till some of the Tech. Schools opened up.

Here is where they sent the guys that enlisted to fly planes. The school they go to are: parachute rigger (Wac's job), bomb sight mech., airplane mech., radio mech, radio operator, teletype operator, teletype mech., camera mech., aerial photography, remote control mech., and stuff like that.

I am shipping out as a remote control mechanic. I will go to Lowrey Field, Denver, Colorado. That is about an 18 week course. I don't bet a delay enroute so I won't get home on leave till Nov. or Dec. If I am lucky then.

I sure hope the weather this summer brings the crop up because the food situation isn't any too good. We don't get much meat or potatoes. We get a lot of greens and stuff like that.

It has been fairly warm down here the temperature has been over 100 degrees almost every day for the last month. The farmers here have most of their grain harvested already. Their wheat average about 16 bushels to the acre, big crop, Oh?

I talked with a soldier from Houston and he said this is the worst part of Texas, just across the border from Oklahoma. He said they have an ocean breeze and it isn't so hot there. We haven't any trees here and the sand really blows. We had a tornado here last Friday. I sent a clipping of it home. It torn the hanger down of the civilian airport here. It wrecked 15 small planes. They had a DC# two engine transport in it that got damaged some. It was torn down to be fixed. They had a two engine transport tied down outside. The wind caught it and got it loose. It took off the ground and flew about a mile at eight to tine feet above the ground then landed just like some one was flying it.

Well, I don't' know much more to write. It will be shipping to Denver within two days so if you get time to write wait till you get my new address.

> Your nephew and cousin,
> Ronald Brinning

April 27, 1945

Dear Violet and Leaguers:

I know that I should have did this a long time ago but really we have been too busy to do any writing. We have been on the go every since we crossed the Ruhr and the Rhine but maybe from now on I will have a little more time.

The weather here lately has really been beautiful but today it had been raining every since we got up. I sure wish that it would stay nice for a good long time. For that is the kind of weather our army's need to end this war in a hurry.

I have been receiving the Messenger every month and I sure hope that they keep on coming for I really enjoy them a lot. You get more news about the home people that may then any other way I know.

Things here with me are going about as good as can be expected and I only hope that is stays this way.

Violet, tell everybody I said Hello and hope they are well.

Will close for this time but will write again soon.

Love,
Stanley Kastel

❧❧❧

May 10, 1945

Hi Violet and Leaguers:

Well, here I am in Texas and it is hot down here. How is the paper coming? I received it and was glad to get it. It is good to hear from those at home. I haven't been away from home long but it seems like a long time here. Cliff is just one barracks away from me and I'm glad of that. How is everyone at home? Tell all the kids I said "hello" for me. This is a bog camp here. I haven't been up town yet. The closest town is 8 miles from here. It is Paris, Texas. It is the size of Adrian. I go out on a march next week, about ten miles. We went on a seven mile march last week with full pack about 60 pounds. It gets heavy before you finish. Red Vessey is on the other side of the road from us and not very far away. Well, that is all for now.

Love to all,
Harold Schadler

May 13, 1945

Dear Violet and leaguers:

I suppose you have figured that I have forgotten you and the paper but I haven't. It is just a single case of time. We have very little time for ourselves. When we do have time we are cleaning our rifle or on some kind of a detail. It's a wonder they don't work us on Sundays.

I will try to explain a little of what they expect of us down here in this barren country. They are trying to cram two years of training into us in 15 or 17 weeks. We are kept busy from morning till night. You now can see what I mean by having time for myself. I am now on detail at the Bn. Headquarters answering the telephone. It so happens that this detail is easy and that I have time to write.

I am very lucky tho, because I have four kids here in my company that are from Lambertville and Temperance. It makes it a lot easier and more fun.

About 3 weeks ago I was very much surprised by running into Red Swyen from Berkey or Metamora. Fritz knows him quite well. He finished his cycle or basic training two weeks ago
and is now in Ft. Benning Ga. Training for the paratroops. He should be home on furlough quite soon.

I also met Jep Creque and Vins Cousino about a week after I was here. We had a great talk for a half house.

I have just had chow. I was relieved by a 2nd Lt. From my telephone detail I wouldn't mind having that kind of detail all the time. Radio, desk, and all the luxuries of home. Well, I think I will get away from the Company area so I don't catch any more details.

Goodbye now until the next time and I hope that I can find time to write more often.

Your fellow Leaguer and friend,
LeRoy Bunge

Feb. 9, 1945

Dear Mom:

I haven't heard from you for a long time so I though I would drop you a few lines to see how everyone is at home. I sure had a streak of luck the other day. They had a drawing for a trip to Paris and my name was drawn. I had a swell time. Paris is a beautiful place to see, there are so many interesting places to go and see.

They have a subway that goes all over Paris and if you aren't careful you can get lost very easily. While I was there I visited the Notre Dame Cathedral, Eiffel Tower and the Trinity Hall. I also bought several souvenirs and will send them home. Things are so high there due to the war. I imagine Paris was a beautiful place before the war. Most of the famous places are closed most of the time.

While we were there we stayed in a hotel that the American Red Cross had any it was a real nice place. We also had our meals there. When we were on our way back we stopped at Nancy and had coffee and doughnuts.

I looked for Elg when I was there but no one seemed to know where his outfit was so I didn't find him. I also lost his address so will you please send it to me.

Tell everyone I am okay and I said "Hello".

Your loving son,
Arthur Whitenburg

෪෪෪

May 16, 1945

Dearest Mom and Dad:

Just a few lines to let you know I am in the best of health and hope this letter finds you the same. Please excuse me for not writing to you sooner but we have been so busy I did not have time. Well, daddy you be ready to go back on a farm when

I come back. You and Dad should see the houses over here. They are nicer than the ones we see at home. The weather over here is very bad. All it does is snow and I mean snow. When it doesn't snow it rains. We are in the Alp Mountains. They certainly are beautiful. I never expected to see them but I have and many other places far from home. Well, Mother, I guess I had better sign off for tonight. It is getting late and I am tired. So good night and God Bless you all and keep you safe always.

Your loving son,
Malcolm Gray

❧❧❧

Dear Mom:

Your welcome letter came last night and I was very glad to hear from home and that Dad is getting better and able to be outside in the fresh air. It will do him a lot of good. The war is over here but there is no way for us to know yet what is on the program for us now. We draw guard once in awhile and the rest of the time we lay around. I will let you know as soon as I can what and where we go. I am sorry to hear Leslie had to come in to the service but he is better off in the armored outfit then the infantry.

The weather is rather warm here. We try to find shade in the afternoon. The hottest part of the day is then. That is about all for now. So long and good luck. Say "Hello" to all for me.

Your loving son,
Floyd Gray, Jr.

❧❧❧

June 8 - Mrs. Gray has received letters from both Jr. and Malcoln that they are both in Austria and will try to see each

321

other through the Red Cross.

❧❧❧

May 18, 1945

Dear Eugene:

Quite sometime has elapsed since either of us has written the other. Well, I was hospitalized more than one month, but am now released from there and awaiting eventual return to my unit. I am gradually improving for which I am thankful.

I am now located in a very fine city of eastern Belgium. I like it very much. It's people are very friendly and hospitable to me wherever I go. I have had an accepted invitations to some of the social and other activities of the community. This means a lot to one over here far from the U.S. and friends.

A friend,
Vernon Packard

❧❧❧

Dear Violet and Leaguers:

I know I should have written before but we were on a move so much. To tell the truth I didn't have any time to write. I received one issue of the Messenger so far since I was over seas. I was in Maronne, France at the time and left for Germany in April 24th and from there to Austria and after the war ended here in E.T.O . We moved back into Germany again across the Rhyne River.

There surely are some beautiful mountains between Austria. I saw the Baravian Alps on the way up we stayed a few days in Austria where you could look at the peaks of them all covered with snow. Well, we got in far enough to earn a Bronze star while we were here overseas and probably get to earn many more the way it looks. I haven't enough points to go back to the States so probably will see more country yet. Thanks a lot for the Messenter and hope they will catch up with me very soon. Am sending all my luck to everyone back home and may God bless us all and this war ends soon.

Yours as ever,
Frank Klauda

❧❧❧

Dear Cliffors: (Whitenburg)

Just a little V-mail to let you know I am fine and hoping you're the same. Received your letter and Valentine okay, dated Feb. 20. Also V-mail from Art. I guess he is stationed nearby here.

I received letters from the folks, Ruth, Ottie, and Inez. We are having nice weather now days. I guess you will be having nice weather too by the time you receive this V-mail. I guess Bonn Annee on that postcard means "good time".

Am sending my best regards to your folks.

Cheerio,
Matthew E. Bieber

❧❧❧

Leroy "Pete" Fischer is still in the Phillipines Islands. He writes that he is fine. Pete has been in service four years being inducted in the Army on June 6, 1941 with Franklin Kummerow. Mr. and Mrs. Chris Fischer received a bouquet of one dozen roses from their three sons in service (Pete, Clayton and Olie) on May 28.

❧❧❧

May 7, 1945

Dear Folks:

Well, I suppose you have heard the good news too by now. We have been expecting it for the last few days and sure was glad to hear it over the radio so we will have to celebrate.

Everything here is the same as before but I am wondering what we will do now.

I went to the dentist a week ago and had three teeth filled. They were the first by an Army dentist and he is pretty good.

Oh, yes, I received a letter from Dale Ballard. He told me where he was and so I hitched hiked there that afternoon and saw him. He looks the same as ever. I was going to bring him back to camp with me to spend the night and next day but he got his shipping orders that afternoon to leave the next morning so we only had a few hours together.

Well, this will be quite short but I wanted you to know I was O.K. and will try to write sooner next time.

Your son,
"Spud: Raymond Shanly

༺༺༺

Pisa, Italy
May 11, 1945

Dear Folks:

They finally lifted the censorship regulations today and so we can write what we want to and seal the letters like we used to back in the States.

When I was in Africa I wrote you about all the places I had visited and most of them we were stationed by but I didn't tell you when we landed in Africa. We landed at Casablanca in

Nov. 1942 and it was quite a town. I would like to see it again as I bet it is nice now.

We didn't have airplanes at first and so had to pull guard duty for a while.

We were about six miles out of town at a gas and supply dump and experienced my first air raid and I will never forget it.

I got off guard at 10:00 p.m. and drank some coffee and fried a couple of eggs and then went to bed in an old building. I was just going to sleep when I heard a lot of shooting and the building shook and I jumped out of bed and dressed and got outside.

They were after Casablanca and not us so we were fairly safe and I had a good chance to see all of it and it was pretty.

We could see the planes in the searchlights and they flew over us and there were so many guns firing that it was real light out where we were and the sky was all red all over. It was prettier than any fourth of July celebration that I had ever seen.

One of the Jerry planes shot back at one of the search lights and one of the fellows there said, Hey, look at those tracers going backward, and we all got a laugh out of that.

We traveled by forty and eights quite aways through Africa but flew from Orleansville to the front there and the country was pretty from the air.

After the war there we dame back to Djilli by truck and it was supposed to be kind of a rest but we were out for air raids for the first ten or eleven nights but they weren't very large ones.

We went from there to Algiers by truck and from there to Ajaccie, Corsica by boat.

I was one of the last to leave Algiers. There were ten of us and one Lieut. In charge of our equipment. The last night before we hit Ajaccio five of us were down in the hold when a bunch of depth charges went off and up the ladder we went and on the deck. We were scared for a awhile as it was dark and we couldn't see anything but after awhile we went down and want to bed. We kept our shoes on and used our life vests for a pillow. The next day they told us that they sunk a German sub about two hundred yards off us. He was just coming up to get a good look at us.

From Ajaccio we went over to Ghisonaccia and a few other towns on that side.

Your son,
"Spud" Raymond Shanly

ঙঙঙ

There is more of Spud's letter which we will print in the July Messenger. Also other interesting letters from Bill Hein (Mrs. Mueller's brother)' Robert Wotring' and Lester Gillhouses. Since we will try to get back on schedule in July it won't be long until the next Messenger will be made.

ঙঙঙ

MEMORIAL SERVICE HELD
A memorial Service in memory of Lt. Melvin W. Dauer was held at Olivet Lutheran Church, Sylvania, Ohio on Sunday afternoon, June 10th. Melvin died near Julich, Germany and is buried in a military cemetery in Holland. He is the husband of Francile Baer Dauer and the son of Mrs. Margaret Dauer Elg. Herman and Fritz sand for the service which was conducted by Rev. Getter.

Again we must print through the pages of our little Messenger that one soldier on our mailing list was killed in action. Also that another was seriously wounded. Delvin Noward, son of Mr. Lester Noward and brother or Roy, Waterville, Ohio was killed on April 26 on the island of Cebu. He was in service 7 months having his basic training at Camp

Wolters, Texas. He was home on furlough in Feb. On June 6 Mr. and Mrs. Robert Nearhood received a telegram saying that their other twin son, <u>Forrest,</u> was seriously wounded on the Negros Island on May 13th.

Dear Mom,

Another nice day has come around. I think the sun might shine if it gets enough encouragement. I used to have fund knocking the Kentucky weather but this beats all.

I believe I am picking up weight here. I'll be as fat as ever if I keep on.

I made a record the other day but I don't suppose you will get it for quite a long while. I mean a voice record not a song.

Everyone writes and says that they suppose we were overjoyed on V-E day. I suppose most people at home think that the war is practically over. Most of the fellows here took the new quite soberly, more as you would when a job is well but done but still a bigger one ahead.

I finally got around to washing some clothes. We have quite a washing machine, consisting of a tub, which a fire can be built under some GI soap and a good supply of elbow grease.

I got the box a few days age. I forgot whether I mentioned that before or not but it was good. They have plenty of recreation here. I went to the Service Club last night. They had a famous movie star and his how. It really was good.

Well, I'll say so long for quite a while

You son,
Norman VanDyke

France
Feb 9, 1945

Dear Mom
     I haven't heard from you for a long time so I thought I would drop you a few lines to see how everyone is at home. I sure had a streak of luck the other day. They had a drawing for a trip to Paris and my name was drawn. I had a swell time. Paris is a beautiful place to see, there are so many interesting places to go and see.
     They have a subway that goes all over Paris and if you aren't careful you can get lost every easily. While I was there I visited the Notre Dame Cathedral, Eiffel Tower and the Trinity Hall. I also bought several souvenirs and will send them home. Things are so high there due to the war. I imagine Paris was a beautiful place before the war. Most of the famous places are closed most of the time.
     While we were there we stayed in a hotel that the American Red Cross shad and it was real nice place. We also had our meals there. When we were on our way back we stopped at Nancy and had coffee and doughnuts.
     I looked for Elg when I was there but none seemed to know where his outfit was so I didn't find him. I also lost his address so will you pleas send it to me.
     Tell everyone I am okay and I said "Hello".
Your loving son,
Arthur Whitenburg

❧❧❧

*****IN LOVING MEMORY*****

When each of us read these few words in loving memory of Jesse Bieber who gave his life abroad the U.S.S. Bunker Hill on June 20th out in the Pacific may we all breathe a silent prayer for our comrade who is sadly missed by all.

WHERE YOU BOYS WERE LOCATED ONE YEAR AGO

- ➢ Horace and Forrest Nearhood – South Pacific
- ➢ Robert Wotring – Little Creek, Va.
- ➢ Stanley Kastel – England
- ➢ Inez Bieber - Italy
- ➢ Harple Gray- Alaska
- ➢ Martin Seits - India
- ➢ Howard Hotchkiss – Corona, Calif.
- ➢ M. Elg Bieber – sSouth England
- ➢ Worthy White – Near Guinea
- ➢ Wilbur Facklam – Fresno, Calif.
- ➢ Verne Jacobs – Alaska
- ➢ Kenneth Brobeck – "Going through Rome"
- ➢ Lee Ahleman – fort Pierce, Florida
- ➢ William Hyde – After furlough – Camp Hueneme, Calif.
- ➢ Clayton Fischer – on the Atlantic or in Italy
- ➢ Kenneth Schmidt – Vancouver, Wash.
- ➢ Edgar Strable – New Guinea
- ➢ Renice and William DeNudt – El Paso, Texas
- ➢ Vernon Bauer – N. Africa
- ➢ Lester Knuth – Southwest Pacific
- ➢ Norman Mueller – Kessler Field, Miss
- ➢ Leroy Fischer – New Gunea

ও৵ও৵

Dear folks,
(Spuds letter continued from June Messenger)
Pisa, Italy
May 11, 1045

I went from there (Ghisonaccia) to Sardinia and then flew back to Corsica and from there flew to Tarquinia, Italy and from there flew up here last Dec. and have been here ever since with no excitement at all. Of course we could hear the guns firing at the front while we lay on our cots at night.
Now that it is all over I don't know what will happen to us.

I told you I saw Dale Ballard. Well, he was about fifteen miles from at Ponte de Deru (I guess that is right) and used to go through here about three nights a week. I can't think of anymore now except that I am O.K. and feel fine. We re having dances three nites a week besides shows that we can go to.

There weren't many people here when we first hit here but there are quite a lot now and still more coming in.

I know a nice little Italian girl and she is a good dancer. She talks a little English and I talk a little Italian and with a little motion of the hands we get along fairly well.

Tell everybody "hello" and I will try to write them a letter as I have quite a lot of time off now. Don't worry about me and write when you can

You son,
"Spud" Raymond Shanly

❧❧❧

In a more recent letter written on June 17th in Naples, Italy Spud expects to return to the States in a couple of weeks. We're glad to hear this good new for him and the Shanly family.

❧❧❧

Dear Leaguers and all,

Well, am finally settled after a very splendid forlough. It sure was enjoyed. I am now stationed at Grant, Michigan. We are guarding German Prisoners. They go out and work on the onion, celery, parsley, and many other vegetable crops.

We have a million little lakes around here. They are all swell little lakes. We have mot any kind of hunting and fishing that a sportsman would e3njoy. The people are really swell to us here. We are invited to church services tomorrow morning in Grant. Most of the fellows are planning on attending the service.

Grant is a town about twice as big as Ottawa Lake so it isn't a bad little community. Well, it is time for me to pull my duty this evening I will write more the next time.

Verne Jacobs

৵৵৵

Liberal, Kansas,
June 7, 1945

Dear Rev. Mueller

I received your Messenger and sure glad to have something to read. I left Monday morning at 7:05 a.m. to Chicago and arrived at 11 a.m. and my train for Liberal, Kansas left at 8:30 p.m. so a sailor and I walked around on the streets of Chicago. We went to the show and art and paintings building. It was a very nice place to visit. We also ate our evening meal there. We had ham and it was the first ham I have had since I left home for service.

I arrived here in Liberal at 9:30 p.m. on Tuesday. I was glad to get off the train. I don't care for train rides.

Today I started to work in the day shift. I received a letter from Don since I've been home on furlough.

We have to have cigarette cards here now. It is something new since I came home. We get six packs a week. This is all till next time.

Yours truly,
Lester Gillhouse

Camp Maxey,Texas
June 24, 1945

Dear Violet and Leaguers,

Well, I finally got around to writing. Time has been passing by quite fast here and we don't have much time off.

I received the second issue of the Messenger last week and enjoyed reading it very much. It is good to hear from those back home and also from other guys in the service.

Today is the ending of the second month of being in the Army. And tomorrow is the beginning for more guys from Ottawa Lake. I wish them all lots of luck.

It has been quite warm here and the sun is shining bright. I have been going to church quite regularly. It isn't quite like the churches back home.

There is going to be speedboat races this after here in Camp on Lamar Lake.

I can hear them now as they go racing around on the lake. I expect to go right after I finish this letter so I will close for now. May God be with us always.

Your friend,
James Christensen

May 28, 1945
near Kassel, Germany

Dear folks,

Quote: The Port of Embarkation was Camp Shanks – group was on a British boat. Landed after Easter at Liverpool from there we went by train to Ashford, Kent and to the field outside the town. We got P-47's and started operating 2 weeks later. (Ashford near Dover and Canterbury).

It was a thrill to hear pilots talk about damage they did and the German defense and to have all the airplanes come back safely, some flak riddled. Then there are days that we really sweat it out, especially when the planes landed. Then we had some nights the German planes gave us a sweat.

Then came the buzz bombs. The first one buzzed at 5 in the morning about 2 weeks before D-Day. That night another came over the field and the ach-ach blew it up in the air over our living area. It made a big explosion with a blinding flash. We thought they were planes at first until one landed and blew up near by killing 200 sheep. I went to the scene on the bicycle.

The buzz bombs were coming over regularly about 200 a day toward London and South Hampton. They were straight on the course so we name each area over the field or vicinity lanes or tracks and we counted about 10 lanes. When we heard a buzz we'd look up and see in which lane they were, sometimes, 3,5, or more in forms formation. You can see and hear them about 20 miles away – a big flash about 30 ft. behind it and all tracer bullets and flak flying thru the air. It looks worse than July 4th every five minutes. All we did was sit tight and sweat them out. Some would get blown up by planes and get the plane too. Others would cut out go into a steep climb and stall out, turn over and go in a dive then the flash and explosion.

One night one of them buzzed the living area at tree top level. About 11:00 P.M. and it vibrated the whole area. After that I rolled over on my bed, and said a prayer and thanked

God. I got a gyro out of the remainder of one of the buzz bombs that landed in back of the field and tent area, landed in a field about 50 yards from two homes which shattered on the side facing the field. Another one got a direct hit on a house where an old couple lived, everything was demolished. The woman was in the house at the time. The man was in the vicinity of the house. He was injured just a little bit.

I will continue this book in the next letter which I will writ tomorrow. I am feeling very good and am now crewing a brand new AT-6F like Mark's brother flew and a German observation plane which I and the fellow who helps me fixed up.
It is a court martial offense to fraternize with German people, that goes for relatives too. We are just north of Kassel on a high hill.

> Your son,
> Bill Hein (brother of Mrs. Mueller)

ৰেৰেৰে

Elsfelth, Germany,
May 22, 1945

Dear Ma, (Mrs. Glen Breese)

Had a little time so I thought I'd drop you a few lines, about time don't you think?

We've had plenty of time to write but I just didn't have the ambition to write. I'll sure be glad when we get some place near home or I'd even settle with any place in the good old U.S.A. Everybody is talking and I'm trying to talk and write at the same time and that isn't so good. So please excuse the mistakes. If I have to wait to get home through the point system I'll be here a year yet. I have only 41 points and that isn't very many. I just read in the paper that there was a guy here that has only 9 points. I've been in the Army 19 months now and have 12 months overseas duty; 11 months of that is combat duty, not bad, eh? We are policing up Germany now, north of Breman. It isn't a bad job but a lot of guard duty and patrol. I guess I can take it though. If it doesn't get any worse I'll never kick. We get to see shows almost every day but today I though I'd stay in and write a few letters. If I don't miss a show I'll never get any letters written. When I get home I'll never write another letter as long as I live. Well, I haven't any more news so I'll close for this time. Hope to hear from you soon.

Love,
Merle Gust

❧❧❧

Wilbert Kastel, son of Mr. And Mrs. Frank Kastel, Riga, is located somewhere in Germay guarding German Prisoners and serving them food. He works from 8 to 2 in the afternoon. He is now in 5F instead of Class 1A. he was hospitalized from Dec. 17th until April 13, 1945. Three of his Messengers (the Dec., Jan., and Feb. issues) were returned and also many letters that his family had written him. We're glad to hear that he is getting his mail now.

❧❧❧

April 27, 1945

Dear Violet and leaguers,

I know that I should have did this a long time ago but really we have been too busy to do any writing. We have been on the go every since we crossed the Ruhr and the Rhine but maybe from on now on I will have a little more time.

The weather here lately has really been beautiful but today it has been raining every since we got up. I sure wish that it would stay nice for a good long time. For that is the kind weather our army's need to end this war in a hurry.

I have been receiving the Messenger every month and I sure hope that they keep on coming for I really enjoy them a lot. You get more news about the home people that way than any other way know.

Things here with me are going about as good as can be expected and I only hope that it stays this way.

Violet, tell everybody I said hello and hope they are well. Will close for this time but will write again soon.

Love,
Stanley Kastel

କଏଷଏ

Camp Maxey, Texas
May 10, 1945

Hi Violet and Leaguers,

Well, here I am in Texas and it is hot down here. How is the paper coming. I received it and was glad to get. It is good to hear form those at home. I haven't been away from home long but it seems like a long time here. Cliff is just one barracks away from me and I'm glad of that. How is everyone at home? Tell all the kids I said "Hello" for me. This is a big camp here. I haven't been up town yet. The closest town is 8 miles from here. It is Paris, Texas. It is the size of Adrain.

I go out on a march next week, about ten miles. We went on a seven miles march last week with full pack about 60 pounds. It get heavy before you finish. Red Vasey is on the other side of the road from us and not very far away. Well, that is all for now.

Love to all,
Harold Schadler

କଏଷଏ

Ft. McClellan, Alabama
May 13, 1945

Dear Violet and Leaguers,

I suppose you have figured that I have forgotten you and the paper but I haven't. It is just a single case of time. We have very little time for ourselves. When we do have time we are cleaning our rifle or on some kind of detail it's a wonder they don't work us on Sunday.

I will try to explain a little of what they expect of us down here in this barren country. They are trying to cram two years of traing into us in 15 or 17 weeks. We are kept busy from morning till night. You now can see what I mean by having time for myself. I am now on detail at the Bn. Headquarters answering the telephone. It so happen that this detail is easy and that I have time to write.

I have been lucky though, because I have four kids here in my Company that are from Lambertville and Temperance. It makes it a lot easier and more fun.

About 3 weeks ago I was very much surprised by running into Red Swyen form Berkey or Metamora. Fritz knows him quite well. He finished his cycle or basic training two weeks ago and is now in Ft. Benning, Ga. Training for the paratroops. He should be home on furlough quite soon.

I also met Jep Cregue and Vins Cousino about a week after I was here. We have a great talk for a half hour.

I have just had chow. I was relieved by a 2nd Lt. from my telephone detail. I wouldn't mind having that kind of details all the time Radio, desk, and all the luxuries of home. Well, I think I will get away from the Company area so I don't catch any more details.

Good-bye now until the next time and I hope that I can find time to write more often.

Your fellow Leaguer and friend,
LeRoy Bung

IN MEMORIAM
Jess Bieber
Harold Jasmund
Kenneth Brodbeck
Clayton Seeley
Leon Harrwald
Melvin Dauer
Cornelius Bloome
Delvin Noward
LeRoy Breier – missing in action

DISCHARGED

Mrs. Lorene Flogle Cunnison, Wac
Robert Luettke, Army
Wilbur Schneider, Army Air Corp.
Wesley VanDyke, Army Air Corp.
John Vanderlaan, Army
Harold Pollock, Marine
Howard Schmidt, Army
Leonard Prisby, Army

HOME ON FURLOUGH

Cpl. Noble F. Woodyard
Pfc. Harple W. Gray
Pvt. Harold Schaddler
Pvt. Ronald Ostrander
Pvt. James Christensen
Pvt. Kenneth Schmidt
Pvt. Lavern F. Nevel
Pvt. Robert J. Vesey

Lt. Inez M. Bieber
S/Sgt. Raymond Shanly
Pvt. Leslie L. Harroun
Pvt. Clifford Papenhagen
Pvt. Robert A. Dietsch
Pfc. Forrest H. Nearhood
Alvin C. Miller, M.M. 1/c

❧❧❧

Dear Rev. Mueller:

I received your Messenger in Saturdays mail and I am always glad to hear from Zion.

I am still working in the fuel system and it is just the same thing with a few news orders to follow.

Tonight it is very cloudy out. You never can imagine how cloudy the sky is. I'm glad that I have to go to work at midnight tonight so if we have a cyclone or something I won't be in the barrack.

A week ago last Wednesday the air force celebrated their 38th years. We had open house here. There were over 10,000 people here that day. They had a Chapel Service for them. Also the people were allowed to inspect the Ground School Radio Training, Link Trainer, Bomb Parachute Dept., Base Shape, the Post Gym, and a display of civilian and military aircraft. Among the group was a giant B-29 Superfort, flown here from the Pratt Army Air Field, Pratt, Kansas. This proved to be a center of attraction.

Cheerio,

Lester Gilhouse
P.S. I'm enclosing a picture.

❧❧❧

August 5, 1945

Dear Violet and Leaguers,

Just received the July Messenger. I am still in communication with one or two Convalescent Depot friends. It's really surprising how one keeps meeting people in ones travels.

The weather is hot now and dust flies around in clouds in the bombed towns of Germany. I am stationed in Neumunster in the North-west province known as Schwelizig Holstein. The other day whilst walking along the street I was amazed to see outside a house an advertisement made of tin and the name "A Fischer" printed on it in block letters and for the moment it made me wonder what I'd see next.

Am afraid there's no news except that Conservatives didn't have an earthly chance in the General Election and suffered a decisive rout as you will probably know.

In the meantime I must close wishing everyone all the Best and God Bless You all.

Yours very sincerely,
Frank Broughton

Norman Eberlin writes from Okinawa: "This place is a little different than what we have been, we have fir trees here, no palm trees, we have hot days but cool comfortable nights. We still have rain and lots of it. Things should grow very well here. The place is terraced all over, we had to cut many of them out in order to have a level place for our buildings. Another thing there are goats all over the place which the soldiers have a lot of fun with.

Charles Belgin, my brother-in-law, is here so we have had some good gabjests. He and the rest of his outfit get a big kick out of every thing as it is new to them. One thing that has helped my stay here is the fact that our pal, Rev. Grotefond from Detroit, is on the island and in charge of the island. He will become a full colonel before long. We have had a lot of fun and some good talks."

Betty McPeek, who is working in the Office of The Inspector General of the U.S. in Washington writes: "It is very interesting work. This town sure is the place to be in right now with all the excitement of the War ending, etc. Never a dull moment – something is going on every day. I got to see General "Ike" when he was here and the day the War was announced as officially over, I was right down there in front of the White House with the rest of the mob going wild. Now I suppose the next great fete to take place will be the big parade they are planning when General McArthur comes home – it is supposed to be the World's largest parade and I sure hope I am here to witness it."

ళళళ

The letter below was written to Don LaPointe by a native of France. Thanks for letting us use it for the Messenger!

My dear friend:

Where are you? That is the question I ask me very often since one year. Where are the generous and friendly soldiers who are passed through my little village and who are so hurried? This was on the first Saturday of September, historical date for us. Where art the two friends I have invited to dine at home? Where are all those who have touched glasses with me?

But naturally, you are at home, are you not? This is I hope, and it is why I write you at your home address. Do you remember always of your first dinner in a France's house. Perhaps. You have seen so many things and so many things are coming after you are pardoned if it is the contrary. But we, we have not forgotten you, and my two little children know Americans are come and dined here and they can show your places at the table. What a poor and piteful dinner my wife had cooked. She is a good "cordon blue" (blue ribbon) I don't know if you have in English the same expression to say a person is a good woman-cook.

I wish you have found your wife in good health and I am sure you are happy as in the first days of your marriage. So life is good and fine. I wish also you will not go to Japan, though you have said me you would go round the world through Germany, Russia, Asia, and throw down Japan into ocean. I think Americans are doing it these days.

In France it is always the same situation the same dearth in all things: food, clothes, shoes, slippers, and so on, and that is heavier to support because they are six years of dearth and the dryness is burning all vegetables. We don't need of that. Every day we are hoping for rain, The south wind is blowing and drying meadows and corn fields have the same color.

We have put the pieces you had given us in our collection. It is a little remembrance of your passage and our deliverance, unperishable remembrance for all frenchies. I am writing you in English but you can perhaps speak and write in French. Do you write us my wife and I? We will be very glad to have your news. I send you all our friendship.

Chambaro Gustituteuss

Cocchignola Redeployment Training Area
5 miles South of Rome, Italy
23 August 1945
Dear Leaguers and friends:

Since the time of publishing the salt issue of the "Messenger" the long awaited VJ-Day arrived. From all reports the celebration in the States and in some cases a bit hilarious and destructive. There was cause for rejoicing. Already we read about the lifting of many rationing restrictions. Gas is unlimited and your greatest care now is to keep tires in running order for a while yet. Less than two weeks ago you were warned that the meat ration for September might necessitate some going a little lighter. Now that conditions have changed there is a possibility of increasing the allowance instead of cutting it. And I am sure that this most recent announcement is good news to all the ladies, namely that nylon stockings will be more plentiful between Thanksgiving and New Years than they ever were in pre-war days.

VJ Day at this Post was similar to a Memorial Day. There was naturally a ceremony in the forenoon but it was rather brief and in addition to a brief address by the Commanding General, various awards were presented to members of the Post by him. Then at 11 o'clock services were held in the Protestant, Catholic, and Jewish Chapels on the Post.

Now the common question to all the Forces naturally is "When do we go home?" Large numbers have already been taken from the European Theater already. Many were over in the States supposedly for a brief stay before they would continue on to the Pacific; and some will do just that thing according to the latest newspaper reports. Likewise many of our group who have never served in a foreign land will soon become replacements in the forces of occupation so that some now there can be returned home

To members and friends of Zion now in the Service may God continue with you and may He hasten the day when can all return to civilian living in a peaceful world.

Sincerely,

Clayton Fischer

೪೪೪

Bad Salzschlirf, Deutschland
19 July 1945

Dear Leaguers:

"Awake! Awake! Put on thy strength", so is the challenge given is in Isaiah 52:1. "How hath the oppressor ceased! The golden City ceased". Isa. 14:4.

Dear friends I feel the above two verses of scripture carry a great meaning for us in this twentieth century of hate, racial prejudice, and bloodshed. Please let us all heed the message therein. The Asiatic oppressor is also forced to now make a last stand to defend his own against those he's killed, robbed, and oppressed. The golden cities of the old World where oppressor sat in luxury and glory while the innocent slaved and starved is now an event of the past. Remember the horrors of Buchenwald. Will this history be repeated? It will not be repeated if the coming generation, you and I, accept the prophet's challenge to awaken and put on our strength and make this world a better place to live in.

An old Prussian axiom, "might makes right" is often criticized as untrue. Truer words were never spoken. Might of the right type is the only assurance to enforce righteousness. This may be termed "Godly might".

Be it highly resolved the costly sacrifices made by us and our allies in Europe and Asia will not be repeated in twenty years hence. Let us all as Luther Leaguers awake and put on our Christian strength. Let us help our fellow young people in other faiths to rally also to the colors of Christ and strengthen their counterparts of our league so that Christian young folk everywhere will invade the troubled world, town, within itself, with a united solid front. What a force toward peace and good will this should be. Remember our church has two decades as we learned in our catechism, "the church militant" and the "church triumphant". First we must be militant before we can ever triumph. We must be triumphant. The graves of our comrades slain in battle and the hospital wards of the maimed and diseased are crying out to us every minute, "Awake, awake, put on thy strength", that we haven't died and suffer in vain.

> Sincerely,
> Pfc. Vernon Packard

In a recent letter from <u>Leroy "Pete" Fischer</u> he enclosed a clipping from their daily paper "Cockatoo" which gave an account of the 6th Division doughboys who were in combat 218 days. They landed on Luzon on Jan. 9 at Linagayen Gulf and were in combat 218 days, a record for any division in the Pacific theater. He doesn't know when he will get home but we sure hope in time for the Christmas holidays.

G. I. WISHES

Here I sit on my G. I. Bed
With my G. I. Hat upon my head.
My G. I. pants, my G. I. shoes,
All is free. Nothing to lose.
G. I. razor, G. I. comb........
G. I. wish that I were home.
They've issued me all I need:

Paper to write on, books to read.
My belt, my soxs, my G. I. tie,
All is free, nothing to buy.
They've issued me food to make me grow.
On furlough G. I. wish I could go.
I eat my chow from a G. I. plate
And buy my needs at a G. I. rate.
It's G. I. this and G. I. that;
G. I. hair-cut, G. I. hat.
Everything is G. I. issue—
O, my darling, G. I. miss you.

❧❧❧

November 1945
Ottawa Lake, Mich.

To Our Loved Ones in the Service
To those discharged and others:

Greetings in the Name of Jesus our Lord and Savior! Perhaps we ought to apologize first of all for not getting the October issue to you. We were caught in the vortex of the extra busy fall season, and it seems that many small things received the attention which at other times has been focused on this project—the Messenger.

We appreciate continued support from the public in the financing of this paper. It is all oil in the machinery!

By now most of us realize that the glorious days of "peace" have resulted only in a greater head-long rush for selfish profits. And the end is not yet! More pay for less work! How ridiculous! We realize that there are two sides to every story, but why can there not at present be a satisfied calm after the storm of war where people the world over join in thankful worship to God who "maketh wars to cease"? The Christian, too, is caught in a wicked snare, so that many times he can only with great difficulty avoid doing things which he knows to be evil. The Christian, truly aiming to follow the Master, knows how the Word of God says "Murmur not!" That is, as the Bible elsewhere declares "having food and raiment, let us be there with content!" What is all this mad chase after money? Have we not yet learned that the love of money is the root of all evil?

How blessed that soul that realizes that if one really and truly seeks first after the Kingdom of God all the necessary earthly things will be added by God Himself! There is still not enough of self-denial in the world for the good of our fellow-men. Men are still far from the realization of the great truth that Christ Jesus died to set them free, —free from the bondage of sin, free to serve God and our fellow-men.

As we write these lines a number of our boys have been discharged. We are happy with them and thankful to them for the service they have rendered their country. Since our last message, several of the boys have been home on furlough, and also we have learned of the death of Leroy Breier. He had been missing in action since March 1st. His death was confirmed in a letter to the parents. Our boys have given their best! What a price has been paid! Surely, we ought to try in every way to prove ourselves worthy. We can only try to do this by being good citizens, by being good Christians, by being faithful in our worship in the house of God, by rearing our children in the Christian way of life.

What we need above all, however, is a complete, personal, unconditional surrender to the Lord Jesus Christ. His program for our life we find in the four Gospels. Christ is the One to Whom we may come with our accusing consciences. He will forgive our sins. Often we must marvel when we behold the arrogance of men, setting up themselves and their will against God. In our own eyes we must decrease. To God alone the glory and the increase of honor!

The challenge is before you. Whom will ye serve, Satan or the Savior? God or the devil? The Church or the world?

Remembering that our life is an eternal destiny, let us say with firm resolve with Joshua "as for me and my house, we will serve the Lord!" Read Psalm 37; Psalm 121; Ps. 51; Matthew 25; John 6; John 14.

Cheerio—
Your Pastor and Friend
(Zion Lutheran Church)
Rev. Marcus Mueller

ৡৡৡ

IN MEMORIAM

Mr. And Mrs. Roy Breier of Stryker, Ohio formerly of Ottawa Lake have received official word from the government that their son, Pvt. Leroy Breier, 21 years old was killed on March 1st in the European theater of war. Pvt. Breier was a graduate of Burnham High School in Sylvania in 1944. He was inducted in the army on Aug. 10, 1944 and went overseas in January 1945. He is survived by his parents, a sister, Juanita and brothers, Richard, James and John. Leroy was a member of Zion and his gold star is the fourth to be placed on the church Service Flag. May God continue to comfort the sorrowing family and his many friends.

DISCHARGED

The following have received their discharges and we hope that many more can be added to this list next month. The two from Zion are Wilbur Facklam and John Wotring.

Mrs. Lorene Flegle Cunnison
Inez Bieber
Willard Gautz

James Clegg
Wilbur Schneider
Charles Fetzer

Frances Creque
Doris Double May
Edward Seeley
Charles McConnell
Robert Luettke
Wesley Van Dyke
Leonard Prisby
Woodrow Reed
Joseph Steiner
Alvin Miller
August Maska
Noble Woodyard
Raymond Shanly
James Grundy
Blair Hertzsch

Martin Schniepp
John Vanderlaan
Howard Schmidt
Edward Cevora
Morgan Mehan
Joseph Merickel
Elwin Beck
William DeNudt
Robert Creque
Carl Schmidt
William Schultz
Henry Cevora
Donald Hahn
LeRoy P. Gray

Jesse Creque is stationed about 50 miles south of Manila.
Virgil Schaedler is located on Guam. Virgil is in the Navy.
Willard Gautz saw quite a bit of Europe while he was overseas.
He was in France, Belgium and Germany but likes the good ole
U.S.A. best.
Worthy White is stationed on Okinawa. We hope that the
locality where he was wasn't hit by the storm over there.
Howard Hotchkiss is assigned to the U.S.S. Franklin Roosevelt
which is an air-craft carrier. He told me many interesting things
about the boat including the information that it is ¼ mile long
and it was to be commissioned by President Truman in New
York City on Navy Day. The boat is too large to go through the
Panama Canal so they will have to go around. Howard looks
fine and we hope you enjoy your time out at sea.

A surprise party was given for Lt. Inez Bieber at her
home on Sept. 19. Many relatives and friends attended.

49th Gen. Hosp.
Manila
8 October 1945

Readers of the Messenger:

Just a few lines to let you know that I am still receiving the Messenger and really enjoy reading it. Again I want to thank all of you who publish this paper as it is no doubt a big job and requires a lot of hard work which has to be done in your spare time.

The present time I am in the hospital again and have been for about a month. I'm feeling fine now but the Dr. said I would be here for another week or so as I have "Hepatitis" and have taken several blood tests but the last was still a little high. I'm hoping the next is down to normal as I should have a chance to start thinking about going home when I get out of here.

A couple fellows from the company were up the first part of last week and brought some good news but being in the hospital it didn't help me. They were down at a camp here waiting to go home and said my name was also on the order but being I was in the hospital it had to be deleted. I talked to Dr. and tried to have him release me but he said he couldn't leave me go out until my blood test was normal. I suppose that is best as I'd hate to go out and in a few days get a relapse and have to spend a couple months more over here in the hospital.

Surely hope to get transferred to the Replacement Depot here so I can get sent home as I may have a chance of getting there before too much longer. Will have to keep my fingers crossed.

I suppose quite a number of the fellows are now wearing those good old "civies" again and can't wait until I can throw a pair on. It's been quite sometime since I last wore them with the exception of the few times I wore them while home on a furlough.

Seeing that our Division is moving to Japan and my address will be changing quite a bit and I may be home shortly I think it best for you who have been writing to me to just remember the news and we'll talk it over when I get back as that will no doubt be sooner than the letter you would send.

Hoping to see all of you before long. Good luck to all.

As ever,
"Pete" Leroy Fischer

&

Birnamwood, Wis.
Oct. 1945

Dear Friends of Zion:

Rec'd the copy of "The Messenger" which was sent to me here at my home. Being the first copy I have rec'd for sometime, I enjoyed it very much.

In the past three years I have greatly enjoyed the friendship of Zion's people, and esp. Eugene and Violet Fischer. I have never and will never regret becoming a member of the Ev. Lutheran Church. It has I feel enriched me with both spiritual blessings and material blessings in the form of a host of fine friends. I appreciate also the extended hands of friendship offered to my British friend, Frank Broughton. We have now increased our circle to include foreign brethren. Frank's brother is a Methodist minister in England, which may be of interest to you also.

Presently I enjoy a 30 day furlough. Will return to Fort Custer, Mich. on Nov. 8th. Goodbye and God bless you.

As ever,
Vernon Packard

&

LeMars, France
Oct. 17, 1945

Dear Violet and Leaguers,

Just a few lines to let you know I am okay except for a little cold. It has been quite cold here thru the nite. Also quite damp living in tents.

I am writing this letter in a 40 by 8 box car. Today marks the day that I am leaving the 156 Inf. and Co. L. Also ends the guard duty at D.T.C. which I am very glad of . I expect to leave LeMars this evening. I may go to Belgium now.

Saw a show the other evening. Also a Red Cross Dance was held last Saturday evening.

Am glad to know you received the snapshot okay of Inez and myself. Am sending my best regards to the folks. Hoping to be seeing you soon.

Your friend,
Matthew E. Bieber

ৰুৰুৰু

Bennie Muntz is in Pearl Harbor but expects to be sent on. He is working there while he is waiting for further orders.

Lester Knuth is back in the States and is able to be with his family most of his free time.

Ellis Rosenbrock is home in Toledo again. After reporting to Texas he was at Fort Jackson, S. Carolina awhile. He's on furlough now.

ৰুৰুৰু

Dear Violet and Leaguers:

Excuse me for not writing sooner but I suppose you know how easy it is to delay writing.

I want to thank you all very much for that good paper "The Messenger". It's always good to hear from some of the boys from the Lake even if I don't know all of them. Their personal experiences here and abroad are very interesting.

I'm still here at Lincoln but not for very much longer and I don't have the least idea where I will go next. Our work is finished here so I'm just waiting.

I only hope that everyone will be able to turn their uniforms in for good.

>   Respectfully yours,
>   Bernard Anger and family

ๅๅๅ

Rheims, France
Sept. 16. 1945

Dear Ma, (Mrs. Glen Breese)
Here is your long lost boy. This is the first time I got up enough ambition to write for about 2 weeks now. We have been pretty busy here lately, driving almost every day. Got a chance to see Paris again about a week ago. We stopped off there for 48 hours on our way back from a trip. That makes the third time I was there 7 days in all. I don't care about going there anymore. I've seen all I want of it there. It takes more than a month's pay to stay there a night.

Tomorrow I'm on K.P. again. The good thing about this place is that if a fellow isn't driving one day they either put him on K.P. or guard.

In another month I'll be in the Army for 2 years. By Christmas I hope to be on my way to the States if everything works out O.K. I have only 60 points but I think its enough so I won't have to stay here.

It's almost time to go to the show. I haven't heard the name of it yet but they usually have good shows here. They have a different one every night. I guess this is about all I have for this time so I'll sign off.

Love,
Merle Gust

❧❧❧

Camp Lucky Strike, France
Sept. 22, 1945

Was very pleased to receive a copy of the August issue of the Zion Lutheran Messenger from Pastor.

Am glad to see what an interesting, newsy and complete newsletter you folks are sending out to those away from home. It means a great deal of work for your staff and much of your time must be spent in preparing it for publication and distribution.

It is a wonderful means of keeping the church close to those away and a valuable source of encouragement, inspiration and cheer, especially to those of us who miss the fellowship of Luther League gatherings.

It is nice to print the letters so the service men and women can also keep in touch with one another as well as the news of activities at home. It is both informal and friendly and must leave in the hearts of those who read it a feeling somewhat like a visit to home.

May God continue to bless this work in every way! Do not use my military address since I am heading for the good old U.S.A.

Faithfully,
Fred Sievert Acts 8:4

❧❧❧

Fort Belvoir, Virgina
Sept. 10, 1945

Hi Everyone,

Received your League paper so I thought I would drop a line and let you all know that I am in the best of health and hope you all are back home in Ottawa Lake. Was glad to hear what the other boys from Ottawa Lake are doing.

I have heard from two of my Buddies that left Detroit with me, Johnny and Lee. They are in the infantry according to their letters. I had a surprise about 3 weeks ago in Washington, I ran into my cousin from near Whiteford, Bill Iott. He had just returned to camp after spending a 30 day furlough at home. He returned from overseas and is now stationed in North Carolina.

I had another surprise the other nite a buddie of mine said he was dancing with a girl at the Service Club that was from Michigan. When he said Michigan I became very inquisitive and asked him if he knew her name and he said Betty McPeek. I was sure surprised. He said she is usually at the dances. It sure makes one surprised to run across friends from back home. Here at Fort Belvoir I am going to an Engineers School. This camp is an Army Engineers Training Camp.

One of the things I like about this camp is that we sure get good chow. Leaguers, I will close now. Tell everyone I said "Hello" and to write.

So Long,
Alvin J. Turk

P.S. Thanks for sending the paper.

Sept. 26, 1945

Dear Violet and friends,

First of all I want to thank you and all the good people of Ottawa Lake who help to put out the paper I enjoy so much. I have been receiving the Messenger every since I've been in the Army.

I left the states Sept. 14 and was a week on the water. I enjoyed the trip mainly because I didn't get sea-sick. As usual there were quite a few fellows standing pretty close to the railing the first day out. The water was really rough. After that it was so calm it was almost like ice. The night we arrived we weren't allowed off the boat so the U.S.O. brought a show (Hula shirts and all) on the boat.

It's nice now that all censorship is off. I'm about 10 miles from Pearl Harbor and Hickam Field. I'm not assigned to any outfit yet but expect to be soon.

I was to Honolulu on a pass last weekend and had a swell time. LeRoy Bunge is stationed the same place as I am and I see him quite often.

We aren't kept very busy here. We have a little physical training and a hike in the morning and play ball in the afternoon.

It seems funny to see pineapple fields and sugar cane instead of corn and the crops we raise at home. I'm with a swell bunch of fellows. Thank God that the war is over and we don't have to go into battle.

As ever,
Ernest W. LaPointe

Japan
Nagasaki, Sept. 27, 1945

Hello Maw and Paw! (Mr. and Mrs. Glen Breese)
Just a few lines to let you all know that I'm still alive and quite busy. I finally arrived in Japan, I have been looking for this day for a long time. I told you folks that I would get here sometime.

Gosh! I sure did travel since I left Ottawa Lake, 2400 miles to Calif., 2450 miles to Pearl Harbor, 3850 miles by plane to Saipan (26 ½ hrs.) and 1500 miles by ship to Nagasaki. 10,200 miles all total.

It's raining all day today and the weather is the same as L.A., Calif. and its all mountains. Boy, oh Boy! I'll have to give the Aviation crew a cigar they didn't miss anything with their bombs. I can't explain what happened here but it's more horrible than people would ever think. I feel sorry for the poor class of Japs. They don't have anything left not even shoes and they make them out of boards.

I saw a 1939 Buick-8 and 3 – 1937 Fords here all in running shape. The Gov. Police are driving them. Tell the gang I said "Hello". Bye now.

Just – Daniel D. Prisby

ശശശ

SERVICE OF THANKSGIVING FOR THE RETURNED VETERANS TO BE DEC. 16, 1945.

A special service to honor the boys and Inez who have returned to civilian life from Zion and the community will be held at 7:30 P.M. on Sunday evening, Dec. 16th. We hope that all of you who have received the Messenger will attend and we wish to give you all a hearty invitation to attend, especially you veterans on our Messenger mailing list. A committee consisting of Geraldine Schmidt, Melva Sieler, Rev. Mueller, Maxine Schaedler and Violet Fischer are in charge. Don't forget the date and come and worship with us at this service of THANKSGIVING.

The printing on the cover page this month was done by Clayton Fischer. Thanks and we're glad for his help and also the way the rest of the boys and Inez who have returned in their ready response to help.

❧❧❧

IN MEMORIAM

Leroy Daniel Breier was born in Toledo, Ohio January 4, 1925, a son of Mr. and Mrs. Roy Breier. He was baptized Feb. 1, 1925 in Bethlehem Lutheran Church, Toledo by the Rev. Boomgarden and confirmed June 4, 1939 at Zion Lutheran Church, Ottawa Lake by Rev. Zeitner. He was graduated from Burnham High School in 1944. He took active part in the work of the congregation here, singing in the choir and also sharing in Luther League work.

He was inducted into the army in August 1944. After his training at Camp Joseph T. Robinson, Arkansas, and after a brief furlough home last Christmas, Leroy went overseas early in January of this year and served with the 302nd. Inf., the 94th Division. He was reported to have died in action March 1, 1945 in the Battle of the Bulge, several miles N.E. of Serrig, Germany. According to Chaplain John Downing of the 302nd Div., "Pvt. Breier was last seen doing his duty under attack in the front lines." It seems this sentence is a fine tribute to a fine soldier. Yet, as fellow Christians, we best remember him as a good soldier in the cross of Christ.

Surviving Leroy are his parents, Mr. and Mrs. Roy Breier of Stryker, Ohio; a sister, Juanita; three brothers; Richard,

James and John; grandparents, Mr. and Mrs. Otto Lenz of Toledo; his fiancée, Miss Lucille Pant; and other relatives and friends.

We commend all sorrowing hearts to the Lord Jesus who said: "Let not your heart be troubled. Ye believe in God; believe also in Me. In my Father's house are many mansions. I go to prepare a place for you.....that where I am, there ye may be also." Jn. 14.

Memorials for Leroy have been given in the following: the Ladies Aid; the Messenger Staff; School District No. 7; the Luther League; Mr. and Mrs. Leonard Harrwaldt and Family; Mr. and Mrs. Roy Bune; Mr. and Mrs. John Olrich; Mr. and Mrs. Kenneth Olrich; C.W. Fischer family; Brotherhood; and an altar desk by the neighbors and friends. To these and all others who have shown their concern the Breier family wishes to express their sincere thanks.

The Breier family also wishes to thank The Messenger Staff for sending the Messenger to Leroy and also the Service Secretary, Miss Geraldine Schmidt for sending the church bulletins.

(Excerpt from a letter written by Chaplain John Downing of the 302nd Inf. Reg. in which Leroy Breier served to Mrs. Augusta Breier, under date of Oct. 25, 1945.

Dear Mrs. Breier,
........Leroy was engaged in an important action across the Saar River, near Serrig, Germany. As his company advanced they were met by terrific mortar and artillery fire. Army investigation has determined that he was struck fatally by an exploding mortar shell during the fighting.

We appreciate fully the pain of loss you feel and pray you may find comfort in the words of our Savior: "In my Father's house are many mansions, I go to prepare a place for you." Eternal rest grant unto him, O Lord!

We hope too, that your natural sorrow will be relieved by the knowledge that Pvt. Breier accomplished much by his unselfish death. Generations will owe to him their freedom and their peace. "Greater love hath no man than this; that a man lay down his life for his friends."

> Sincerely,
> John L. Downing
> Chaplain (Capt.)

Leroy's gold star is the fourth to be placed on Zion's service flag. The other three being placed for Jess Bieber, Kenneth Brodbeck and Leon Harrwaldt.

Memorial Services were held at the church Nov. 25, 1945. The Sermon: "He Shall Rise Again" was delivered by Rev. Mueller and Mrs. Arthur Bischoff and Melvin Bischoff gave two musical numbers: "My Faith Looks Up to Thee" and "Near To the Heart of God".

WELCOME BACK HOME!!!

The following have received their discharge who are members of Zion:

Wilbur Facklam	Inez Bieber
Horace Nearhood	John Wotring
John Fisher	Matthew Elg Bieber
Leroy Fischer	Clayton Fischer
Frank Schumacher	

Last issue of the Messenger had a list of 34 who had received their discharge. These people were on the Messenger mailing list. We're happy to add the following names to that discharge list and hope that all of you are enjoying your civilian life again. It really seems grand to see you fellows around again and we know all of you are really happy to be back home again.

Harold Pollick, Jr.
Ralph Reger
Stanley Kastel
William Hyde
Malcolm Gray
Harple Gray
William Hein

Elwood Brenke
Bernard Anger
Vernon Root
Raymond Berry
Paul Bruns
Edgar Strable

പ്പപ്പ

ZION LUTHERAN MESSENGER
Ottawa Lake, Michigan
January 1945

THIS ISSUE OF THE "MESSENGER" IS DEDICATED TO THE NINE YOUNG MEN ON THE "MESSENGER" MAILING LIST THAT GAVE THEIR LIVES IN THE SERVICE OF OUR COUNTRY.

Cornelius Blome, Jr., son of Mr. and Mrs. Cornelius Blome, Sr., Blissfield, Michigan and brother of Mrs. Bertha Lievens and Mrs. Linda Papenhagen was born Feb. 1, 1921. He died Dec. 2, 1943 on his ship the result of an air attack on the coast of Italy. He was a Merchant Marine.

Jess Bieber, son of Mr. Frank Bieber, was born Aug. 19, 1924 and died June 20, 1944 on his aircraft carrier the "Bunker Hill". He was buried at sea.

Harold Jasmund, son of Mr. and Mrs. William Jasmund of Route 10, W. Toledo, Ohio died in England on July 23, 1944 from a subdural hemorrhage as a result from a fall from a bicycle. He was in the Army in the Medical Corps.

Clayton Seeley, husband of Mrs. Nellie Vanderlaan Seeley died in France Sept. 25, 1944 of wounds he received the same day. Besides his wife he is survived by a daughter Elsie and a son Raymond.

Kenneth F. Brodbeck, son of Mrs. Ida Brodbeck was born Aug. 2, 1919. He died Nov. 20, 1944 in Southern France. His burial was in an American Cemetery in France at which a Protestant Chaplain officiated.

Leon Harrwaldt, son of Mr. and Mrs. Leonard Harrwaldt, was born Dec. 26, 1925. he died on Feb. 5, 1945 in the Belgium-Luxembourg sector. He was buried in an American Military Cemetery at a Protestant Service in Foy, Belgium.

Melvin Dauer, husband of Francile Baer Dauer and son of Mrs. Margaret Dauer Elg died near Julich, Germany on Feb. 24, 1945. He is buried in Margareta, Holland. Besides his wife and mother he is survived by a daughter Janet.

Leroy Breier, son of Mr. and Mrs. Roy Breier was born Jan. 4, 1925. He died on March 1, 1945 in the battle of the Bulge, several miles N.E. of Serrig, Germany. According to Chaplain John Downing of the 302nd Regt. "Pvt. Breier was last seen doing his duty under attack in the front lines."

Delvin Noward, son of Mr. Lester Noward and brother of Roy of Waterville, Ohio died on April 26, 1945 near the city of Tabuelon on Cebu Island of the Philippines. He is buried in Cebu City.

LEAVES FOR SERVICE

Charles DeVriendt, Jr., son of Mr. and Mrs. Charles DeVriendt, Sr. enlisted in the Navy and left Dec. 27th for Cleveland, Ohio to receive his orders. This will be the 30th star to be placed on Zion's Service Flag. We wish you health and happiness in your new work, Charles and hope that it won't be too long before you return home.

The past two issues of the Messenger had a list of 53 who had received their discharge. These people were on the Messenger mailing list. We're happy to welcome the following back home and into civilian life again:

Shurley Sackett	Kenneth Korth
Daniel Mueller	Vernon Packard
Donald LaPointe	Norman Mueller
George Dannecker	Henry Metzger
Albert Mueller	Don Gillhouse
Fred Ernst	Eugene Hart
Gilbert Harre	Franklin Kummerow
Willis Harre	Martin Seitz
Vernon Bauer	Edwin Crots

❧❧❧

Fukuoka, Japan
Dec. 10, 1945

Dear friend Rev. Mueller,

I'm going to take a few minutes of my spare time this morning to thank you for sending me the Messenger. Even though I'm not so well acquainted with most of the boys I still enjoy reading all the news.

One of your members, Clifford Papenhagen and myself have been together all through our army career until just recently we were separated. At present I do not know where he went to.

The climate here in Japan is rather mild. It doesn't seem possible it's so near Christmas and the weather so nice. The Japanese all have nice gardens and are working in them every day. Some have started to sow rice, which is their main living.

The place where I'm at now used to be quite a good size city but since it was bombed there isn't much left here. It's hard to picture a scene like this until you actually see it. I have a very nice place to live in and our work is very easy.

It's almost time for me to go to work so I'll have to close my letter. Thanking you again and my God bless us and be with us till we can meet again. I remain,

Sincerely yours,
Pvt. Lavern F. Nevel

❧❧❧

Oaho Island
12/4/45

Dear Mom and Dad:

I told in my last letter that Willie (Willie is the boy from the East side a member of St. John's Church near the Orphans home) and I planned to go to Honolulu to Sunday School and church. Willie knows the minister over there.

Willie, his navy friend from Toledo and I left here about 8 arrived there about 9:30. Willie introduced us to both ministers. The minister in charge of the church is Dr. Harmann. Pastor Kock is in charge of the Lutheran Service Center. They are both good speakers. Dr. Harmann is 75 years old. His wife teaches German in the University of Hawaii, his son works as an engineer at Pearl Harbor and his daughter works at the library in Honolulu.

Every first Sunday of the month they have communion. It so happened it was the first Sunday so Willie, his navy friend and I communed. Every first Sunday in the month they serve a dinner. We had dinner there and visited awhile. In the Service Center they have a pool table that was practically new. We played pool with some of the fellows most of the afternoon. About 3:30 they served cake and coke which was good. At 5:30 they served hamburgers and coke. It was very good, the hamburgers were spiced just like your sausage, it was really delicious. At 6:30 they had a vesper service which we attended. After the services we were invited to a wiener roast sponsored by the Mission Synod. We had hot dogs and marshmallows and sang songs. We really enjoyed ourselves all day.

One thing that amused me was when Willie introduced me to Dr. Harmann. He seemed to know the name Bunge. He said "Bunge that's a good ole German name". He knew the correct pronunciation and spelling without asking any questions. He is a fine minister. He has been over here 30 years, quite a long time I'd say. We got back about 9:30.

Well, I'll say Good-night. It's about time to retire.

Your loving son,
LeRoy Bunge

ๆๆๆ

Nagoya Base, Japan
Dec. 11, 1945

Dear Violet and Leaguers,
I received the Messenger today. I was glad to get it and I can't begin to tell you all how much I enjoy it. There's not much doing here. I drive truck for the Officer Mess. They have

Jap girls that work in the Mess Hall. All we do is go get them and get rations so it's not very hard work. This was a big city before the bombers came. Nagoya is just like most of the big Jap cities. The city is crowded that you can't get one foot on the sidewalk. Cliff Papenhagen left me out at the 11th replacement depot. I don't know just where he is. He was going to write me when he got settled. I hope to hear from him most any day. I got a camera but I can't get film. I would like to take some pictures of the factories.

Well, there it goes, every time I get a letter started I have to go some place. So will say Bye for now.

As ever,
Harold Schaedler

1946

WELCOME BACK HOME !!!!

The following have received their discharge who are members of Zion: Garld Holmes; Merle Harroun; and Vern Jacobs. This increases the discharge list from Zion to 13 members. There are still 13 members from the church that are still in Service.

In previous issues of the Messenger we have listed 72 who had received their discharges. These people were on the Messenger mailing list while in Service. We're happy to welcome the following back home and into civilian life again:

Roland Wotring
Carl Clegg
Arthur Loomer
Victor Logan
Verne Jacobs
Harold Bunting
Norman Eberlin
Donald Hart
Lawrence Metzger

Willard G. Behm
Russell L Creque
Dale Viers
Kenneth Myers
Worthy White
Arnold Nearhood
Howard Miller
Arnold Kummerow
John McMahon

Edgar Strable sends this little note to James Christensen who is located at Kobe Honshu Island, Japan: "Is the 11 piece all Japanese Band still playing all American music at the Club Kabuka at Osaka and are the girls still appearing in their nylon formals? Do they have the Kobe water front clear of mines for shipping? When I left they were in the process of making it a separation center. Write me when you have time and give me the latest news on the old place. Good luck, Ed." Ed was stationed at Kobe when he was in Japan.

Berlin, Germany
Jan. 4, 1946

Dear Violet and Leaguers:

 Just a line to leave you know where I am. I am way over here in Berlin, and no longer in the Infantry. I got transferred to the Quartermaster the day before New Years. We are staying in a factory right now in Berlin. It was a medicine factory before the war. There are 3 men to a room. My buddy, another fellow, and I are staying in where the office rooms to the factory used to be, because they are real nice. We have German women that come in every morning and make our beds, clean our room up, and shine our shoes. We have German women that do the cooking for us too. We work in a big warehouse across the road from where we stay, but we don't do much work. We tell the Germans what to do. I am working in the metal shop where they fix stoves and things like that. But all I do is see that the Germans work, and do the bookwork. Some day when it isn't so cold the Lt. is going to take us in the truck and take us around Berlin and show us a few things. The German people that work in this warehouse seem like very nice people and a few of them speak English, but the only thing that I don't like is that you can't understand what they are saying and they can't understand us. My Grampa taught me how to count to 10 in German when I was little and that helps out a lot, but I'm picking a lot of German up by just hearing the people talk. We can get $10 for a pack of cigarettes over here in Berlin.

 Well I guess I had better close for now. Write when you can.

   As ever, a Leaguer
   Leo Bexten

      ৡৡৡ

Dear Violet:

Just to announce that I am at last beginning to take advantage of the GI Bill of Rights education. I arrived her yesterday and enrolled today at Wartburg College.

Classes begin Monday. Until then I can't voice any opinions as to whether or not I will like it here. I have some premature conclusions but time alone can tell.

How are you all? I hope with sincerity that all is very well with you. Will write more later when I'm settled down.

Vernon Packard

෨෨෨

DISCHARGED

Two more discharge emblems have been added to the Service Flag at Zion. They are for Curtis (Olin) Fischer and Kurt Durst. To our list of 90 discharged servicemen who have received the Messenger we are happy to add the names of Frank Klauda, Bernard Myers, Joe Perry and L. Paul Freeland.

WELCOME HOME.

Also Carl Ernst, Jr. from Ann Arbor, Mich.

HOME ON LEAVE

Charles DeVerindt, Jr. enjoyed a 7 day furlough at home the last week in February. He looks grand in his navy blue. He will report back to the Great Lake, Ill. Hope you get home again real soon.

෨෨෨

Berlin, Germany
Jan. 30, 1946

Dear Violet and Leaguers,

I thought I would drop you a line and leave you know how everything is coming over here in Berlin. My buddy and I went to an opera last night. The Red Cross girls took us. We got out of work at noon and ate our dinner, then they took us over to the Red Cross girl's house. We spent the afternoon over there and at 4:00 P.M. they took 12 of us GI's to the opera. I enjoyed it very much. I am sending Mother the program and I will tell her to show it to you. After the opera they took us back to their house and gave us a nice supper. It was hard to figure out what the opera was all about, because it was put on by German people. Before we went to the opera the Red Cross Girl read the story to us.

They did some very good acting in the opera and some very good singing. My buddy and I go on furlough Saturday, and we are planning on going to England. My buddy has an aunt in England and we are to stay with her. There isn't much to do over here during the week. I either go to the show or else stay home and write letters. I got 3 Valentines all ready, so I think I'm doing OK. I guess I'd better close for now, as it is getting late. Write when you can.

As ever,
Leo Bexten

ഏഏഏ

Feb. 17, 1946

Dear Violet, Leaguers & Friends,

I want to congratulate the League on their fine work of sending me the copy of the Messenger (hot off the press) and the Mighty Fortress, Bulletins, and especially all the Christmas Cards and Valentines. You have been editing or publishing the Messenger for several years now and have been doing a wonderful job. I received the last copy several days ago and as I was reading it, I was wondering how long you expect to continue to publish it. Have you any idea? I have heard that the Mighty Fortress is going to be discontinued. Is that right? (In answer to the questions before we forget; the Messenger has been published 3 years this month, and hope to continue publishing it as long as there are members of Zion in service. As for the discontinuing of the Mighty Fortress, to the best of our knowledge, it is to be discontinued soon.)

Usually the fellows write in their letters the type of work they are doing, so as to stick to the S.O.P., I'll also tell you a few of my duties.

I was just recently promoted to the job of Chief Clerk in the Personnel Office here at the 13th Pepple Depple. It is more interesting and a lot easier than what I was doing. My old job as section chief was a headache. I now handle AWOL cases, Court Martials, Dependency Discharges, and last but not least, which is a large concerning yours truly, Marriage Requests. My most numerous and difficult work is AWOL cases which later result in Court Martials. Sometimes they are very interesting, as you no doubt can guess.

Besides my work during the day in the office, I work at night as cashier in the theater. All in all, I have received a good break here at the Depple. I don't have much spare time and the days seem to fly fast.

The weather on the rock has been rather bad the last few weeks. We are in the rainy season which results in quite a bit of rainfall. During this season it rains better than 50% of the time.

I was very sorry to hear that the Temperance School burned. Our school and Temperance were always rival schools and it meant a lot to both schools who won the football games. We did have some rough times with them a few years ago.

Again I thank you for the Messenger and all the other things that the League and Church has done for me while in Service. Until we meet again, Adous Folks.

As ever,
LeRoy Bunge

ويويوي

Ellington Field, Texas
Feb. 13, 1946

Dear Rev. Mueller,

Received the Zion Messenger in Tuesday's mail and very glad to receive it. It sure is good to receive it to see how things are going back home. This field is going to close very soon and we are hauling our furniture from Sq. K now and everybody else is also. Quite a few men are getting discharged. So that makes a difference. Right now we have three officers and two enlisted men left. We did have four officers and seven enlisted men. They cut all P.T. and drilling.

I spent last weekend down in Galveston, about 35 miles from here. My buddy who lives a block from me at home is stationed down there in the Navy. I had the best time of my life when I was down there. We was to Church Sunday, and had a nice Service from the Navy Chaplain. In the Navy the wear the Robe, but the Army don't.

We slept on a tugboat with four beds and a kitchen right on. We took a four hour boat ride also.

The weather is raining as usual here in Texas, and still trying to rain. It is pretty chilly and windy. This seems to take care of the news at present.

As ever,
Lester Gillhouse

ೋೇೋೇೋೇ

Feb. 7, 1946

Dear Violet,

Just received a letter from Russell. He is stationed at Shanghai, China. He left San Francisco Jan. 4th and arrived at Shanghai Jan. 28th.

He says he enjoyed every day of his first ocean voyage. He is very proud of the fact that he was not seasick. The rails were lined with boys for about 3 days who were very sick. The people and everything he has seen so far are very dirty and crummy.

He says he is with about 7 boys from Toledo. They have a grand bunch of men (crew and officers.) The food is good and all in all he thinks the Navy is swell. He went across on the USS Napa, but is on the Casa Marina now.

We enjoy the paper and hope you can keep up the good work.

Mrs. Russell McGlenn

ೋೇೋೇೋೇ

Miami Springs, Fla.
Feb. 25, 1946

Hi Folks,

How is the skating on Ottawa Lake these days?? I have been flying with TACA Airlines as co-pilot for a week now and like it very much. Flying between Miami and Havana Cuba. Making two round trips a day. Evening flights on other days. I fly one day and off the next. We are flying "Lockheed Lodestors" and they are faster than the Douglas airlines. We are flying passengers. I may be based in San Jose, Costa Rica later.

Dan Mueller

Waverly, Iowa
Feb. 13, 1946

Dear Violet and Leaguers:

I have received the Feb. issue of the Messenger and glad to receive the same. I promise to write more, so please accept my humble ambitions in that direction. In as much as Wartburg College represents the American Lutheran Church, of which Zion's Congregation is a constituent
Portion, I feel my few words herein will find some interest in your minds.

Some few weeks have now passed since I arrived on Wartburg Campus. Oh! What a contrast to a "Campus" and a "Camp" despite the linguistic derivation of these words and their consequent similarity in spelling. Anyone in the service, or a discharge as I am will certainly verify this statement for me.

I have found this Church College to possess a fine Christian Campus overfilled with enthusiastic young people who are all friendly with one another. A true Christian brotherhood exists among us all. The faculty are all well versed in their respective courses and true educators therein. My personal curriculum includes Chemistry, Christianity, German, Speech, History, and Prin. of Secondary Education. In all of these classes I receive adequate instructions and kind consideration from my professors. Being an ex-elementary teacher, now pursuing a course for secondary teaching, I find this college of our Lutheran Church, is really laying in my soul a supreme storehouse of knowledge and Christian experience to lead me in my future career when mine will be the responsibility to mould the minds of members of our nations' future. Be proud you are members of a great Church which sponsors such fine educational institutions as Wartburg College.

How are you all? I hope you are all well and happy in your service for your Lord and his cause. I am doing fine and know I am truly blessed with opportunities here. I look for even greater ones to come in the coming years before I take the final leave of college days on the Commencement day. This will be in January 1948. Having had two years at a secular Teacher's College I entered here as a Junior. Two years will pass rapidly and before I realize, the parting hour will have crept upon me. So I herby resolve to get the most out of it in my short two terms I will be here. Fortunate are those whose entire four years will be spent here.

Sincerely,
Vernon Packard

₮₮₮

Virgil A. Schaedler is still on Guam and is working on refrigeration.

Lt. Arthur Shanley is now at Dayton, Ohio. He was at Luke Field, near Glendale and Phoenix, Arizona and while in Phoenix he saw Owen Trowbridge, formerly from Sylvania, Ohio.

Curtis (Olin) Fischer started back to college at Bowling Green, Ohio.

Taking peeks into a brief diary with the title, "Life in a German Kriegio Camp" or "Hell on Earth," gives the reader a bare glimpse of the life led by former Sgt. Clarence Smith, son of the late Harry and Mrs. Louella Smith, Ottawa Lake.

Mr. Smith had been in service for 2 years and 10 months when received his discharge, and the high-light of that experience was undoubtedly the miraculous escape from death when his plane received a direct hit by Ack fire.

The former Staff Sergeant was a tail gunner on a B-17, which was named, rightly or wrongly, F-4. He was one of the nine crew members and on the plane's 19th mission on Sept. 19, 1944, while over Darmstaedt, Germany, and flying at over 25, 000 feet, the plane was struck by anti-aircraft fire and blew apart. Smith, being the tail gunner, found himself falling in the tail of the plane like a leaf, twisting, whirling and then leveling off in a glide, then repeating the whole routine again and again. He says it seemed to take about fifteen minutes for the plane to reach the ground, during which time he was conscious and with his mind in a whirl he is not sure of the time spent in the descent, but he felt he lived his lifetime over again while waiting for the crash.

When the tail of the plane hit the ground, it was in an open grain field which had been harvested. The crash knocked him unconscious and when he came too, it was to find a German civilian pointing a pistol at his head. A German soldier took the gun away from the would be killer however and he was taken by ambulance to a hospital in Kreusnach. X-rays showed three broken bones in his right foot and a cracked jawbone. Removal to another hospital in the same town.

On Sept. 29, he was moved back to the original hospital and had a cast put on his leg. Bones had not been set. He remained there for five and one half weeks.

To quote from the diary now: Oct. 27, 1944, two German Luftwaffe guards came after me in the evening, but we did not leave until the next morning. Oct. 28, took a train to Frankfurt and then to the interrogation center at Oberussel, where I was put in cell number 77 (no windows). After about two hours, guards called for me and I was photographed and questioned. Oct. 29, taken from the cell early in the morning and questioned all day by a German Captain. Threatened to call Gestapo. Oct. 30, taken from cell in the afternoon and proceeded to the "Hohemarke" along with 5 other fellows. These were the first "Yanks" I had seen since we were shot down. Became good friends with Hubert Garlock, a second louie P51 pilot from Lansing, Mich. There were about 50 Americans and British prisoners there. We were given 50 cigarettes when we came in plus a hot bath (my first in 6 weeks). Nov. 2, left Hohemarke with about 20 others for Wetzlar, a temporary P.W. camp about 40 miles from Frankfurt. After a search and a short interrogation we were given a Red Cross capture parcel, a hot shower and a bed. Nov. 6, left with 150 others for a permanent camp. There were about 35 men to a car and it was very crowded and uncomfortable. Had a Red Cross food parcel in addition to Jerry "black bread" and sausage.

Nov. 11, arrived at "Cross Tipchow," a permanent camp of some 9000 strong. The camp was about 60 miles from Stettin. There I was searched again, and put in barracks 5, room 1. The camp was divided into four compounds. I was put in D Compound. I was the 23rd man in the room. As there were only 16 bunks, I had to sleep on the floor.

The boys put on several stage productions at this camp and they had a very good dance band led by Frank Del Grado. A minstrel show was put on at Christmas time and the Red Cross provided a special Christmas parcel in addition to one half of the regular parcel.

On Jan. 30, the diary notes of a removal of 1500 of the men by boxcar, jammed 50 to 55 men to the car, to another camp at Barth. The Russians were getting very close and was the cause of the removal.

The last entry in the book is enlightening. March 8, 1945, writing this today. We had very little food lately and the situation doesn't look too good. Our fingers are crossed.

March 18, 1945. Two men shot this morning for being outside during air raid. Oatmeal for dinner.

Mr. Smith explained that the two men were foolhardy and failed to comply with the rules which demanded that all prisoners were to go inside if any Allied planes were to come over. This they refused to do and less than a month later the prison camp was liberated by the Russians.

At the time of the liberation, the Russians, some of whom were mere children, such as these pictured, who were 14 and 15, and wives and babies, celebrated by taking anything they saw such as bicycles, motorcycles, or anything else which appealed to them. Sgt. Smith is pictured on a motorcycle which he "found". The conditions at the time of liberation were so riotous that eleven American prisoners were killed by trigger happy Russians who thought them Germans.

Sgt. Smith was flown to Lyons, France by American pilots and he has a story to pass on to his grandchildren. He fell five miles and lived to tell it.

❧❧❧

The following is a letter diary written by Kenneth Schmidt, son of Mr. and Mrs. George Schmidt, Sr. aboard the S.S. Monterey, which also carried the missionaries from the States en route to Mission Fields in New Guinea and India.

Sat. Jan. 26, 1946

Dear folks:

Well, here I am way out in the ocean a whole day and a half. We are headed for Australia and New Zealand, this trip is supposed to last 8 weeks so that means that much closer for my discharge and home.

I haven't been seasick as yet but this old ship sure does rock back and forth. We are carrying civilians over that have married in the States and then we will bring back all the war brides over there and their children.

I have been working pretty hard every since I've been on this ship.

I certainly eat good. The water is so blue and pretty. It hasn't been too rough but once in a while there are a few big waves.

I heard this is supposed to be a 16,000 mile round trip so that will add a few more miles to my mile chart.

There is one boy with us that has been sick almost all the time. We are living in a stateroom and it is so nice. There are six in this room and we are having a swell time.

Jan. 30, 1946

Back again only a few days later but it doesn't matter now because it will be sometime before I can mail this letter; at least two more days.

If you have a hard time to read this it's because the ship keeps rocking back and forth. More fun trying to walk sometimes.

It is getting hot here now. We have gone 2200 miles or by this time it is a lot more so that least I'm about 5000 miles from home.

I am glad that I'm not in the navy because I have seen enough water to last me a long time. It never changes out here; all you can see is water and more water.

We are supposed to get back to the States about March 7.

We have a show about every nite which I have to run. There are two of us and we take turns to run the show. I don't have to work very hard any more. I didn't do a thing so far today but wash some of my clothes out and that is about the hardest work I know of.

I heard we are going to stay at Sidney, Australia for 7 days so maybe I'll get to see a little of Australia.

Jan. 31, 1946

Here it is the next day and that much closer to some land. I'll be glad to see some once again. Did I only get a sunburn today. I was only out in it for about 45 minutes but my back is just as red as it can be so I had to go to the medics and have them put some cream on it now I'm all greased up. I hope it will turn to tan soon.

We crossed the equator today at 11 a.m. The first place we are supposed to land is Pago Pago, some little Island off of New Zealand.

I washed my only shirt tonight. I have only 1 suntan shirt with me the other ones are in the laundry back in the States.

I saw some birds today, the first for a long time. We have been on the water one week today and haven't seen land.

It is fun to hear some of these Australian people talk. They sound so funny you can't understand them sometime.

Feb. 2, 1946

I am writing this letter on the sixth but it is only the fifth back there. You see we have crossed the date line so we lost last Monday.

Now about the island we were at last Saturday and Sunday. It was the most beautiful place I have ever seen. We were at Pago Pago on the Island of Samoa. We got there about 4 on Saturday afternoon. I was on CQ for the first 8 hours but the next day Sunday I had off so 4 of us took off to see the Island. It was so pretty and I can't explain it in writing. We got to know one of the sailors that was stationed there. He is in charge of all the fuel and trucks and jeeps so he took us around and showed us the Island. He took us about 10 miles out to the farm that the Navy has there. It is only used for experimental to see what they can raise there but the natives are very lazy.

The natives do go to church 3 times on Sunday. There are a few that do a little work but not those that live way back in the village. I would have liked to stay there for about a week. The sailor that took us around said he would take us out to some more of the villages and have a dinner with the Chief. At that time we heard we were coming back to that Island on the way back by now we hear we aren't.

We got two big stocks of bananas from that farm we were at. Also all kinds of fruit. They gave them to us. If we had bought them from the natives it would have cost us $20.

I heard we might go to Boston to dock instead of San Francisco that is if the strike is still on.

Feb. 11, 1946

We are supposed to get to Sidney, Australia tomorrow early. We stayed the day and a half at New Zealand. What I saw of it I didn't like at all. I am getting a little tan. This is the end for this one, God Bless You all.

Your son,
Kenneth Schmidt

❧❧❧

The total of Service-men and –women who had received the Messenger while in Service was 97. Six more names have been added during the past month although two of these, Herbert Kodelman and Kenneth Never were discharged sometime ago. Dale Ballard is at home in Toledo, Ohio. Bert Vesey, son of Mr. and Mrs. Wade Vesey is home and discharged returning from Alaska. John C. Guatz is home and says "Thanks for the Messengers". Merle Gust was discharged on Feb. 8th and is making his home with Mr. and Mrs. James Mehan. We hope that we can add your name to our discharge list in June. Also Harry Hill is a veteran now.

WATCH FOR DATE OF PARTY TO HONOR SERVICE-MEN AND –WOMEN TO BE HELD AT ZION THIS SUMMER.

Sometime during the summer we hope to have a "Get-to-gether" of you veterans who have received the Messenger and also all of you who have received the Messenger so you can see and chat with your friends. No definite plans have been made but we hope to get committees working on the program for a gathering of this kind to be held some Sunday afternoon this summer at Zion. Plan now to attend. We hope that the majority of our Messenger Readers will be there for an afternoon of fun.

We were glad to see <u>Paul Freeland</u> and his mother back at Ottawa Lake again. They visited several days in the Geo. Halter home and then left for Montreal, Canada to visit relatives. Paul was a Warrant Officer with the Marines. He hopes to attend college this fall. He hopes to visit back here again this summer.

∾∾∾

Berlin, Germany
March 6, 1946

Dear Mom and everyone:
My buddy and I got back from our furlough yesterday afternoon. (They had been to England). I didn't have time to write yesterday so I thought I would write the first thing tonight. We was gone one month yesterday. We didn't get back on time as we were delayed because they had a hard snow storm in Paris and the trains didn't run. The Lt. didn't say a thing because we didn't get back on time after we told him everything. Boy, I bet you can't guess how many letters I had when I got back. I had 51. So I spent all last night reading them. I got some that you wrote to me in Dec. I sorted them all out and read the oldest ones first. After getting 51 letters I thought I better get busy and write tonight.
So Betty thinks she will get married in June. I wish I could be there but I know I can't. It seems like everybody is getting married or having children back home. I took some nice pictures when I was in London. But I am sorry I can't send them home, because I had them stole on me. They took my

camera and everything but I didn't lose very much because I only gave 7 packs of cigarettes for it and that is 35 cents. I am going to try and get another one. I am very sorry about this but tell Doris not to be looking for that package every day as it is so hard to send something from here. You have to have it inspected by an officer and go through so much red tape. Don't worry I will get it sent home one of these days. Guess I better close as I'm running out of paper.

> Your son and brother,
> Leo Bexten

P.S. Did you notice anything different on my address? (Yes, we did Leo, congratulations on your rating of Pfc.)

❧❧❧

Reims, France
May 17, 1946

Dear Leaguers,

I didn't have much to do tonight so I thought I would write you a letter. I am moving around so fast that my mail can't keep up with me. Two weeks ago I was in the heart of Berlin and now I am way over here in France. Reims, France is about 100 miles from Paris because it is off limits to all American troops. We went through there when we went on furlough. We had to change trains there and it looked like a very pretty city.

Now I will tell you a little about Reims, France is a very old city. You can tell by the roads and the buildings. The roads are all made out of stone and the buildings are too. You never see a wooden building over here. Reims is a large city but it don't have many factories. It is more of a market place. All the farmers bring their crops in and sell them. The city is down in a valley and there is farming land all around. It looks so funny out in the Country because all the farmers live close together. It looks just like a little town and then for miles you don't see a house. Then you come to another little town of farmers.

I guess I'd better close for now. Write whenever you have time. I would like to hear from all of you.

God Bless You all,
As ever,
A Leaguer, Leo Bexten

❧❧❧

GOOD NEWS

As we type these lines we have just learned that Rolland Schmidt is in the States and will be home the end of the week. Also William Fischer has landed in Norfolk, Va. and is at Parris Island in Carolina. Both of these young men should be home soon with their discharges. Both are members of Zion. Rolland is the son of Mr. and Mrs. Leon Schmidt and William (Bill) is the son of Mr. Dan Fischer. Welcome home boys! Hope all the rest of you still in Service get home soon.
LESS HARROUN is in Nurnberg, Germany. He is fine and seems to be getting along O.K. ALVING TURK is now up in the far north of Alaska. He says that he had a nice trip up.

❧❧❧

Dear Servicemen:

It is a privilege for me to write you a few lines. The other day Violet Fischer came to me and told me about this paper which had been put out during the war. She brought along samples of the papers which have been published and I sat down and looked over them. I can see why the paper was a popular one because it contained so many things of interest.

It is not pleasant to be away from home and friends. Nobody likes it. But war brings with it many unpleasant things. We know however, that God goes with us wherever we are and He provides for us in our every need. He shows us ways of serving Him by serving others. He brings us in contact with new friends. Often He tests our faith by putting us through fiery trials. But He will never try us beyond what we can stand.

Many of you have seen places and things you would not have seen, if you hadn't been in the army or navy. You have made friends you never would have known. You have had the opportunity to let your light shine and to be the salt of the earth. May God help you to continue this glorious work. In all your thoughts, words, and deeds, may God be glorified.

As yet, I do not know any of you to whom I am writing. I am looking forward to meeting you sometime in the future. At the present time, I am trying to get acquainted with the people here in Ottawa Lake. My family and I arrived here on September 30. We got straightened around here in the parsonage by October 6, on which Sunday I was installed. Last evening, October 13, the congregation had a reception for us and what an enjoyable time it was too. After the program, they started carrying in boxes of groceries and canned foods and we began to open all the packages. What an assortment of items it was - everything from soup to soap. We certainly have enjoyed our stay here already, and look forward to many happy hours together.

In closing, let me wish you God's blessing, and express the prayer that God will keep you safely under His protection and in His good time, permit you to return home again to stay.

Your pastor and friend,
Rev. Dallas Adler

✿✿✿

REV. AND MRS. MUELLER, DAVID AND TEDDY MOVE TO NIAGARA FALLS, NEW YORK

On August 25th, Rev. Mueller preached his farewell sermon and after the service played a few numbers on the new pipe organ. That same evening the congregation gathered in the church basement for a farewell party in their honor. It was after prayerful consideration that Rev. Mueller accepted the call extended to him to be a parochial school teacher and organist at his home congregation at Niagara Falls, New York. They drove to their new home on August 31st. It was quite a weary trip since they had two flat tires and did not arrive until 3:30 a.m. Sunday morning September 1st. He was installed on that day.

We were all glad to see them back on October 6th for the big celebration which you will read about in the next item. They are all looking fine and the Reverend enjoys his work very much. David says he expects to come back to Ottawa Lake and be a farmer but perhaps when he's a young man he might change his mind. Reverend has 44 children in his school. On September 20th part of the Falls caved in and he felt the shake and rattle in the school about 8 miles away. The building shook as in a heavy blast. We hope the Mueller's will return often to visit all of us.

❦❦❦

CELEBRATIONS AT ZION ON OCTOBER 6TH

On October 6th an entire day of celebrations was held. At the morning service, Rev. Dallas F. Adler was installed as our new pastor. The installation was conducted by Rev. Menter, president of the Michigan District of the American Lutheran Church. He was assisted by Rev. Marcus Mueller. The Junior Choir sang.

At noon a pot-luck dinner was served to about 100 people in the church basement. At three in the afternoon the 85th Anniversary of the congregation was celebrated. Speakers at this service were Rev. A.O. Zeitner and Rev. Mueller. Eugene Fischer sang a solo. All the people that were confirmed at Zion were invited.

After a pot-luck supper the congregation and their guest assembled at 8:00 p.m. and the new Schantz two manual pipe organ was dedicated by Rev. Mueller. An organ recital was given by Mr. James Hunt, organist at Salem Lutheran Church of Detroit. The following people were in the program of vocal numbers: Melvin Bischoff, Mr. and Mrs. Arthur Bischoff, Mrs. Dawson Kortier, Eldora Fischer, Mildred Shoemaker, Herman Nieman and Eugene Fischer. They were accompanied by William Whitney of Sylvania.

It will be of interest for you to know that $2,259.45 was received for the Organ Fund so that clears our organ debt and we are very thankful for the wonderful cooperation by everyone present.

A beautiful set of Deagan Chimes were installed in the Pipe organ. They are the gift of Mrs. Ida Brodbeck in memory of her son Kenneth, who gave his life in the war. An organ light was given by Mr. and Mrs. John Rosenbrook.

FOUR YOUNG MEN FROM ZION ARE DISCHARGED

William Fischer, son of Mr. Dan Fischer received his discharge since the last Messenger and is home to stay. Bill is working on the road construction gang up near Flint, Michigan.

Rolland Schmidt, husband of Helen and daddy of Diana, is also home to stay. He is the son of Mr. and Mrs. Leon Schmidt.

Relmond and LeRoy Bunge, sons of Mr. and Mrs. Roy Bunge are both home since we last made the Messenger. Both are looking fine and it's a pleasure to see these boys back with us again.

With the four above discharge emblems on the Service Flag at church that leaves only nine boys still in service from Zion. They are the following and we'd like to comment so you know why some of their addresses will not appear on the last page as usual:

Leo Bexten, is still in France and hopes to be home in the spring. Let's write Leo, send Christmas cards and packages too if you'd like to.

Ronald Brinning, last report that he was at the replacement depot waiting for his turn to get on a boat bound for the good old U.S.A. It'll be swell seeing you back in these parts, Ronald.

Charles DeVriendt, is still in the Hawaiian Islands. Without a doubt he too will be glad to get the usual Christmas treats from us, cards, letters, packages and etc.

Clifford Papenhagen, is waiting for his boat and hopes to be home soon.

Forrest Nearhood, is at home in Ottawa Lake.

LaVern Schmidt, is at Camp Campbell, KY.

Curtis and Courtland Timming, are both at Camp Lee, VA.

 જ્ઞજ્ઞજ્ઞ

Shanghai, China
July 25, 1946

Dear Violet and Leaguers,

Well, to start with, this is one of your Messenger receivers and one that enjoys the paper very much. Yesterday I received your May-June issue and I was glad too. I have been here in Shanghai several months now and I have received the Messenger pretty regular. I want to thank you and all the staff for making the paper so interesting.

The weather over here is very hot at times and it usually rains about every third day. Most people claim that China is so far behind in modern things. But they should come over once and see for themselves. I will admit that it isn't a wonderful place but it is fair.

Our barracks are about one mile from the center of downtown but even out here it is crowded with people. That is the main thing wrong with Shanghai, just too much population. Most of the Naval Reserves have left here and it seems like the place is deserted. About the only reason I don't mind it is that there are so many different things that a kid like myself can learn.

I can talk a little Chinese just in the seven or eight months that I have been here. My work is very easy. I am a storekeeper striker. I might be lucky enough to get a rating in a month or more. But that's the question for now.

I am with a kid that is from Toledo. He and I went through boots together and have been lucky to stay together. He also reads the Messenger and enjoys it as much as I do.

Our mail comes through about three or four times a week and that's our happiest days of the week. The time is getting short now so I guess that this is the time to close and hope and pray for another Messenger. I wish to thank you and all for the Messenger. We all pray that God will see us all home safely in the time to come.

> As ever,
> Russell McGlenn

∾∾∾

Dear Violet and Leaguers,

Quite sometime has lapsed since I wrote any of you. However, I haven't forgotten you. I sincerely hope all is well with you as I am at this writing.

I just received a communiqué from Georges Paquay, your little Belgian reader of the Messenger. How long he'll be with us on mortal earth seems to be to be only a matter of time. His attending physicians are unable to diagnose his condition. I am informed he has just regained consciousness after a deep coma of several days duration. I can see by his correspondence that his mental capacities are affected by the long illness. He just had an operation, as if he wasn't in enough peril, without that. He has asked me to inform Violet, it is quite impossible for him to concentrate on letter writing. He writes me very short messages because I am his personal friend, and can inform the others. If you can decipher his metaphor, he said his head is a "material etna".

I am indeed grateful to all of you who have written him to cheer him in his hour of trial. He is as my own little brother to me. I met many persons in Europe, but this lad was my favorite among them all. Whatever anyone has done for him, has been done for me also. In the light of his condition, I have no hopes of ever seeing him again. I only wait for the seemingly inevitable news, that his suffering is all over. When it comes it will be a blow to me but I'll be satisfied that he is no longer lingering in a slow "living death". Since June 1945 he has suffered severely.

I am now attending Milwaukee State Teacher's College. I like it here very much in this large city and the classes are superb in scholastic qualities and achievements. I always did prefer larger cities with their evidence of bustling life and diversions from the monotony of duller environments. We have over 1,800 students this year at the college. So it is quite a lively place. Not much news so I'll close.

As ever,
Vernon Packard

Camp Lee, Virginia
August 7, 1946

Hello Violet and Leaguers,

I thought I would drop you a few lines this afternoon before I go to work. I am working nights now and Courtland is working days now. We are having lots of cool weather and a little rain. Glad to hear that some of the boys are home on leave and that some are home with discharges too.

I like it much better here at Camp Lee than in Texas and it is closer to home. We'll be coming home on furlough soon. The people are very nice to us here too.

It sure is interesting to read all the other boys letters that are printed in the Messenger and I see that my two were in it too. That way the boys will know what we are doing here in Virginia. I suppose everybody is busy back there these days with the farming and getting the crops harvested. I hope you have some rain by now and that the ground isn't too dry for the crops.

I guess I'll have to close for now as it's about time to eat and then go to work again. Tell everybody we said Hello and hope to see you all in the near future. So for this time I will say good-by and God bless you all.

As always,
Curtis Timming

❧❧❧❧

Reims, France
September 20, 1946

Dear Violet and Leaguers,

I haven't written to you for some time so I thought I would write you a letter tonight.

My buddy and I went to the show this afternoon. We saw the "Spanish Main". We both had seen it back in the States but we thought we would go and see it again because it is a very good show. We just got back from the show and boy, did it rain. It rained so hard that the cars had to stop on the road because they couldn't see to drive. It only rained for about a half hour and then it stopped.

My buddy and I have been going over to the Chapel every Wednesday night. A bunch of fellows go over there every Wednesday night and we sing songs and discuss the Bible. We have a good time all the way around. It is a good way to pass the time away. The first time we went over there were only five of us. The T/5 that was in charge made us all sing a solo. I sang the first verse of "Rock of Ages". They all said it was very good. I showed them the Messenger and they all said it was a very good paper. They thought it was a wonderful idea to make a paper like that and send to the men in the service. I sure am glad that you kids are still making the paper and sending it to us that are still in the service.

I have been receiving all the church papers that Jerry and Mildred have been sending me and I do enjoy reading them.

Boy, it sure is going to seem funny when I get home not to have Rev. Mueller for our minister.

I receive letters from the National Lutheran Council very often. They always send me some papers to read. They always tell me if I need a prayer book or New Testament or any kind of book I want they would be glad to send me some. I think it is nice of them to do things like that for us.

Well, I can't think of anything else to write about now so I guess I will close.
Write when you can
  And I will do the same
    May God bless you all and
    Keep you always the same.
    Leaguers

                 As ever, a Leaguer
                 Leo Bexten

❧❧❧

JESS BIEBER, son of Mr. Frank Bieber, was born Aug. 19, 1924 and died June 20, 1944 on his aircraft carrier the "Bunker Hill". He was buried at sea.

KENNETH F. BRODBECK, son of Mrs. Ida Brodbeck, was born Aug. 2, 1919. He died Nov. 20, 1944 in Southern France.His burial was in an American Cemetery in France at which a Protestant Chaplain Officiated.

LeROY BREIER, son of Mr. and Mrs. Roy Breier, was born Jan. 4, 1925. He died Mar. 1, 1945 in the battle of the Bulge, Several miles N.E. of Serrig, Germany. According to Chaplain John Downing of the 302nd Regt. "Pvt. Breier was last seen doing his duty under attack in the front lines."

LEON HARRWALDT, son of Mr. and Mrs. Leonard Harrwaldt, was born Dec. 26, 1925. He died on Feb. 5, 1945 in the Belgium-Luxembourg sector. He was buried in an American Military Cemetery at a Protestant Service in Foy, Belgium.

CORNELIUS BLOME, JR.

HAROLD JASMUND

CLAYTON SEELEY

MELVIN DAUER

DELVIN NOWARD

Printed in the United States
23222LVS00001B/222

9 780974 408453